Pornography
and the Justices

Pornography and the Justices

THE SUPREME COURT AND THE
INTRACTABLE OBSCENITY PROBLEM

Richard F. Hixson

SOUTHERN ILLINOIS UNIVERSITY PRESS
Carbondale and Edwardsville

Library of Congress Cataloging-in-Publication Data

Hixson, Richard F.
     Pornography and the Justices : the Supreme Court and the
intractable obscenity problem / Richard F. Hixson.
          p.   cm.
     Includes index.
     1. Obscenity (Law)—United States—History.   2. Free-
dom of speech—United States—History.   I. Title.
KF9444.H69   1996
345.73′0274—dc20
[347.305274]   95-42412
ISBN 0-8093-2057-6 (alk. paper)   CIP

For Terry

Contents

Preface

In the end, Justice John Marshall Harlan was probably right when he concluded, in a letter to a friend just months before his death in 1971, that the "obscenity problem [is] almost intractable, and that its ultimate solution must be found in a renaissance of societal values." But nothing ever comes to an end at the U.S. Supreme Court, least of all societal values that touch upon obscenity and pornography. Such controversial issues seem never to be resolved. They take on a life of their own, as this book attempts to show in its chronological treatment of the many obscenity cases that have reached the Court and in the analyses of the justices' views.

Issues involving the constitutional protection of obscene material have long been the source of controversy within the judicial system, as well as within public discourse in general. The traditional hierarchy of protected free speech, and of the press, as guaranteed by the First and Fourteenth Amendments, ranks political and social expression highest, followed by personal and aesthetic expression, then moral and religious expression—"pure speech," in other words. Obscenity's position on the chart continues to be debated, but it is generally said to rank somewhere near the bottom with "fighting words" speech, libelous speech, and commercial speech—"impure speech." While the Constitution itself does not single out obscene material for exceptional First Amendment treatment, most Supreme Court justices have followed this assumption, casting the Court in the role of "Super Censor" of low-status speech. It's a dirty job, but someone has to do it.

"The subject of obscenity has produced a variety of views among members of the Court unmatched in any other course of constitutional adjudication," said Justice Harlan in 1968 in *Interstate Circuit v. Dallas*. It was then that he first alluded to the obscenity problem's intractability. But the subject of obscenity, which is what pornography is called when it is proscribed by law, is more than a problem for the courts. Obscenity is also an issue for society at large, for whether viewed as a struggle against repression or as a fight to prevent harmful expression, the issue is permanently on the public agenda of modern democratic society. Elizabeth Fox-Genovese's view, expressed in *Feminism Without Illusions*, is as much to the point: "Each society gets the pornography it deserves." Justice Harlan could not have said it better.

Judge John M. Woolsey, author of the original *Ulysses* decision in 1933, spoke for the judiciary in general when he said he thought the courts had defined obscene as "tending to stir the sex impulses or to lead to sexually impure and lustful thoughts." Obscenity, according to the Rosewater Law, is "any picture or phonography record or any written matter calling attention to reproductive organs, bodily discharges, or bodily hair." The law was named after Senator Eliot Rosewater of Kurt Vonnegut's *God Bless You, Mr. Rosewater or Pearls Before Swine*, which, though fictional, is as close a concept as the Supreme Court itself has been able to frame.

Anthony Burgess introduced wit to the debate when he wrote in "What Is Pornography?": "A pornographic work represents social acts of sex, frequently of a perverse or wholly fantastic nature, often without consulting the limits of physical possibility."

Peter Gay, author of the ongoing historical series, *Education of the Senses*, added: "Pornography, while it boasts of an impressive repertory of acrobatic feats, is the most monotonous kind of literature extant." W. H. Auden, as if addressing the Supreme Court's penchant for restricting "prurient interest" pornography that arouses sexual desire, asserted in *The Dyer's Hand and Other Essays*: "One sign that a book has literary value is that it can be read in a number of different ways. Vice versa, the proof that pornography has no literary value is that, if one attempts to read it in any other way than as sexual stimulus, to read it, say, as a psychological case-history of the author's sexual fantasies, one is bored to tears."

Finally, the questioning voice of writer Robertson Davies is also incisive. In *A Voice from the Attic*, he wrote: "A concept of obscenity appears to be as necessary to one's view of life as a concept of purity. If we seek to encompass all that we can of the spectrum of human intellect and feeling, we cannot confine ourselves to the reds and oranges; we must know the violets and indigos as well. Which is the wiser course—to attempt to suppress a large part of what occupies the human mind, or to examine and cultivate everything in the mind that can be reached?"

On his retirement from the Supreme Court in 1981, Justice Potter Stewart mused that his enduring legacy would be a throwaway line he wrote in an obscenity case. He had remarked years earlier that he could not really define obscenity but he knew it when he saw it.

Despite Stewart's commonsense approach and Justice Harlan's belief that the solution lay outside the judicial system, the Supreme Court has grappled with the intractable problem for fifty years, first by defining *obscenity* in more elaborate terms than Stewart, then by casting its opinions in terms far more complex than those suggested by Harlan. Justices William O. Douglas and Hugo Black, the only First Amendment absolutists on the Court for many years, were even more straightforward, but they were so blasé on the politics and morality of obscenity that their opinions hardly counted for more than honest statements. Justice William J. Brennan Jr., early on, and John Paul Stevens, more recently, have emerged as consensus builders, as have the conservative chief justices Warren E. Burger and William H. Rehnquist.

To say any more in the preface would only give away the

plot, that is, what I learned in the process of research and what I suggest as ways to alleviate the intractability of the obscenity problem.

This volume is in many ways a sequel to my earlier *Privacy in a Public Society* (1987) in which I examined the constitutionalization of personal privacy and the ways the Supreme Court justices have interpreted the phenomenon. The present work looks in much the same way—case studies in historical context—at another area of law affected by America's highest judicial body. A third project, tentatively called "The Fourth Estate," will explore how the Court has interpreted the First Amendment's shortest clause, "and of the press."

As with previous research, I continue to enjoy the support of friends and colleagues, from those with simple encouragement to those recruited as research assistants. Always present in my work is the hand, now unfortunately invisible, of Alfred McClung Lee, friend, scholar, and gentle mentor. Of much the same variety is Brent D. Ruben, a longtime friend and Rutgers colleague who is always available when I need advice. On this project I am especially indebted to Hartmut Mokros, a Rutgers colleague who critiqued part of the manuscript while on vacation with me in Maine; Hilary Crew and Vincent Fitzgerald, doctoral students, who helped with bibliogaphical discovery and, in Ms. Crew's case, provided me with a better understanding of the feminist point of view; and the many students, both undergraduate and graduate, who educated me along the way. Friends in various academic departments across the country, but especially those at home, have assisted in this project and in my work generally. They know who they are, and I thank them profusely. I also want to thank James D. Simmons and Carol A. Burns at Southern Illinois University Press and Rebecca Spears Schwartz, who carefully edited the manuscript.

As always, my children, Sommer and Todd, continue to inspire me and keep me in check as friend, parent, and teacher. Terry, my wife, allowed selflessly for the time it takes to complete such a large design. She also read every word, a gesture of love if I ever heard one. In the end, however, there is no sharing of the responsibility for any errors of interpretation or misstatements of fact, not with the other First Amendment scholars whose publications have informed me, nor with the justices upon whose opinions I ultimately relied.

Pornography
and the Justices

1

Isolated Passages

PORNOGRAPHY—called "obscenity" when proscribed by law—is largely defined by efforts to regulate it. But the question of pornography—called the "intractable obscenity problem" by one U.S. Supreme Court justice—is more than a question of definition or a problem for the courts. It is also, and perhaps more so, an issue for society at large. Richard S. Randall's observation is accurate: "Whether viewed as a struggle against repression or as a struggle to prevent offending, possibly harmful expression, the pornography issue has an unavoidable and probably permanent place on the public agenda of modern liberal mass democratic society."[1] Randall's book, *Freedom and Taboo*, is a recent, and reasonable, attempt to understand pornography in its many overlapping dimensions, especially the psychological.

For example, the cause-and-effect relationship, where harm is said to stem directly from pornography, has been hotly debated throughout human history, despite the clear absence of empirical evidence. "Sexual murder, rape, and child molestation are universally condemned," writes Randall, "but agreement over the harmfulness of promiscuity, the subordination of women, or masturbation . . . is much more problematic." But, if an effect were proved and widely agreed to be harmful, Randall notes, we might still prefer to realize free-speech values. Conversely, even if an effect were agreed not to be harmful, we might still prefer to give greater weight to considerations of privacy or decency.[2]

Most views assume pornography to have "compelling temptations" as well as more subtle "subversive properties." After all, as Randall points out, psychodynamically the pornographic is an expression of forbidden and, therefore, usually repressed sexual and aggressive impulses and wishes. "The pornographic thus remains essentially fantastical, a kind of hallucinatory realm where everything is possible, and where we were all once originally supreme." The pornographic is inviting because its fantasies promise gratification of the kind reality seldom affords, the infantile counterparts of which were once ardently sought—yet, because forbidden, it is often perceived as threatening or dangerous.[3]

Randall labels this overall phenomenon the "pornographic within"—an interior sexuality of forbidden impulses, wishes, and fantasies that forms the psychological basis of pornography. Such a distinction needs to be kept in mind, Randall suggests, in order to separate pornography as a *psychological* element from pornography as a *social* designation. The former describes an "imaginistic product of a normatively modified sexuality," the latter a "normative judgment on an expression of that product." One needs always to be aware of the two pornographies—the *psychological* and the *sociological*—not to mention a third, the *legal*, which has been society's ultimate instrument in the social control of sexual expression. For example, to borrow again from Randall, the anthropomorphic description of Jerusalem's corruption in the Old Testament Book of Ezekiel might be functionally pornographic for some persons yet not be pornography. And Molly Bloom's soliloquy in James Joyce's

◆ ISOLATED PASSAGES

Ulysses might be designated pornography yet for some not be psychodynamically pornographic.[4]

"If the human capacity for pornography is universal," writes Randall, "the human interest in censoring it is no less so." But, equally, liberal notions of free speech, individual rights, equality, and popular rule must coexist if modern liberal democracy is to be sustained. Such conflicting, if not opposing, views are nowhere more apparent than in pornography, where, on the one hand, there is the fact of no appreciable effect beyond immediate and rather short-lived arousal and, on the other, the widespread belief that pornography is indeed harmful. Empirical data pitted against belief structure seldom wins the day. For example, when the President's Commission on Obscenity and Pornography was confronted with evidence that repeated exposure led to lowered levels of arousal, it concluded that ending legal restraints might also lead to a diminished interest in pornography.[5] However, it would be unthinkable for Americans, who have always felt a need to regulate obscenity, to cease and desist.

There are several such wrinkles in the battle over causative agents and influences. Randall notes that, while there is not much support for the fear that exposure leads to new or higher levels of sexual activity or to changes in an individual's established sexual behavior, in a reverse cause-and-effect relationship, sexual experience and higher levels of sexual activity may account for greater and more regular use of pornography. Real sex may be more addictive than pornographic representations.

On the immediate impact of pornography on criminal activity and antisocial behavior, the President's Commission concluded that there is "no evidence . . . that exposure to explicitly sexual materials plays a sizable role in the causation of delinquent or criminal behavior among youth or adults." Randall notes that ideological bias toward the question of pornography may also play a part in the entire effects debate. In the end, the various studies—retrospective surveys, aggregate-data analysis, and experimental research—are inconclusive on whether pornography is causally linked to antisocial or criminal behavior. "Pornography is in fact likely to be less arousing than one's own imagination," posits Randall, who concludes:

> The capacity of the human mind to eroticize is nearly limitless, and almost any depiction, symbol, idea or object can be transformed into a source of pornographic or near-pornographic stimulation. Pornography may feed a prurient interest and is designed to do exactly that, but it neither creates that interest nor is vital to it. The attractiveness of pornography is precisely that it violates our taboos and norms. Such license is bound to portray the subordination and degradation of women and aggression about them. Our quarrel with the disturbing, mean-spirited, sometimes frightening, often infantile images of pornography is largely a quarrel with an eroticized human sexuality that creates a fantastical pornographic within, which, in turn, both invents and responds to a pornography without.[6]

Restrictions on the public portrayal of sexuality—"sexual expression," for clarity—had been lifting gradually since the turn of the century. By at least mid-twentieth century, American courts had steadily narrowed proscribable obscenity, and by the mid-1960s, few legal barriers remained against sexual expression. "The veil of nineteenth-century reticence was torn away, as sex was put on display."[7] The Puritan strain that runs through all of American history—from the apocalypse-fearing settlers and property-aspiring immigrants to freedom-seeking refugees—may help to explain why Americans have always insisted on the surveillance of personal morality in order to regulate, if not outlaw, deviant behavior.

The varying degree of community involvement in the sexual lives of others is nowhere better reflected than in the U.S. Supreme Court's persistent struggle, as this book discusses, with having to determine community standards by which obscenity may be measured. The Court is also expected to decide, of course, what is obscenity in the first place. The justices, individually and collectively, have tried on many occasions to describe what Justice John Marshall Harlan called the "intractable obscenity problem." William J. Brennan Jr. said obscenity was "utterly without redeeming social importance." Harlan said it had to be "fundamentally offensive," "prurient," and "inherently sexually indecent." Potter Stewart always looked for "hard-core" pornography before he decided what was obscene and unprotected by the Constitution. Admitting his inability to formulate a coherent test for obscenity, Stewart claimed "I know it when I see it." Thurgood Marshall, who rejected the notion that watching obscene materials in the privacy of one's home might lead to criminal conduct, compared such illogic to the prohibition of chemistry books on the ground that they may lead to the making of homemade spirits. John Paul Stevens, proponent of the Court's sliding-scale theory of First Amendment values, believed that obscene expression is of a lesser magnitude than political debate, thus requiring less protection.

Before evolving its own framework, however, the Supreme Court first had to dismiss an old nemesis, the Hicklin Rule, so named from the nineteenth-century English case, *Regina v. Hicklin*, which stipulated that the test for deciding obscenity was "whether the tendency of the matter . . . is to deprave and corrupt those whose minds are open to such immoral influences, and into whose hands a publication of this sort may fall."[8] Applying this broad test, the court held obscene an old anti-Catholic tract entitled *The Confessional Unmasked; Shewing the Depravity of the Romanish Priesthood, the Iniquity of the Confessional and the Questions Put to Females in Confession.* There was no question that the treatise was political and religious, not sexual. Nevertheless, Lord Chief Justice Cockburn ruled it obscene because "it is quite certain that it would suggest to the minds of the young of either sex, or even to persons of more advanced years, thoughts of a most impure and libidinous character." This work, he said, is circulated on street corners, where it falls into the hands of all classes, young and old, "and the minds of those hitherto pure are exposed to the danger of contamination and pollution from the impurity it contains."[9]

Obscenity was to be decided on the basis of the impact of certain parts, or isolated passages, of the offending material—rather than the work as a whole—on susceptible individuals. The author's intent was irrelevant, but an improper

7

Isolated Passages ◆

motive could be implied if the work itself was obscene. *Hicklin* meant that all readers, young and old, were reduced to the level of the most intellectually and emotionally defenseless readers. Evaluation of a work was based on the work's possible effect on children, the mentally weak or immature, or "a particularly susceptible" subclass of the community. This is the way—not all that far removed from the present zealousness to rid the air of verbal impurities—that isolated passages became the criteria for censorship and the innocence of youth became the yardstick for determining a work's potential to corrupt.[10]

On this side of the Atlantic, meanwhile, another not-so-moral force was at work, "sexual commerce," which by the mid-1890s had become a disturbing (for some) part of the American way of life. The market for pornography—called "cheap and licentious" literature in those days—had been expanding since the Civil War. "The congregation of men in the army apart from families created a demand for sexual commerce and constituted an easy market for purveyors to target," surmise the historians John D'Emilio and Estelle B. Freedman.[11]

Almost as if they were destined to meet, two sides emerged in the sex wars of the late nineteenth century: the one, led by Anthony Comstock, called for direct government involvement in the suppression of obscenity; the other, led by anarchists and free lovers, called for exposing all sexual matters to the light of day. The question then, as now, was whether sex was best regulated by expanding or restricting its public discussion. Comstock's crusaders won most of the battles, but by the early twentieth century, the expansive mode, supported by free lovers, suffragists, and sex educators, would begin to win the war.[12]

D'Emilio and Freedman also note in their history of sexuality in America that an increasing commitment to freedom of the press as well as the limited circulation of obscene publications slowed any movement for censorship. Only rarely, they observed, did the states express concern about the potential of art and literature to corrupt the morals of youth.[13] Before 1800, governmental concern with immorality was limited largely to blasphemous and other antireligious matter, and it was not until 1815 that an American court upheld a conviction on a specific charge of obscenity. In that case, *Commonwealth v. Sharpless*, the Pennsylvania Supreme Court said that, in the absence of explicit legislation, "Any offence which in its nature and by its example tends to corruption of morals, as the exhibition of an obscene picture, is indictable at common law."[14]

In 1821, a Massachusetts court sentenced a bookdealer to six months in jail for selling the eighteenth-century English novel, John Cleland's *Memoirs of a Woman of Pleasure*, better known as *Fanny Hill*, to local farmers. The Customs Act of 1842, in effect our first federal obscenity law, prohibited the importation of "all indecent and obscene prints, paintings, lithographs, engravings and transparencies" but excluded printed matter from regulation. In 1865, Congress passed the first statute prohibiting the shipment of obscene books and pictures through the mails. In 1873, Anthony Comstock, grocer's clerk turned antipornography crusader, was instrumental in getting through Congress an omnibus anti-obscenity bill, aided by the Committee for the Suppression of Vice. Congress amended the "Comstock Act" in 1876 to label obscene publications "nonmailable." Comstock was recognized for his lobbying efforts with a special agent appointment by the postmaster general to enforce the new law, a post he held until his death in 1915. Walter Kendrick, in his study of pornography in modern culture, is mindful of Comstock's forty-year reign as one of the most striking oddities of American history, when problems of public morality were entrusted almost wholly to the discretion of one man, an agent of the U.S. Post Office.[15]

In 1896, the U.S. Supreme Court first confronted the legal issue of obscenity when it reviewed two lower-court convictions. In the first, *Rosen v. United States*, the Court upheld the conviction of New York publisher Lew Rosen for mailing "indecent" pictures of females in violation of the Comstock Act. Justice John Marshall Harlan, the first, and grandfather of the second Justice Harlan to serve on the Court, reiterated the trial judge's use of Lord Cockburn's definition of obscenity in *Regina v. Hicklin* as that which has a tendency to deprave and corrupt the most susceptible person.[16]

9

In the second decision, handed down six weeks later, the Supreme Court *overturned* the conviction of Dan K. Swearingen, who had been found guilty in a federal district court in Kansas of mailing a newspaper that contained an "obscene, lewd and lascivious" article. The offending piece, which appeared in Swearingen's *Burlington* (Kansas) *Courier*, charged an unnamed—but apparently an easily identifiable—person as being "meaner, filthier, rottener than the rottenest strumpet that prowls the streets by night," a "red headed mental and physical bastard," and a "black hearted coward" who would "sell a mother's honor with less hesitancy and for much less silver than Judas betrayed the Saviour, and who would pimp and fatten on a sister's shame with as much unction as a buzzard gluts on carrion." While agreeing that the language was extreme and "plainly libelous," the Court ruled that no obscenity had been committed. Obscenity, the Court said, does not apply to language that is simply "coarse and vulgar," but it does concern words that "signify that form of immortality which has relation to sexual impurity."[17]

The *Rosen* and *Swearingen* decisions were not major cases, but they were important steps, as Thomas L. Tedford notes, in the evolutionary development of controls on sexual speech. In *Rosen*, the Court interpreted the Comstock Act as to make it illegal in the United States to mail anything that a jury might find sexually provocative to a child. And in *Swearingen*, the Court, perhaps without realizing it, ended three centuries of evolution of the Anglo-American concept of the obscene. That which began as a seventeenth-century church punishment for the sin of communicating an immoral or blasphemous thought had now become the state crime of communicating an erotic one, according to Tedford.[18]

For life outside the legal sphere, meanwhile, sexual desire became a selling device not only for the popular entertainment industry but for mainstream businesses as well. "More and more of life . . . was intent on keeping Americans in a state of constant sexual excitement," according to D'Emilio and Freedman.[19] Changes in literary styles moved even quicker, as, in the words of Cole Porter's Broadway parody,

◆ ISOLATED PASSAGES

"Good authors who once knew better words / Now only use four-letter words / Writing prose / Anything goes!" Older definitions of obscenity were being challenged at all levels of society, and in the courts, too, of course, where the Hicklin Rule had long been the standard for dealing with obscene matter.

Its armor showed signs of wear in 1913, when district court judge Learned Hand wrote that the Hicklin Rule, "however consonant it may be with mid-Victorian morals, does not . . . answer to the understanding and morality of the present time." He continued:

> I question whether in the end men will regard that as obscene which is honestly relevant to the adequate expression of innocent ideas, and whether they will not believe that truth and beauty are too precious to society at large to be mutilated in the interest of those most likely to pervert them to base uses. Indeed, it seems hardly that we are even to-day so lukewarm in our interest in letters or serious discussion as to be content to reduce our treatment of sex to the standard of a child's library in the supposed interest of a salacious few, or that shame will for long prevent us from adequate portrayal of some of the most serious and beautiful sides of human nature.[20]

A major break with the judicial past did not come, however, until 1933, when district judge John M. Woolsey suggested that a better test than that in *Hicklin* would be the impact or dominant effect of the whole book on the average reader of normal sensual responses and an evaluation of the author's intent. The book in question was James Joyce's *Ulysses*, which the judge went to great pains to study before giving his verdict. He revealed that for many weeks, including spare time and vacation time, he had read the book once in its entirety and parts of it several times, especially "those passages which the government particularly complains." In the end, the judge held that *Ulysses* "in spite of its unusual frankness," was not pornographic, that is, written for the purpose of exploiting obscenity.[21]

The meaning of the word *obscene*, Judge Woolsey said, had been defined by the courts in a number of cases as "tending to stir the sex impulses or to lead to sexually impure and lustful thoughts." Whether a particular book would tend to excite such impulses and thoughts, the judge said, must be tested by its effect on a person with average sex instincts. "I am quite aware that owing to some of its scenes 'Ulysses' is a rather strong draught to ask some sensitive, though normal, person to take. But my considered opinion, after long reflection, is that, whilst in many places the effect . . . on the reader undoubtedly is somewhat emetic, nowhere does it tend to be an aphrodisiac."[22]

Judge Woolsey's opinion, remarkable for its clarity, was upheld by Judge Augustus Hand of the Second Circuit Court of Appeals and cousin of Learned Hand, who added to this newly evolving "work as a whole" doctrine: "That numerous long passages in 'Ulysses' contain matter that is obscene under any fair definition of the word cannot be gainsaid; yet they are relevant to the purpose of depicting the thoughts of the characters and are introduced to give meaning to the whole, rather than to promote lust or portray filth for its own sake."[23]

Literary critics seemed generally to rejoice over Judge Woolsey's decision that *Ulysses* was legal, and they applauded Attorney Morris Ernst's successful handling of the case, his latest score, as Ben Ray Redman put it, in the cause of enlightenment. But Redman, among others, did not believe that either the embattled lawyer or the learned judge had dug down to the roots of the obscenity problem. He said that, despite the recent triumph over censorship, the situation remained precarious. Redman believed that the "black brood of censors" was in full retreat and that authors were enjoying a "liberty of expression" equal to, if not greater than, that enjoyed by a Petronius, a Chaucer, or a Wycherley. However, nothing less than a radical revision of certain widely held ideas would ensure a continuance of literary freedom.[24]

Specifically, Redman took issue with the legal definition of obscenity, as used by Judge Woolsey and implied by Judge Hand, though Woolsey said that *Ulysses* was not to be deemed obscene simply because the narrative may tend to stir the sex impulses or lead to sexually impure and lust-

◆ ISOLATED PASSAGES

ful thoughts. "To deny literature the right of stirring the sex impulses of man is to deny it one of its prime and proper functions; for these impulses are fundamental, necessary and energizing, and there are no strings within us more vital and more vitalizing upon which art can play." Redman's views are typical of those held by critics then and now. He concluded, prophetically: "Fashions fluctuate and manners change, laws come and go according to the dictates of embattled minorities or aroused majorities; but literature continues in beauty and in power."[25]

Meanwhile, it was Judge Learned Hand who put the Hicklin Rule to its final resting place. "This earlier doctrine," he wrote in 1936, "necessarily presupposed that the evil against which [a] statute is directed so much outweighs all interests of art, letters or science, that they must yield to the mere possibility that some prurient person may get a sensual gratification from reading or seeing what to most people is innocent and may be delightful or enlightening. No civilized community not fanatically puritanical would tolerate such an imposition, and we do not believe that the courts that have declared it, would ever have applied it consistently." He concluded, bluntly, that the isolated passages theory was dead and that an accused book or picture must be judged as a whole. "If it is old, its accepted place in the arts must be regarded; if new, the opinions of competent critics in published reviews or the like must be considered." What counts, Judge Hand said, is the work's effect, not upon any particular class, but upon all whom it is likely to reach.[26]

The next important Supreme Court decision affecting obscenity law was *Chaplinsky v. New Hampshire*, the famous "fighting words" case that had dealt with the weighing of social value against social order and morality. With *Chaplinsky* in 1941, it is said, the constitutional law of obscenity begins. Actually, *Near v. Minnesota* in 1930 had suggested that obscenity did not fall within the First Amendment. Chief Justice Charles E. Hughes said in that case that, while censorship of speech and press were generally prohibited, such freedoms did not constitute an absolute principle. One exception, he said, involved the "primary requirements of decency," in other words, the problem of obscenity. The other exceptions involved national security and the endangerment of public order by the incitement to violence.[27]

With *Chaplinsky*, the Court established a rationale that distinguished unprotected from protected speech. Obscenity and lewdness, libel, and fighting words should not be protected by the Constitution because, in the words of Justice Frank Murphy, who wrote the Court's unanimous decision, "such expressions are no essential part of any exposition of ideas, and are of such slight social value as a step to truth that any benefit that may be derived from them is clearly outweighed by the social interest in order and morality." In upholding the conviction of Chaplinsky, a Jehovah's Witness who in anger cursed the police of Rochester, New Hampshire, the Court created a new two-level standard for judging protected expression, which eventually would help it deal specifically with sexual expression. At the first level is *worthwhile* speech, the "exposition of ideas," deserving of First Amendment protection. At the second level is *worthless* speech of "such slight social value" as not to deserve any protection. This distinction provided lower courts a strategy for dealing with erotic materials. Those judges who wanted to censor "worthless expression" could do so out of hand without having to prove any degree of threat to society. Others, such as Judge Curtis Bok in Pennsylvania, could demand more than a showing of appeal to lusts. In *Commonwealth v. Gordon*, Judge Bok found a number of books not obscene and said that, in addition to the excitement of sexual desire, a work to be legally obscene must create a danger of incitement to criminal conduct. "The causal connection between the book and the criminal behavior must appear beyond a reasonable doubt," he wrote.[28]

So, while the isolated passages doctrine of *Hicklin* gave way to more liberal legal theories regarding speech and press, the Supreme Court was still not headlong on a journey of freeing up all kinds of speech. Nor were courts in general free from the moat of society surrounding them but not protecting them from their worst repressive instincts. "The *Ulysses* decision impressed the literary world, but not the other courts," Charles Rembar learned during his successful

14

defense of such literary works as *Lady Chatterley's Lover,* *Tropic of Cancer,* and *Memoirs of a Woman of Pleasure* (*Fanny Hill*).[29]

On the other hand, despite the fact that the *Ulysses* decision had indicated that more open and frank fiction might survive the courts after 1933, literature did not change radically in the succeeding decade. Some four-letter words appeared as well as a few anatomical references that had not previously been seen outside of *Ulysses* and the classics. One study of literature and obscenity during the period reported that the sex act was seldom depicted, and then not at length. Characteristically, sexual acts were implied or reported as having taken place without being described. "After World War II," reports Felice Flanery Lewis, "a trend toward either an increased use of four-letter words and other unusually frank language or a more detailed description of sexual relationships is noticeable in the fiction known to have been involved in obscenity litigation." Several books also depicted a much wider acceptance of extramarital liaisons. Thus, the sexual revolution in literature advanced on the heels of war, as it had many times before.[30]

Following the war, according to D'Emilio and Freedman, pornography, as well as other media products that titillated males by "sexually objectifying women's bodies," moved beyond its customary place in a marginal underground world. Soldiers carried pornography home from Europe and Asia, and their acquired tastes were soon satisfied by a new genre of pulp literature, *Playboy,* for example, and scandal magazines such as *Confidential* and *Keyhole. Playboy's* first issue appeared in December 1953 with Marilyn Monroe's barely concealed breasts on the cover, announcing, in effect, the dawning of a new voyeuristic age. After Pocket Books initiated the "paperback revolution" in 1939, Bantam issued its first "beefcake" cover in 1948, and by the 1950s "lurid designs and suggestive copy" dominated the paperback field. While World War II may have diverted the attention of purity crusaders, its aftermath provoked a resurgence of resistance to sexual frankness. Antismut campaigns emerged in a number of cities, including New York City, where police raided distributors of "girlie" magazines and pulp novels; campaigns were directed against retail outlets in Times Square as well. By the end of the 1950s, fourteen states had tightened their obscenity laws to prohibit the sale and distribution of sexually suggestive comic books.[31]

"The rhetoric of the purity campaigns of the 1950s reveal both continuity and change in America's sexual history," D'Emilio and Freedman note. "Like the anti-vice crusaders at the turn of the century, opponents of pornography tended to ascribe all manner of evil to sex." But also by the 1950s, with the mores of the middle class having changed profoundly since Anthony Comstock's successes in the late nineteenth century, purity crusaders were more and more operating outside the mainstream. Their victories, though effective from time to time, were fewer. Ironically, the battlefield shifted from the neighborhoods to the courtrooms. Zealous law enforcement efforts to suppress pornography provoked wave after wave of litigation, which in turn forced the U.S. Supreme Court near the end of the 1950s to address the obscenity question directly.[32]

Edmund Wilson's *Memoirs of Hecate County* was among the more famous fictional works prosecuted during the decade or so after the war. The book, a series of six interrelated stories told by the same unnamed male protagonist, is noteworthy for its graphic sexual descriptions and for the legal decisions that followed its publication in 1946. While it represented the last vestige of Comstockery in America, it also served pointedly as a harbinger of the thorniest problem ever to face the country's highest judicial body.

Almost immediately upon publication, the book was banned in Boston in April 1946. One hundred and thirty copies were confiscated by the police from four bookstores owned by Doubleday, the publisher, after the New York Society for the Suppression of Vice, Comstock's old group, charged that it was salacious and lascivious. The New York Public Library removed it from circulation. Yet fifty thousand copies had been sold in the four months since publication. The Court of Special Sessions of the City of New York, a now-defunct municipal court which heard such misdemeanor cases, found the book obscene in a two-to-one decision and fined the publisher and its local shops $1,000. The district attorney warned that anyone who sold a copy could be sentenced to a year in prison.[33]

In Los Angeles, merchants were fined for selling the book. A San Francisco bookseller who had sold the book was acquitted on a second trial after the first had resulted in a hung jury. Police in Philadelphia confiscated copies, and the publisher stopped shipments to Massachusetts because of that state's strict censorship law. Nationwide, the Hearst newspaper chain used *Memoirs of Hecate County* as the focus of its ongoing campaign against indecent books. Lionel Trilling, English professor at Columbia University and a leading literary critic and essayist, testified at the nonjury trial that the stories were not only related but that together they constituted a study of good and evil. He said that the sexually frank passages in "The Princess with the Golden Hair" contributed to the "very moral" theme of the book, a view shared by other notable critics. But it appears that neither literary merit nor judgment of the book as a whole were given serious consideration in reaching a decision.

Significantly, the three-judge panel determined, but without writing an opinion, that Doubleday and Wilson had violated the New York Penal Code, Section 1141 of which provided:

> A person who sells . . . or has in his possession with intent to sell, lend, distribute or give away, or to show . . . any obscene, lewd, lascivious, filthy, indecent or disgusting book . . . or who . . . prints, utters, publishes, or in any manner manufactures, or prepares any such book . . . is guilty of a misdemeanor.[34]

The New York statute, prohibiting mainly the circulation of obscene matter, recited a number of synonyms for *obscene* but failed to even suggest an obscenity test and gave no hint of pornographic intent. Perhaps it was the vagueness of the law and the uncertainty of the judicial tests of obscenity that caused the dearth of opinions. Apparently, the judges were unwilling to hazard a guess as to what standard should apply. They settled for a "personal taste" standard that, however conscientious it may have been, put publishers and authors in a worse state of constant jeopardy, not knowing whether they were acting within the law or in violation of it.

Meanwhile, the old Hicklin Rule, astir in its grave, was believed by the prosecution still to be the test for New York. Doubleday, the publisher, had urged, however, that the controlling factor was whether the motive of the book was designed to excite erotic images in the mind of a reader. Conversely, if a work was primarily pornographic and other incidents and qualities merely ancillary, both sides appeared to agree that the work could then be suppressed. Other courts, in New York and elsewhere, had been using the criteria that the proper test of obscenity was the motive of the writing, not its remote tendency.

While special sessions judge Nathan D. Perlman conceded in his dissent that "The Princess with the Golden Hair" was properly set apart from the rest of the book, and upon which the conviction alone rested, he nevertheless maintained that the court was wrong in considering the impact of the story upon the young and emotionally immature rather than upon the bulk of the adult reading population. Rejecting the test offered by the prosecution, the judge suggested that any possible evil effects on the youthful and immature were far outweighed by the story's helpful insights into social problems that readers, as members of the community, must solve. In his opinion for the majority in an earlier case, Judge Perlman said, "The normal person must serve as a criterion, not the abnormal."[35] In *People v. Doubleday*, the case of Edmund Wilson's book, Judge Perlman said:

> To adopt a standard of obscenity which would disregard the interests of the mature and ignore the positive and vital contribution which books can make in their lives, is to needlessly sacrifice the welfare of a vast portion of our community. I am confident that such was not the intent of the legislature. Section 1141 of the Penal Law, as every other statute, is fundamentally intented to benefit and protect society as a whole.
>
> The writer of the story is evidently and honestly concerned with the complex influences of sex and of class consciousness on man's relentless search for happiness. That is

◆ ISOLATED PASSAGES

a problem which is also of deep concern to the matured reading public. That public is entitled to the benefit of the writer's insight and that right may not be lightly disgarded by excluding from consideration all interests but those of the young and immature.

To suppress what may appear bad in a book is also to suppress what is good therein. The court's primary duty is to interpret all laws in the terms of the general welfare.[36]

John S. Sumner, executive secretary of the Society (formerly the Committee) for the Suppression of Vice, and Comstock's successor, said that officers of the society were gratified with the decision and hoped it would act as a deterrent to publishers and writers. He said it came at an opportune time, "because of a tendency of publishers and writers to go to extremes in the matter of obscenity in productions."[37]

The New York conviction of *Memoirs of Hecate County*, after being upheld in 1947 by the New York Court of Appeals, the state's highest court, reached the U.S. Supreme Court in 1948. In the first constitutional test of a state obscene-literature statute as it applied to a book, the Court split four to four, with Justice Felix Frankfurter not participating in the *per curiam* opinion. The conviction was therefore allowed to stand, although a new edition of the book was published in 1959, followed by one in Boston in 1960, and met with no legal problems. Because the justices were divided down the middle in an unsigned opinion, the Court did not publicly address the claim that literature attacked as obscene was entitled to constitutional protection. The justices did not again face that issue for nearly ten more years.

II

Dominant Theme

The subject of obscenity has produced a variety of views among the members of the Court unmatched in any other course of constitutional adjudication.

—Justice John Marshall Harlan, *Interstate Circuit v. Dallas*

JUSTICE Harlan called it "the intractable obscenity problem." In thirteen decisions with signed opinions between 1957 and 1967, easily the most active and the most chaotic obscenity years for the Court, the nine justices filed fifty-five separate statements of their views. Moreover, they put themselves at odds with state legislators, local prosecutors, and juries when they reversed thirty-one lower-court convictions between 1967 and 1973. In this chapter, we look at the major Supreme Court decisions between 1957 and 1963.

First came the little-known but important *Butler v. Michigan*, a unanimous decision written by Justice Felix Frankfurter that threw out a state obscenity statute prohibiting the distribution of material "tending to incite minors to violent or depraved or immoral acts." Frankfurter said that the Michigan law was not restricted "to the evil with which it is said to deal, but, instead, in its overbreadth reduces the adult population to reading only what is fit for children. "Surely," the justice wrote, "this is to burn the house to roast the pig." *Butler* was the last nail in the *Hicklin* coffin.[1]

Soon after the decision, which had been announced in February 1957, the American Law Institute, a group of judges, lawyers, and scholars, proposed as part of its Model Penal Code a new standard for identifying obscenity. The Institute argued that "society may legitimately seek to deter the deliberate stimulation and exploitation of emotional tensions arising from the conflict between social convention and the individual's sex drive." The goal of the Institute was to establish a new "rational" obscenity law which would "reflect changes in men's views of the importance of freedom of expression."[2]

Consistent with this end, the Model Penal Code defined obscenity as follows: "A thing is obscene if, considered as a whole, its predominant appeal is to prurient interests, i.e., a shameful or morbid interest in nudity, sex, or excretion, and if it goes substantially beyond customary limits of candor in description or representation of such matters."[3] As it turned out, ironically, Justice William J. Brennan Jr. was already at work on a draft of a decision on the subject and would draw upon the proposed code. On 24 June 1957, the Supreme Court reported three important obscenity rulings, one written by Frankfurter and the others by Brennan.[4]

Frankfurter wrote for the majority of five in *Kingsley Books Inc. v. Brown*, upholding the constitutionality of a state statute permitting municipal injunctions against the sale or distribution of certain books and magazines judged "obscene." Under New York state law, towns could also seize and destroy obscene material. Frankfurter, joined by Harlan, Harold Burton, Tom Clark, and Charles Whittaker, viewed the statute as a valid regulation of obscenity, but they allowed for no restraint on material not yet published and not yet found offensive. Frankfurter wrote: "If New York chooses to subject persons who disseminate obscene 'literature' to criminal prosecution and also to deal with such books as deodands of old, or both, with due regard, of course, to appropriate opportunities for the trial of the underlying issue, it is not for us to gainsay its selection of remedies."[5]

But that was not the issue that most concerned book publishers. They were not looking for protection specifically for the book under question—*Nights of Horror*, a collection of words and pictures depicting primarily sadistic sexual tortures of women by men that, in the words of two critics, "might have chilled the blood of De Sade." What the publishers wanted, and needed, was some recognition that such statutes posed a threat of court censorship, which could operate to inhibit, if not prohibit, the sale of marginal books and magazines, those not legally obscene but nonetheless controversial. Instead, Justice Frankfurter said, "It is not for this Court . . . to limit the State in resorting to various weapons in the armory of the law." He said, borrowing from *Near v. Minnesota*, that liberty of speech and press is not an absolute right nor is the protection of prior restraint without limits. Prior restraint is not per se unconstitutional, according to Frankfurter, although any such restraint must be "closely confined so as to preclude . . . licensing or censorship."[6]

Chief Justice Earl Warren, in dissent, insisted that the case was not one of criminal obscenity at all. "It is a case wherein the New York police . . . located books which, in their opinion, were unfit for public use because of obscenity and then obtained a court order for their condemnation and destruction." Thus, while the state law puts the book on trial, Warren said, there is no standard in the statute for judging the book in context. Justices William O. Douglas and Hugo Black also dissented, noting, "The regime approved by the Court goes far toward making the censor supreme [and] substitutes punishment by contempt for punishment by jury trial."[7] Their objection, with this case as well as a spate of others, also hinged on the First Amendment as a block to censorship in any form, but especially that which is inspired by government.

Justice Brennan, who wrote the majority opinion in the other decisions of 24 June, *Roth v. United States* and *Alberts v. California*, dissented in *Kingsley* on grounds that the decision did not take into account the absence of a jury determination of obscenity. Drawing upon *Roth* and *Alberts*, Brennan opined that a trial provides "a peculiarly competent

◆ DOMINANT THEME

application of the standard for judging obscenity which, by its definition, calls for an appraisal of material according to the average person's application of contemporary community standards."[8] No book, in Brennan's view, should be proscribed unless, or until, a jury has had an opportunity to decide its legality. Justice Harlan, who waited to explain his rationale in *Roth* and *Alberts*, simply voted with the majority because *Kingsley Books* concerned state rather than federal law. Throughout the years, Harlan maintained that states might use criminal or civil sanctions but that the national government could not.

A New York "purveyor of distasteful material," Samuel Roth, had been convicted under federal law for advertising and mailing the book *American Aphrodite* and the magazine *Good Times*.[9] Despite his reputation as a purveyor of obscene matter and his several arrests and convictions in state and federal courts since 1928, Roth was also the victim of the reign of Postmaster General Arthur E. Summerfield during President Eisenhower's administration. Summerfield's term in office was known as the high point of Comstockery.[10]

In 1956, meanwhile, Roth had been indicted and charged with "mailing books, periodicals, and photographs (and circulars advertising some of them) alleged to be 'obscene, lewd, lascivious, filthy, and of an indecent character.' " He was convicted in New York federal district court on four counts of a twenty-four-count indictment, and his conviction was affirmed by the U.S. Court of Appeals, where Judge Jerome Frank concurred but protested, as he had in an earlier case, that the "clear and present danger" doctrine might apply to obscenity cases. He said that even trash should be left alone unless, or until, it can be shown persuasively that the social impact is more than a mere transitory, psychic response without overt misconduct. "Obscenity dissemination, a ridiculously vague crime, punishes people for selling books or pictures which may only 'evoke thoughts' and nothing more," Judge Frank wrote. "This is carrying government suppression too far. Just as with the soapbox political zealots, so with 'publishers' like Roth: let them alone as the price we pay for freedom, unless and until we can show that they have produced some tangible danger to society, a danger more 'clear' and more 'present' than mere stimulation of 'lustful thoughts.' "[11]

Roth's appeal was argued before the Supreme Court on 22 April 1957 and was supported by an impressive array of *amicus curiae*, friend of the court, briefs, including ones from the American Book Publishers Council, *Playboy* magazine, Authors League, and the American Civil Liberties Union. The Court joined Roth's case to that of David S. Alberts, who had been accused of violating an antismut statute in California.

A Beverly Hills mail-order merchant, Alberts, waiving a jury trial, was found guilty in municipal court for "lewdly keeping for sale obscene and indecent books, and with writing, composing and publishing an obscene advertisement of them" in violation of the California Penal Code. His conviction was affirmed by the state superior court. When the U.S. Supreme Court also affirmed his conviction, and that of Roth, it endorsed the constitutionality of obscenity legislation at both the federal and state levels.[12]

While on numerous occasions the Court had assumed that obscenity was not fully protected by the freedoms of speech and press, the *Roth-Alberts* decision was the first time the question had been squarely presented to the Court. In neither case was there a question about the alleged obscenity of the material, though Justice Brennan, who wrote the majority opinion, hinted at a definition. He referred to the American Law Institute's definition: "Obscene material is material which deals with sex in a manner appealing to prurient interest." But sex itself, he said, is a great and mysterious motive force in human life, the subject of absorbing interest to mankind through the ages.[13]

The Court rejected the old Hicklin Rule, long used by courts for judging obscenity by the effect of isolated passages upon the most susceptible persons. Obscene material, Brennan maintained, is material that deals with sex in a manner appealing to prurient interests. The test of obscenity was to be a more modern application of Judge Woolsey's ruling in the 1933 *Ulysses* case. It was whether "to the average person, applying contemporary community standards, the dominant

◆ DOMINANT THEME

theme of the material taken as a whole appeals to prurient interests."[14] Hence, the Court said that neither the federal law, under which Roth was convicted, nor the state statute under which Alberts was found guilty, offended any constitutional safeguards or failed to signal adequate notice of what speech is prohibited. The federal obscenity law, the Comstock Act, was found a proper exercise of the postal power delegated to Congress, and the California statute "in no way imposes a burden or interferes with the federal postal functions."

Justice Harlan, who concurred in *Alberts* but dissented in *Roth*, feared that the "broad brush" used by the majority might loosen the tight reins that he believed state and federal governments should hold on the enforcement of obscenity statutes. Seeming to scoff, the justice averred: "The Court seems to assume that 'obscenity' is a peculiar genus of 'speech and press,' which is as distinct, recognizable, and classifiable as poison ivy is among other plants." Since every communication has an individuality and value of its own, Harlan argued, the suppression of a particular writing or other tangible form of expression is an individual matter.[15]

"I am very much afraid that the broad manner in which the Court has decided these cases will tend to obscure the peculiar responsibilities resting on state and federal courts in this field and encourage them to rely on easy labeling and jury verdicts as a substitute for facing up to the tough individual problems of constitutional judgment involved in every obscenity case." And Harlan believed that the constitutional limitations on federal power should be far more stringent than those imposed on the states. Except for hard-core pornography, which to the justice was not speech, in the constitutional sense anyway, the U.S. government lacked the power to enforce anti-obscenity statutes. "Congress has no substantive power over sexual morality," he said, but the states "bear direct responsibility for the protection of the local moral fabric."[16]

Chief Justice Warren, though concurring in the result, also doubted the wisdom of the broad language used by the majority. "The conduct of the defendant is the central issue, not the obscenity of a book or picture." Warren said it was okay in these cases for the state and federal governments to punish Roth and Alberts, because they were "plainly engaged in the commercial exploitation of the morbid and shameful craving for materials with prurient effect." However, that was all the cases presented, and that was all the Court needed to decide, the chief justice believed.[17]

Justice Douglas, joined by Justice Black, strongly dissented. He said that by sustaining the convictions "we make the legality of a publication turn on the purity of thought which a book or tract instills in the mind of the reader. If we were sure that impurity of sexual thoughts impelled to action, we would be on less dangerous ground in punishing the distributors of this sex literature." Douglas captured the essence of his, as well as Black's, ongoing pragmatism about First Amendment issues when he continued: "Government should be concerned with antisocial conduct, not with utterances. Freedom of expression can be suppressed if, and to the extent that, it is so closely brigaded with illegal action as to be an inseparable part of it." He concluded: "I have the same confidence in the ability of our people to reject noxious literature as I have in their capacity to sort out the true from the false in theology, economics, politics, or any other field."[18]

Despite the fact that the Supreme Court had upheld the obscenity statutes, the *Roth-Alberts* decision was said to have opened the floodgates for mail-order pornography. The definition of obscenity was a liberal one, conservatives believed, and the test itself required that material had to be taken as a whole, that it must be judged by community standards, and that the effect was on average adults rather than the most susceptible. Also the material in question had to be, in Brennan's indelible phrase, "utterly without redeeming social importance." That left but "hard-core" pornography assailable, the term Justice Potter Stewart later used to describe obscene matter underserving of constitutional protection.

Most lower-court judges interpreted *Roth-Alberts* liberally. Efforts to bar from the mails *Confidential* magazine and *Playboy* failed, for example, as did other such attempts by the post office under Postmaster General Summerfield. For

26

the first time, the country had, as a matter of federal constitutional law, a standard of obscenity that was applicable in both federal and state courts and which rendered invalid any more stringent standards created by legislators or judges.[19]

Roth-Alberts, in contributing a workable definition of obscenity, also made it clear that postal censorship, as then practiced, was unconstitutional. From the different Supreme Court opinions, we also can begin to learn of possible solutions to Justice Harlan's concern over the intractable nature of obscenity in general. First, Douglas and Black maintained there can be no suppression of any sexual expression, even that viewed as obscene, without evidence of a clear and present danger of harm. According to Harlan, the states can use criminal or civil sanctions but the federal government cannot, except against hard-core pornography, which is what the justice preferred as a guide for the states as well.

Brennan's compromise, a kind of balancing act, is more complicated. Rather than undermine the statutes, he would seek jury trials to ensure fair enforcement of the law and to determine community standards. Chief Justice Warren, meanwhile, said that it is the manner of use that should determine obscenity, not simply the quality of the art or literature. "To do otherwise," he said, "is to violate the First Amendment."[20] The recommendations of Warren and Harlan have serious merit, since together they would limit the scope of state regulation to cases where the pornographer's purpose is clearly exploitation. They would also require judicial surveillance to ensure that no work otherwise protected by the Constitution would be suppressed by legislation aimed at obscenity.

The *Roth-Alberts* test, with its five clear stipulations, hardly meant that obscenity law had become definite and precise: (1) average person; (2) community standards; (3) dominant theme; (4) whole work; and (5) prurient interest. Since the test applied to movies as well as to printed material, it would have to seek legal precision as individual situations arose. The Court in 1952 brought motion pictures under the ambit of the First Amendment, as was noted in the previous chapter. The Court now faced the task of refining the *Roth-Alberts* test. In some cases, like *Kingsley Interna-*

tional Pictures Corp. v. Regents of the University of New York, that meant extending protection to "ideological obscenity." In other cases, like *Smith v. California*, it meant adding more variables to the *Roth-Alberts* test.[21]

The immediate consequence of *Roth-Alberts* was a series of *per curiam* reversals of obscenity convictions, that is, opinions by the entire court rather than those of any one justice.[22] But the next full treatment by the Court continued to reveal strong differences among the justices. In *Kingsley International Pictures*, they wrote five separate opinions in considering a new problem—"ideological obscenity."

New York's motion picture censors had banned exhibition of a French film based on *Lady Chatterley's Lover*, the novel by D. H. Lawrence. The state's motion picture licensing law forbade permits to films that depicted, in whole or in part, "acts of sexual immorality, perversion, or lewdness, or which expressly or impliedly present[s] such acts as desirable, acceptable or proper pattern of behavior."[23] The film was banned, not because it was obscene, but because it portrayed adultery as desirable, acceptable, and proper behavior. The justices reversed unanimously, because the statute, they said, violated the First Amendment's basic guarantee of freedom to advocate ideas, even those which to some are immoral and unacceptable. Obscenity law per se was not an issue, so the ruling left to speculation what might have transpired had the justices agreed that the film was obscene and unprotected, therefore, by the Constitution.

Justice Stewart, who wrote the Court's opinion, said that the motion picture could not be suppressed merely because it advocated an idea, even advocacy of adultery, as proper behavior, "no less the advocacy of socialism or the single tax." The Constitution, he said, protected expression which is eloquent no less than that which is unconvincing. Justice Tom Clark found the prohibition of ideas impermissible and the statute itself vague. Black and Douglas reiterated their view that all prior censorship of motion pictures violated the First and Fourteenth Amendments. Frankfurter found less problem with the law than with its application in the *Lady Chatterley* case. He recommended case-by-case determinations.

28

To this, Black responded that the justices seemed especially unsuited to make such individualized value judgments.[24]

Harlan, too, found the law's application to the film unconstitutional, but not the law itself. He viewed the film, as was his custom in such cases, and saw it as a depiction of nothing more than a "somewhat unusual, and rather pathetic, 'love triangle,' lacking in anything that could properly be termed obscene or inciting the commission of adultery." Frankfurter, who also watched the movie, confessed: "As one whose taste in art and literature hardly qualifies him for the avant-garde, I am more than surprised . . . that the New York authorities should have banned 'Lady Chatterley's Lover.' To assume that this motion picture would have offended [even] Victorian moral sensibilities is to rely on the stuffiest of Victorian conventions."[25]

Kingsley International Pictures, in sum, resulted in the nine justices agreeing that the law simply did not apply to the film under question. They said the ban was illegal and should be lifted. A five-member majority also declared that the censorship standard—banning films portraying immoral conduct as acceptable behavior—was unconstitutional. They said that the New York statute was invalid under the First Amendment as it applied to the states via the Fourteenth Amendment. Black and Douglas, absolutists on First Amendment issues, wrote separately to say that *all* prior censorship of motion pictures violates the Constitution. Clark, on the other hand, thought the law too vague, and Harlan, whose view Frankfurter joined, thought the film's depiction of triangular love "pathetic" but neither obscene nor corruptive of public morals. Frankfurter, alone, added that, apart from the constitutionality of the statute, the law could not be applied to the film in question. Theirs was a narrow view of the case. What one learned from *Kingsley International Pictures* is that any antiexpressive sex law had to be confined to a serious infraction of the *Roth-Alberts* standard. The Court simply upheld existing constitutional law.

Meanwhile, on the opposite end of the country, Los Angeles had an ordinance making it unlawful for anyone to possess an obscene or indecent book in a place of business where books were sold or kept for sale. Eleazer Smith was one such bookseller. When Smith was prosecuted under the city ordinance, he objected on the ground that it was an imposition of "strict liability," that is, mere possession with no requirement of *scienter*, knowledge of the contents of the books he offered for sale. Smith protested that a bookseller could be convicted with no showing that the material was in fact obscene. The county court said that the city, acting within the scope of its police powers, had a right to protect its citizens against the sale of articles dangerous or deleterious to the public or contrary to public morals. The Supreme Court reversed in December 1959 and thereby added to the *Roth-Alberts* test the requirement that, before a person can be convicted for selling obscene books, the state must first prove that the bookseller had knowledge of the contents of the books.[26]

Smith v. California generated five opinions, but the entire Court was in agreement that the Los Angeles ordinance, though aimed at obscene matter, had such a tendency to inhibit protected expression that it could not stand. The ordinance imposed criminal sanctions on a bookseller if an obscene book were found in his store. The strict liability feature—"sell at your peril"—imposed an undue inhibition on book vending, declared the Court's majority. "We think this . . . would tend seriously . . . to restrict the dissemination of books which are not obscene, by penalizing booksellers, even though they had not the slightest notice of the character of the books they sold." The justices said that such self-censorship, compelled by the state, would be censorship affecting the whole public. "Through it, the distribution of all books, both obscene and not obscene, would be impeded."[27]

Justice Black wanted the opinion more sweeping, urging separately that no government agency, including Congress and the Supreme Court, had the power to subordinate speech and press to what it thinks are more important issues. "If, as it seems, we are on the way to national censorship, I think it timely to suggest again that there are grave doubts in my mind as to the desirability or constitutionality of this Court's becoming a Supreme Board of censors—reading

30

books and viewing television performances to determine whether, if permitted, they might adversely affect the morals of the people throughout the many diversified local communities in this vast country." Douglas, relying on his dissent in *Roth-Alberts*, added that neither the Court nor legislatures had power "to weigh the values of speech or utterance against silence." While he found the book in question repulsive, efforts to suppress its publication and distribution were repugnant.[28]

Frankfurter, concurring, said the trial court had violated the Fourteenth Amendment's due process clause by excluding the testimony of qualified witnesses on prevailing literary standards and moral criteria by which comparable works were deemed not obscene. Harlan found the conviction defective because he, too, believed the trial judge had denied attempts to introduce evidence of community standards. However, neither justice offered a definition of community standards, but each put this part of the *Roth-Alberts* test at the center of the entire obscenity dilemma.

Frankfurter, whose argument for community standards is the strongest and longest of the justices, went so far in *Smith v. California* as to assert this test criterion as "a right implicit in the very nature of the legal concept of obscenity" in order "to enlighten the judgment of the tribunal, be it the jury or as in this case the judge, regarding prevailing literary and moral community standards and to do so through qualified experts." He continued:

> Community standards or the psychological or physiological consequences of questioned literature can as a matter of fact hardly be established except through experts. [To] exclude such expert testimony is in effect to exclude as irrelevant evidence that goes to the very essence of the defense and therefore to the constitutional safeguards of due process. The determination of obscenity no doubt rests with judge or jury. Of course the testimony of experts would not replace judge or jury in determining the ultimate question whether the particular book is obscene, any more than the testimony of experts relating to the state of the art in patent suits determines the patentability of con-

troverted device. There is no external measuring rod for obscenity. [I] would make the right to introduce such evidence
a requirement of due process in obscenity prosecutions.[29]

Harlan, who agreed, tied this part of the *Roth-Alberts* test
directly to the "substantive right" of due process, essentially
Frankfurter's position. "The community cannot, where liberty of speech and press are at issue, condemn that which it
generally tolerates," Harlan said. While the government may
not be debarred from regarding trial courts as the embodi-
ment of community standards, he noted, it is not privileged
to rebuff all efforts to enlighten or persuade the trier of fact.
But neither did he believe, however, that expert testimony
should be compelled, although that is normally the most
convenient and practical method of acquiring proof. The
judge, in *Smith*, had denied every effort to introduce evidence bearing on community standards.[30]

Frankfurter's concurring view implies, as does Harlan's,
that the Court had yet to clarify, and would leave for the
future, the meaning of its requirement that a book be judged
obscene on the basis of contemporary community standards.
One detects in Harlan's opinion the need for the convergence
of two factors, public taste and artistic merit, the former to
be determined by the judge and jury and the latter by the
testimony of experts. Unsuitable, it appeared, was the judgment solely of the court and its assorted members.

Roth-Alberts and its progeny turn out to have been satisfactory in liberalizing obscenity regulation, but not so satisfactory in dissipating confusion on finding a legal test for
obscenity. Justice Brennan had, in effect, withdrawn constitutional protection from obscenity on the basis of what has
been called the two-level theory of free speech—freedom for
the thought we hate, no freedom for the candor we deplore,
speech, that is, "utterly without redeeming social importance." Black and Douglas advocated no suppression unless
there was a clear and present danger that antisocial behavior
would result. A test of the "common conscience of the community" was repellent to them, for that could not be applied
as well to religion, economics, and politics. Chief Justice
Warren said it was the conduct of the purveyor, not only the

content of the material, that should be judged; Frankfurter wanted adjudication on a case-by-case basis, and he emphasized the need for community standards, popular ones as well as professional. Harlan and Stewart urged protection of all but hard-core pornography, and Harlan also nearly always supported a state's right (but not the federal government) to regulate obscenity.[31]

By the end of the 1950s, the U.S. Supreme Court had reasserted its authority and, in the words of one historian, "no longer could be viewed as the mincing, acquiescent, issue-dodging body it had been under [Chief Justice Fred M.] Vinson."[32] Led by a Republican, Earl Warren, sitting under a Republican president, Dwight Eisenhower, who had appointed him, the Court's activism produced criticism in the civil rights area in general and with freedom of expression in particular. But its actions in the area of speech also produced some precision as manifested in *Roth-Alberts* and progeny.

Hard-core pornography—verbal or pictorial expression without any redeeming social importance—became better defined and, possibly, better understood. A work's dominant theme, not its isolated passages, became the focal point for judging. Ignorance became bliss, indeed, for booksellers unaware of alleged obscenities on their shelves. Most important, independent judicial review, including expert testimony, was to be made available. What appeared to some as liberal activism, seemed to others as more precision on the part of the Court in dealing with obscenity.

In January 1961, the Court attacked broadside all motion picture censorship. But, instead of addressing the question of obscenity or the issue of censorship, the five-to-four Court in *Times Film Corp. v. Chicago* hinged its decision on whether an issue is even capable of judicial resolution, an abstract question of law. Courts deal with "justiciable controversy" as distinguished from hypothetical situations.[33] The issue in *Times Film Corp.* was if the ambit of constitutional protection included absolute freedom to exhibit any kind of motion picture at least once. Justice Clark, for the majority, said that Chicago's ordinance requiring submission of films prior to their public showing was not "void on its face," adding that the claim of absolute privilege against prior restraint under the First Amendment was "without sanction in our cases." Because the filmmaker had refused to submit the film, *Don Juan*, to the board of censors, obscenity questions were not in question; the Court, instead, ruled solely on the basic authority of the board.[34]

Justice Harlan joined the majority, but he cautioned Clark against "conveying the impression that we are saying that this sort of prior restraint is good in all circumstances, that is, whatever may be the character of the superior state interest, vis-à-vis First Amendment rights (e.g., obscenity, national emergency, subversive activity, etc.) and no matter what the subject matter of the restraint is (e.g., movies, newspapers, etc.)." Then he added: "I suggest that it would be well to make clear in the last paragraph that we are dealing only with obscenity and movies." Such a statement, while appearing to endorse selective prior restraint, was more likely an appeal for stricter procedural standards on state and local censorship codes. Harlan liked to follow legal precedent and was always a stickler for administrative precision.[35]

Chief Justice Warren, joined by Black, Douglas, and Brennan, said that the constitutional guarantee of freedom of speech prohibited unlimited censorship of films before exhibition through a system of licensing. Warren's dissent is one of the more comprehensive ever written by a member of the Court on the subject of censorship. It includes quotations from a number of historic sources, including John Milton, who wrote in *Areopagitica*: "If he [the censor] be of such worth as behooves him, there cannot be a more tedious and unpleasing journeywork, a greater loss of time levied upon his head, then to be made the perpetual reader of unchosen books and pamphlets . . . we may easily foresee what kind of licensers we are to expect hereafter, either ignorant, imperious, and remiss, or basely pecuniary."[36]

Warren said censorship tended to engulf everything, which in Chicago alone included newsreels of policemen shooting at labor pickets, films criticizing Nazi Germany, the movie *Anatomy of a Murder* because it contained the words *rape* and *contraceptive*, and a scene from Walt Disney's *Vanishing Prairie* showing the birth of a buffalo. And he noted cases in other cities, for instance, the one-man

◆ DOMINANT THEME

board in Memphis that banned all of Ingrid Bergman's movies because the censor judged her soul "black as the soot of hell." Warren concluded: "The censor's sword pierces deeply into the heart of free expression."[37]

Times Film Corp. was pivotal four years later in a ruling that dealt primarily with obscenity, *Freedman v. Maryland*, when a unanimous Court found that the First Amendment had been violated by a Maryland law that required exhibitors to submit films to a board of censors before their public showing. Three years after *Freedman*, a revised version of the Chicago censorship ordinance came before the Court in *Teitel Film Corp. v. Cusack*. Seven justices in a *per curiam* opinion agreed that the Chicago procedures violated both the Constitution and judicial safeguards against the dangers of such a system.[38]

Meanwhile, *Roth-Alberts* underwent more technical refinement in 1961, when the Supreme Court struck at the coercive tactics of public officials in seizing allegedly obscene publications. In *Marcus v. Search Warrant*, the justices questioned Missouri's procedure for the search and seizure of matter deemed obscene. Five retail newsstand operators and a wholesale distributor of books, magazines, and newspapers in the Kansas City area sued when a judge issued search warrants without looking at any of the publications and upon only cursory police knowledge of their contents. Approximately 11,000 copies of 280 publications were removed from the shops. The hearing was not held for two weeks, after which the judge took another seven weeks to decide that 100 of the seized magazines were obscene and ordered the remaining 180 returned to their owners.[39]

Justice Brennan, for seven members, reasoned that the seizure of obscene publications is a matter so potentially injurious to freedom of expression as to be tolerated only when "hedged about" with safeguards. While the use of search-and-seizure power to suppress publications is not novel or new, it was used so sweepingly in the Missouri case, Brennan said, as to withhold from the market for more than two months publications not found obscene. Unlike *Kingsley Books v. Brown*, which allowed for limited injunctions against obscene books and magazines, Marcus dealt with a "mass seizure" of a "broad range" of items, "far more thoroughgoing and drastic" than any such restraint previously upheld by the Court.[40]

Marcus also brings to mind *Smith v. California*, which held that before a person can be convicted for selling obscene books the state must prove *scienter*—that the seller had knowledge of the contents of the books. Thus, *Marcus*, like *Smith* before it, adjusted, but did not outlaw, state search-and-seizure procedures in keeping with the new *Roth-Alberts* guidelines.

Beset by such niggling in its attempt to settle the intractable obscenity problem, the Court in 1962 decided to give a plenary, or full, review of the constitutional and administrative problems. *Manual Enterprises Inc. v. Day* dealt with three fundamental issues: (1) authority of the post office to bar obscene matter under the Comstock Law; (2) effect of the act's declaring unmailable magazines that carry advertisements for obscene merchandise; and (3) meaning of the *Roth-Alberts* definition of obscenity.[41]

The justices could not agree on a single opinion, but six of them concurred that the Comstock Act did not permit the postmaster general to exclude matter from the mails on his own determination of what is obscene. Specifically, the justices said that the post office could not bar a magazine without proof of the publisher's knowledge that the advertisements inside promoted obscene merchandise.[42]

Justice Harlan, joined by Stewart in the decision's central, and most substantive, opinion, said that the magazines designed to appeal to male homosexuals were not patently offensive and that the government had failed to show that the publishers knew that advertisers were offering obscene matter for sale. Harlan added yet another prong to the *Roth-Alberts* test when he maintained that patent offensiveness, along with prurient interest, must be demonstrated in order to declare a work obscene.

Brennan, joined by Chief Justice Warren and Justice Douglas, said that the Comstock Act did not authorize the post office to determine obscenity; that had to be decided at a trial. Clark, the lone dissenter, believed that Congress had authorized the post office to remove obscene matter, even

36

advertising matter with or without a *scienter* requirement. Black concurred without an opinion. Frankfurter and Byron White did not participate in the decision. But it is Harlan's long opinion that is important for the light it sheds on the question of obscenity in general and on the *Roth-Alberts* test in particular.

In March 1960, the postmaster at Alexandria, Virginia, withheld delivery of six parcels containing some four hundred copies of magazines consisting largely of photos of nude, or "near-nude," male models, their names and the name and address of the photographer. The magazines— *MANual, Trim,* and *Grecian Guild Pictorial*—also contained advertisements by other photographers offering nudist pictures for sale. Copies were seized and the post office judicial officer found them obscene under the Comstock Act. The district court and the court of appeals for the District of Columbia upheld the seizure and ban.

Justice Harlan, in applying *Roth-Alberts*, said that the magazines could not be "deemed so offensive on their face as to affront current community standards of decency." He found the magazines "dismally unpleasant, uncouth, and tawdry," appealing only "to the unfortunate persons whose patronage they were aimed at capturing." But he could not label them legally obscene. As for determining offensiveness, Harlan advocated a "national standard of decency" for a country whose population, he said, reflects many different ethnic and cultural backgrounds. He found "intolerable" the denying of some sections of the nation access to material on the basis of the community standards prevailing in another area. But he left open the question of whether Congress could legally defer to a smaller geographical area.[43]

Justice Harlan described the limits of such congressional deference as if they were incontrovertible. "We need not decide whether Congress could constitutionally prescribe a lesser geographical framework for judging [obscenity] which would not have the intolerable consequence of denying some sections of the country access to material, there deemed acceptable, which in others might be considered offensive to prevailing community standards of decency."[44]

The Harlan approach, which perhaps is nothing more

than a rearranging of the *Roth-Alberts* test, is worth remembering for what it suggests as well as for what it actually says: that community, whether local or national, is a matter to be decided by the offending material's *primary* audience. To hold so might protect even hard-core pornography, which may disgust the average person but appeal to a narrow group that seeks it out. In fact, it was not but two years later that Justice Brennan seized upon Harlan's language as support for a national approach to defining obscenity.[45]

Among the reactions to Harlan's community standards exhortation in *Manual Enterprises* was an interesting exchange of letters in 1962 between the justice and Dean Joseph O'Meara of the Notre Dame law school. "I have the greatest skepticism as regards the possibility of identifying community standards or mores, that is, the public morality," wrote Dean O'Meara. He said that some moral issues, like divorce, provoke a rather universal response, but others, such as segregation, may not elicit the same response in all parts of the country. Harlan admitted that the community standards test was far from ideal, but that much of the difficulty would disappear were the Court to adopt, at least in federal cases, a hard-core pornography test for judging obscenity. "The concept [a yardstick for deciding the constitutionality of suppression of challenged material] is not a novel one in our jurisprudence, as witness, for example, the prudent or average man test for judging of conduct in negligence cases."[46]

Though obscenity itself may receive no protection from the First or Fourteenth Amendments, the Supreme Court has several times passed on the constitutionality of procedures used to ferret out obscene materials. Procedures were in question in *Kingsley Books Inc. v. Brown, Smith v. California*, and *Marcus v. Search Warrant. Bantam Books v. Sullivan*, the last decision to be discussed in this chapter, raised the question of whether a state may informally regulate allegedly obscene materials by circulating publicly lists of such magazines and books. With only Justice Harlan dissenting, the Court ruled in February 1963 that a system of informal sanctions employed by the Rhode Island Commission to Encourage Morality in Youth abridged First Amendment freedoms.[47]

38

The state legislature had created the commission "to educate the public concerning any book, picture, pamphlet, ballad, printed paper or other thing containing obscene, indecent, or impure language, or manifestly tending to the corruption of the youth."[48] In practice, the commission notified book and magazine distributors in a series of official letters that certain publications had been declared objectionable by a majority of the body for sale or display to youths under eighteen. The letters solicited cooperation, but they also intimated that police action and prosecution might follow. Max Silverstein and Sons, exclusive wholesaler of Bantam Books throughout Rhode Island, had received at least thirty-five such notices, and each time stopped further circulation of the listed publications.

When the case made its way to the Supreme Court, Brennan, for eight brethren, wrote that "informal censorship" may sufficiently inhibit the circulation of publications as to warrant relief because the commission, acting under the color of state law, stopped circulation of publications to many parts of the state. While the dealers were "free" to ignore the notices, the blacklists, Brennan said, plainly served as instruments of regulation independent of laws against obscenity. The commission's operation was a "scheme of state censorship affectuated by extralegal sanctions; [it] acted as an agency not to advise but to suppress."[49]

Harlan criticized his colleagues for their failure to fix principles for the state court to follow on remand of the case. Harlan and Clark, who concurred in the result, advised the commission to abandon its pretensions of power, but thought that the Constitution permitted it to identify publications as obscene or objectionable, communicate its views to distributors and anyone else, and enlist the aid of police officials against law violators. Harlan's plea was for more precision on the part of the Supreme Court.

Justice Harlan appeared also to want to help Rhode Island deal with the problem of juvenile delinquency. He said that none of the majority's concerns—government censorship, absence of safeguards for protecting nonobscene material, and adult access to tainted though protected material—is of "overriding weight" in the context of what to him seemed not an effort to obstruct free expression but an attempt to cope with a "most baffling social problem." He found controlling the absence of legal consequences, unlike the licensing system upheld in *Times Film Corp. v. Chicago* and the injunction procedure sustained in *Kingsley Books v. Brown*. The Rhode Island index of offensive material did not bar or penalize "in any way" continued distribution of a tainted work. And judicial review remained available to anyone aggrieved by a commission decision or in a prosecution by the state for obscenity.[50]

Precision in law generally as well as in "the intractable obscenity problem" specifically was Justice Harlan's consistent plea. The justice's biographer, Tinsley E. Yarbrough, believes that, while Harlan never made his position on obscenity entirely explicit, his various opinions indicated the search for a "workable means by which the Court could partially extricate itself and inferior tribunals from a continuing constitutional quagmire." Under his hard and fast standard, federal obscenity regulations would be presumed invalid and few, if any, prosecutions upheld. On the other hand, under the broad leeway he believed states should be accorded by the Fourteenth Amendment due process guarantee, virtually no state obscenity convictions would be overturned. "In neither federal nor state cases under Harlan's formula, therefore, would the outcome of individual disputes have turned on the sorts of subtle determinations the inherently vague obscenity formulae made it exceedingly difficult to make or predict." Whatever the thinking underlying his position, Harlan adhered to the end that, as he wrote a friend, "the preservation and assertion of state authority [held] the best promise for effective legal measures" in the obscenity area.[51]

40

III

Community Standards

I shall not today attempt further to define the kinds of material I understand to be embraced within [the] shorthand description ["hard-core pornography"]; and perhaps I could never succeed in intelligibly doing so. But I know it when I see it, and the motion picture involved in this case is not that.

—Justice Potter Stewart,
Jacobellis v. Ohio

WITH THIS now-famous definition, Justice Stewart joined Harlan and Brennan as a serious player in the Supreme Court's unfolding, and never-ending, obscenity drama. He said in *Jacobellis v. Ohio* that, while it was possible to read the *Roth-Alberts* decision in a variety of ways, he thought that the Court had confirmed, "at least by negative implication," that the Constitution limited criminal laws in this area to hard-core pornography. Brennan, meanwhile, returned to center stage in the Court's 1963 term, when the justices wrote ten different opinions in deciding three cases, *Jacobellis v. Ohio, A Quantity of Copies of Books v. Kansas*, and *Grove Press v. Gerstein*, all reported the same day, 22 June 1964.[1]

Brennan, who had written the Court's landmark rulings seven years before, reaffirmed *Roth-Alberts* in *Jacobellis*. He noted that the community standard for judging obscenity should be national, then stressed that the primary test for determining censurable material was whether it was "utterly without redeeming social importance." Although six justices voted to reverse the Ohio courts, they again were unable to agree on a single opinion. With Brennan in calling for reversal were Arthur Goldberg, Black, Douglas, White, and, as noted, Stewart. Clark and Harlan dissented with Chief Justice Warren. In *A Quantity of Books*, the Court narrowed the range of material that could be branded obscene and struck down a procedure for curbing such material. In *Grove Press*, five justices reversed without opinion a Florida conviction of Henry Miller's *Tropic of Cancer*. What is more important, *Jacobellis* marked the justices' first full discussion since *Roth-Alberts* of the specific merits of a work called obscene.

The makeup of the Court had changed in the interim. The majority in *Roth-Alberts* consisted of Brennan, Burton, Clark, Frankfurter, and Whittaker. By the time of *Jacobellis*, President Eisenhower had replaced the retiring Harold Burton with Potter Stewart in 1958; and President Kennedy had replaced the disabled Charles Whittaker with Byron White, and Felix Frankfurter, who retired after twenty-three years on the Court, with Arthur Goldberg, both in 1962. However, none of the changes signaled much alteration in the Court's overall liberal direction, at least not at that juncture.

Nico Jacobellis, manager of a motion picture theater in Cleveland Heights, had been convicted on counts of possession and exhibition of an obscene film in violation of Ohio law. *Les Amants* (The Lovers) told the story of an unhappy marriage, the wife's falling in love with a younger man, and depicted an explicit but brief love scene toward the end. (Justice Goldberg said of this scene that it was so fragmentary and fleeting that only a "censor's alert" would make an audience conscious that something "questionable" had been portrayed.) Jacobellis was fined $2,500 and sentenced to the workhouse if the fine was not paid. His conviction by three judges in Cuyahoga County was upheld by the Ohio Supreme Court.

Brennan, joined by Goldberg, reiterated the constitutional test as first enunciated in *Roth-Alberts*, that "whether to the average person, applying contemporary community stan-

42

dards, the dominant theme of the material taken as a whole appeals to prurient interest." He added that obscenity was excluded from protection only because it was "utterly without redeeming social importance."[2]

On the equally important question of the appropriateness of independent judicial review, the justice reaffirmed the principle that, in obscenity cases, as in all others involving rights derived from the First Amendment guarantees of free expression, the Court "cannot avoid making an independent constitutional judgment on the facts of the case as to whether the material involved is constitutionally protected." He said the due process clause of the Fourteenth Amendment required such high court review; to do otherwise would be an "abnegation of judicial supervision in this field . . . inconsistent with our duty to uphold the constitutional guarantees."[3]

But the most important new wrinkle was Brennan's clarification of what he called an "incorrect reading" of *Roth-Alberts*, that the test had to be determined on the basis of the "national community," as first expressed by Judge Learned Hand in 1913 in *United States v. Kennerley*. Brennan believed that Judge Hand had not referred to state and local communities, but, rather, to the community in the sense of " 'society at large . . . the public, or people in general.' " The concept of obscenity for Judge Hand would have a "varying meaning from time to time"—not from county to county, or town to town. Some things will always be shocking to the public taste, Judge Hand said, but "the vague subject matter is left to the gradual development of general notions about what is decent."[4]

In order to reinforce his position, Brennan called upon Harlan's point in *Manual Enterprises Inc. v. Day*, that a standard based on a particular local community would have "the intolerable consequence of denying some sections of the country access to material, there deemed acceptable, which in others might be considered offensive to prevailing community standards of decency." Brennan said the Court had consistently refused to tolerate a result whereby the limits of free expression would vary with state boundaries and create

43

Community Standards ◆

barriers for localities where a work might not be held obscene. "It is, after all, a national Constitution we are expounding," he concluded.[5]

Justice Black, joined by Douglas, concurred on the broad ground that a conviction for exhibiting a motion picture abridges freedom of the press, safeguarded by the First Amendment and made obligatory on the states by the Fourteenth. Justice Stewart accused the Court of trying to define, in *Roth-Alberts* and elsewhere, what may be indefinable. He had himself come to the conclusion that obscenity laws were limited to hard-core pornography, which he could not describe but which he recognized upon sight.

Chief Justice Warren, in a dissent with Clark, went further. "I believe that there is no provable 'national standard' and perhaps that there should be none. At all events, this Court has not been able to enunciate one, and it would be unreasonable to expect local courts to divine one." But he recommended that "community" implied local community, which is the "only way . . . to obviate . . . this Court sitting as the Super Censor of all the obscenity purveyed throughout the Nation." Simply, Warren and Clark wanted *Roth-Alberts* to stand unaltered.[6]

Justice Harlan, predictably, said that he would make the test one of rationality for the states and that they should not be prohibited from banning any material which, taken as a whole, had been found in judicial proceedings "to treat sex in a fundamentally offensive manner." After years of frustration, Harlan had come to a conclusion: "The more I see of these obscenity cases the more convinced I become that in permitting the States wide, but not federally unrestricted, scope . . . , while holding the Federal Government with a tight rein, lies the best promise for achieving a sensible accommodation between the public interest sought to be served by obscenity laws and protection of genuine rights of free expression." And he said that the application of general constitutional tests must "necessarily be pricked out on a case-by-case basis."[7]

While *Jacobellis* of 1964 contributed little new law beyond that already suggested, if not settled, by *Roth-Alberts* of 1957, it was nevertheless valuable as a vehicle for the justices to reexamine, and refine, their previous opinions and definitions. Brennan's view of obscenity, for example, seemed to approach Stewart's hard-core category. One was still left, however, with little guidance for determining the obscenity of a specific work. When applying Brennan's test, the first thing to decide was a work's merit, its lack of social importance, and, next, its degree of prurience. At what point in the scheme did *Les Amants* become *not* obscene? Brennan's answer came in one short paragraph at the very end of his opinion. He said that the film had been favorably reviewed in a number of national publications and had been rated among the best films of its year "by at least two critics of national stature," that it had been shown in approximately 100 large American cities, and, finally, that nearly all the objections were directed at the one brief, though explicit, love scene. Justice Goldberg, who may have come closer than Brennan in applying the *Roth-Alberts* formula, said he found the film not obscene because of its "dominant theme."[8]

As the first revisiting of the landmark *Roth-Alberts* decision, *Jacobellis* still left its share of unanswered questions. There remained, for instance, the validity of the average person in deciding obscenity. Brennan had suggested in his final comments that this hypothetical person might include an expert, but that was not made an explicit part of either *Roth-Alberts* or *Jacobellis*. As one observer noted after the *Jacobellis* ruling, "Taken as a whole, the . . . decision represents a progressive step in the evolution of obscenity standards . . . and at least defines methods for approaching an area which intellectually and practically defies any concrete delineation."[9]

In *A Quantity of Books*, reported the same day as *Jacobellis*, a state law authorized prosecutors to obtain warrants for the seizure of allegedly obscene material prior to any adversary hearing to determine obscenity. As they had with *Jacobellis*, the seven justices, led by Brennan's central opinion, did not agree on a single view. Brennan, with Goldberg, White, and Warren, deemed the Kansas procedure unconstitutional for failure to prescribe a hearing. Black and Douglas found the procedural issue irrelevant, and said that book burning, so to speak, violates the First and Fourteenth Amendments, pure and simple. Stewart found no fault with the procedures, but agreed with Brennan because the books were not hard-core pornography. Harlan and Clark dissented on the grounds that Kansas could find the books obscene and that the Constitution does not require an adversary hearing before seizure. Harlan accused Brennan of straitjacketing a state's legitimate attempt to protect what it considers an important societal interest.

During the 1960s, as the Supreme Court barely managed to keep its head above water over obscenity, the "culture war" of that decade, so named by social historian Loren Baritz, turned out to be a threat to more than one cultural convention. Sometimes overlapping, sometimes not, but mutually supportive, the war was fought over morality, radicalism, civil rights, and alienation. All were in repudiation of middle-class values, demanding reevaluation of the past's usefulness (the anti-intellectualism that lingers still), suspicion of established institutional and personal authority, trust only in peers, refusal to accept previous middle-class dictates of living, dressing, eating, and loving, and a commitment to greater democracy and equality. "Most upsetting to the culture's custodians was the new morality and its fashions," according to Baritz, who argues convincingly that, while the civil rights movement of the 1960s, though stunted, also had durable impact, the least impactful was political radicalism. But the changes in morality, a rekindling, as it were, of the sexual assaults of the 1920s and the post–World War II period, dominated the social scene.[10]

"The pill," approved by the FDA in 1960, marked the decoupling of sex and procreation. John D'Emilio and Estelle B. Freedman, historians of sexuality in America, note that the contraceptive revolution moved hand in hand with changes in both sexual behavior and attitudes. While the advent of oral contraception, and the other devices that followed, brought some stability to the rate of premarital sex, which had jumped sharply in the 1920s, it also altered the code of sexual ethics to make such behavior morally acceptable in the 1960s. "What was daring and noncomformist in the earlier period appeared commonplace a generation later." To marriage itself, couples brought new expectations of plea-

◆ COMMUNITY STANDARDS

sure, satisfaction, and mutual enjoyment, encouraged by a more explicit "advice literature that emphasized the sexual component of conjugal life."[11]

The lasting effect of these societal changes, certainly more fixed than litigation affecting pornography, became clearer in 1965, when the Supreme Court invalidated a Connecticut law forbidding the dissemination of birth control information as a violation of a right to marital privacy. This was *Griswold v. Connecticut*, which overturned *Poe v. Ullman* of 1961, which in turn had upheld a challenge to the old Comstockian statute making it a crime to use contraceptives. Connecticut also had a general accessory law allowing for the punishment of any person who aided another in committing an offense. *Poe* had been an attempt to get the law removed from the books, but the Court said that the law was never enforced and thus a moot issue. Meanwhile, the chronology of events, from the arrival of the pill to the Court's reversal on birth control, is somewhat less than causal, yet, one suspects, more than coincidental.[12]

Among Loren Baritz's several inspired generalities about the 1960s, this one captures a bit of the sociology within which the legal community functioned:

> The new fingering of sensation repudiated the entire universe the middle class had constructed for itself, the buttoned-up loving and living and working of the past. It celebrated what could be if people would only breathe freer, love easier, and follow the lead of spontaneity and joy. These refugees from the middle class sought release from crippling adherence to conventional values, including the value of work, competition, marriage, the family, patriotism, democracy, and equality. They sought freedom from oppressive social institutions and conventional authority, including the law, police, universities, politicians, and corporations.[13]

And these refugees detested the middle-class obsession with privacy, a more-than-interesting development since it was the various privacy rulings by the Supreme Court that enhanced, if not enabled, such antisocial behavior. Individualism, it seems, has a price.

Meanwhile, the Supreme Court justices addressed only one obscenity case in their 1964 term, *Freedman v. Maryland*, which dealt mainly with legal procedures rather than philosophical issues but the effect was to restrict even further the movie censor's authority. By the mid-1960s official censorship of motion pictures had been fast disappearing. As a friend of the court in *Freedman*, the American Civil Liberties Union pointed out that New York, Virginia, and Kansas were the only states with statutes similar to Maryland's and also that Chicago, Detroit, Fort Worth, and Providence were the only cities with similar ordinances. The *Freedman* decision necessarily affected those censorship laws as well as Maryland's.

Ronald L. Freedman, a Baltimore theater operator, was convicted in Baltimore criminal court of publicly exhibiting a film before submitting it to the board of censors. The Supreme Court held that the procedural aspects of Maryland's movie censorship law did not contain adequate safeguards against undue restrictions on otherwise protected expression. Without dissent, the justices struck down the procedures because (1) if the censor disapproved a film, it was up to the exhibitor to start judicial proceedings and prove the film was protected; (2) once the board had acted against a film, it could not be exhibited until after judicial review, no matter how protracted; and (3) the law contained no assurance of a prompt judicial decision. For these reasons, the conviction was unanimously reversed. More important, the decision probably hastened the death of all state and local film censorship boards.[14]

Brennan wrote for seven members, while Black and Douglas added their own concurrence. "I would put an end to all forms and types of censorship and give full literal meaning to the command of the First Amendment," said Douglas, leaving no doubt once more as to the absolutist position he shared with Justice Black over the years, especially on obscenity matters that, to them, seemed to defy judicial remedy.

Richard S. Randall, whose fine treatise on the psychological contradictions in the obscenity problem was used in chapter 1, provides insight into the judicial dilemma: "Argu-

48

ments abound over where to draw the lines for sexual expression: hence so many dissenting opinions. There are also many arguments about how those lines are best rationalized: hence so many concurring opinions." For example, in addition to the Brennan "prurient interest" requirement, the Stewart "hard-core" interpretation, and the Warren "intent" approach, the justices pursued throughout the 1960s other interesting, and sometimes creative, ways of controlling the intractable problem.[15]

But, in the decade since *Roth-Alberts*, despite their brave attempts, it had been impossible to obtain any Court consensus on obscenity. The three 1965 cases proved no exception. They produced fourteen opinions. Earl Warren and Abe Fortas were the only justices who did not write separately. Nevertheless, with three important cases decided during the term, the justices implied that obscenity might also vary with the circumstances of the material and the nature of the audience.

The first to be announced on 21 March 1966, *A Book Named 'John Cleland's Memoirs of a Woman of Pleasure' v. Attorney General of Massachusetts*, mainly reaffirmed the three-part *Roth-Alberts* test but emphasized the need to satisfy each criterion independently before the material could be condemned. The second, *Ginzburg v. United States*, developed the idea of variable obscenity by identifying obscene materials as those marketed to the public in a pandering way. And the third to be announced, *Mishkin v. New York*, warned that books appealing to "deviant" prurient interests and sexual practices may also be deemed obscene.[16]

Cleland's book, commonly known as *Fanny Hill*, was published originally in England in two volumes in 1748 and 1749 and contains repeated and extended descriptions of male sexual organs and acts of sexual intercourse. Sex between men is mentioned but condemned. With *Fanny Hill*, Cleland created the genre of the prostitute's confession or autobiography. His novel became eighteenth-century Europe's most notorious pornographic work, perhaps even the single most read pornographic novel of all time. It was translated into French only two years after its English publication and into many other languages during the nineteenth century.

And the book had been in the Massachusetts courts before, in 1821, in what is recorded as America's first literary obscenity case. A celebrated work, indeed!

Litigation involving *Fanny Hill* on its homecoming to these shores dated from when the book was reissued by G. P. Putnam's Sons in 1963. A large number of orders were placed by universities and public and private libraries, including the Library of Congress, which requested permission to translate the volume into Braille. According to Justice Douglas's tongue-in-cheek version of events, "The Commonwealth of Massachusetts instituted the suit . . . praying that the book be declared obscene so that the citizens of Massachusetts might be spared the necessity of determining for themselves whether or not to read it."[17]

Putnam's defended the book in three court cases. In New York it was cleared by a trial court, held obscene in an appellate judgment, then declared not obscene by the court of appeals. In Hackensack, New Jersey, a decision was handed down against the novel after trial. The Boston case was finally appealed to the Supreme Court after *Fanny Hill* was condemned in a lower court and in the Supreme Judicial Court of Massachusetts. Charles Rembar, Putnam's legal counsel in all three locales, remembers how the novel was much more vulnerable than either *Lady Chatterley's Lover* or Henry Miller's *Tropic of Cancer*, both also represented by him.

Rembar believes Cleland's book may have been victimized by censorship's dual tradition, one symbolized, for example, by *Ulysses* and *Tropic of Cancer*, the other by *Lady Chatterley's Lover* and *Fanny Hill*; the former because they are offensive; the latter because they arouse lust. "For most people *Ulysses* and *Tropic* are not enticing; *Lady Chatterley* and *Fanny* are." Also, in the one line of cases, public decency, rather than private morality, is at stake; in the other, it is sin, rather than the proprieties. "The one book is attacked because it repels, the other because it attracts; the one because it disgusts, the other because it allures." Rembar continues to illuminate the problem:

> The taboo against illicit sex is much stronger and more
> deeply rooted than the taboo against bad manners. Where

◆ COMMUNITY STANDARDS

the book makes sex unattractive, the court is able to say that it will hardly affect anyone's morals. Thus Judge Woolsey concluded his famous opinion by disapproving the aphrodisiac and approving the emetic.[18]

In a footnote to his memoir of pornography battles, both won and lost, Rembar opines that Lenny Bruce, if he had wanted to win his cases, would ultimately have prevailed against his tormentors because, in reality, offensiveness was the entire charge against him. The value of his social comment and the absence of eroticism would have won for him an appeal.

Fanny Hill went to trial in Boston in the spring of 1964, the prosecution arguing that the book was no more than a collection of sexual episodes, written to sell to those seeking titillation, without any social value, and, because of its continuous emphasis on sex, prurient and patently offensive. Rembar, for the defense, countered with the testimony of a number of literary authorities, all professors of English literature, among them John M. Bullitt of Harvard; Fred Holly Stocking of Williams College; Robert H. Sproat of Boston University; and Norman Holland of M.I.T.

Ira Konigsberg of Brandeis testified that *Fanny Hill* was "obviously more healthy" than certain contemporary novels. When challenged, he explained that of the three associates of Fanny in prostitution, one ends up married and the other two end up happy. "Various aspects of their professional life are attacked by Fanny at various times in the novel as being perverse or in bad taste or without love." Rembar also used "good reviews" by the critics V. S. Pritchett and Bridget Brophy.[19] Witnesses' testimony was summarized by a member of the court:

> In view of one or another or all . . . the book is a minor "work of art" having "literary merit" and "historical value" and containing a good deal of "deliberate, calculated comedy." It is a piece of "social history of interest to anyone who is interested in fiction as a way of understanding society in the past." The book contains no dirty words and its language "functions to create a distance, even when the sexual experiences are portrayed."[20]

Community Standards ◆

In New Jersey, meanwhile, the trial closed with the testimony of two Rutgers University professors of English, Paul Fussell Jr. and David Burrows. Rembar recalls that each managed to make some literary comments that sounded fresh despite anything that had gone on before. Ronald Picinich, who tried the case for the prosecution, devoted a great deal of cross-examination to Fussell, who, in Rembar's words, was "cool and resourceful" and, with the possible exception of Professor Stocking in Boston, knew *Fanny Hill* better than any other witness in any of the trials. Fussell said he had read the book twelve times.

> "Did it," Rembar asked, "improve or diminish in your eyes as you reread it?"
> "It improved as a literary work," he answered, "it diminished as an erotic work."[21]

Judge Morris Pashman took six months to render his verdict—against *Fanny Hill*. After the New Jersey trial, and before Pashman had arrived at a decision, the Court of Appeals in New York held the book not obscene, making the third reversal in that case. Later, however, and still before the New Jersey decision, Judge Donald M. Macaulay in Boston held the book obscene. The net effect of all this, according to Rembar, was pretty much an equilibrium—eight judges had ruled against the book, and seven had ruled in its favor. "The conclusion that the New Jersey judge eventually reached was probably no different from what it would have been if none of the other cases had taken place." By the time Pashman issued his opinion, the matter was largely academic. The Boston case was already on appeal to the state's Supreme Judicial Court, and it was the Massachusetts decision that eventually made its way to the U.S. Supreme Court.[22]

Optimism was running high. After *Jacobellis*, a year earlier, the belief was that it was now extremely difficult, perhaps impossible, for a book to be declared obscene. It was assumed, if nothing else, that the social-value theory enunciated in *Roth-Alberts* and confirmed and expanded in *Jacobellis* was firmly established. Attorney Rembar, however, was fearful that the justices would be overly cautious and too much influenced by the companion cases, *Ginzburg* and

52

Mishkin, both highly vulnerable if a pattern of conduct, such as Ginzburg's pandering, rather than a book, was the issue. "I was uneasy at the thought that *Ginzburg* and *Mishkin* might furnish the Justices their next opportunity to speak on the interaction of the First Amendment and anti-obscenity laws." After all, the Court had recently ruled without opinion on a Florida judgment against the publisher of Henry Miller's *Tropic of Cancer*, another Rembar case. There were neither briefs nor oral argument, and the decision was made simply on the papers filed with the petition for *certiorari*, the directive to the court below to send up the case. While the Florida judgment was summarily reversed, and the novel cleared of obscenity, only five justices chose to address the merits of the case and felt that an appeal should be granted. They did not write their customary opinions but referred instead to their simultaneous ruling in *Jacobellis*.[23]

Rembar, in arguing *Memoirs* before the Court, urged that if qualified critical opinion believed that a book had literary merit—the social value theory—it could not be considered legally obscene according to *Roth-Alberts*: "Where you have highly qualified witnesses who come to court and stake their professional reputations on their analysis of the book and its values—where you have published reviews and critical essays, by people who have no interest in the outcome of the litigation, which also establish that value—then, on the record, the book is entitled to the protection of the First Amendment."[24] This newfound respectability for questionable works, bestowed by expert witnesses, gave added status to literary criticism in obscenity cases. Earlier in the century, as Felice Flanery Lewis recalls, such critical judgment had sometimes been allowed in a court hearing, sometimes not. "Even when judges permitted critical reviews or testimony to be introduced, they generally indicated that such opinions were considered as limited 'aids to the court.' " With events that culminated in the *Roth-Alberts* decision and its interpretations, the views of literary authorities indirectly became, for a time at least, the decisive factor in an obscenity case.[25]

Fanny Hill, the popular title of Cleland's novel, is the story of a penniless orphan, aged fifteen, who goes to London and enters the bordello of Mrs. Brown thinking that she will earn her keep legitimately. She has no intention of becoming a prostitute, but her curiosity is soon piqued and her sensuality aroused as she witnesses others in the house having sex. She is nearly raped when Mrs. Brown, in Fanny's words, arranges to secure "a good market for my maidenhead." Before she loses her virginity, Fanny falls in love with Charles, who subsequently takes her maidenhead in Mrs. Brown's house. Eventually, they are happily married but soon parted when Charles is sent to sea by his father. After countless other adventures—including those at Mrs. Cole's very exclusive house of prostitution—and after living for several months with an elderly man who leaves her his fortune when he dies, Fanny is reunited with Charles.

So the second part of Fanny's memoir is more positive and upbeat, at times lyrical, with Fanny learning from the old "rational pleasurist," as she calls the elderly man, the pleasures of the mind are superior to those of the body. At the same time, "they were so far from obnoxious to, or incompatible with each other, that . . . the one serv'd to exalt and perfect the taste of the other to a degree that the senses alone can never arrive at."[26]

Randolph Trumbach, a historian of sexual life in eighteenth-century England, attributes much of the novel's sexual excitement to Cleland's use of narrative realism, but it was not an especially realistic representation of the average prostitute's life. "Fanny does not become pregnant; she avoids disease and drunkenness; and she marries her first customer for love. Most importantly, she fully shares the pleasure of her customers." Cleland may have wanted to end his rendition on the joys of sex on a note of optimism. "Cleland's idealization of sexual pleasure may have broken with . . . traditional Christian suspicion, but his ideology of sexual liberation was firmly contained within the new structures of romantic love."[27]

Memoirs v. Massachusetts generated five separate opinions, including three in dissent. Joining Brennan were Chief Justice Warren and Abe Fortas, whom President Johnson had appointed in 1965 as Arthur Goldberg's replacement when Goldberg became U.S. ambassador to the United Nations.

54

Brennan argued that under *Roth-Alberts* a work may not be deemed obscene "in the abstract" unless the three elements coalesce. It must be established that: (1) the dominant theme of the material taken as a whole appeals to a prurient interest in sex; (2) the material is patently offensive because it affronts contemporary community standards relating to the description or representation of sexual matters; and (3) the material is utterly without redeeming social value. Brennan said the Supreme Judicial Court of Massachusetts had erred in holding the book obscene even though it found that the "testimony may indicate this book has some minimal literary value." Brennan said that for a book to be proscribed it must be found to be *utterly* without redeeming social *value*, even though it may possess the requisite prurient appeal and patent offensiveness.[28]

Attorney Rembar had argued that the prurient interest prong, "standing alone," left the law to deal with "grave yet delicate questions in terms of judicial responses that must remain largely subjective." The determination of whether the dominant appeal of the material is to prurient interest is a matter of personal reaction, he said in the brief he presented to the Supreme Court. Social value, on the other hand, Rembar insisted, provided a criterion that could be subjectively applied. "Judges and jurors are no longer committed to a total reliance on their individual responses. Traditional judicial techniques come into play. There is evidence to be considered." He cited the testimony of qualified experts, for example, and such documentary evidence as book reviews and critical essays. "Opinion as to value is quite different from opinion as to whether a book is prurient or not prurient, or obscene or not obscene." In his oral presentation before the Court, Rembar focused on the importance of the social-value test and affirmed Justice Brennan's suspicion that the critical testimony of acknowledged experts in the field should end any obscenity case without the justices ever reading the material.[29]

The degree to which Rembar may have influenced Justice Brennan's plurality opinion is seen in the justice's change from "utterly without redeeming social importance" to "utterly without redeeming social value." Presumably, a work's value had a better chance of being objectively verified by the courts than a work's importance. However, Brennan allowed for an exploitation loophole when he conceded that a book commercially exploited for the sake of prurient appeal might qualify the work as utterly without social value. "It is not that in such a setting the social value test is relaxed so as to dispense with the requirement that a book be utterly devoid of social value, but rather that, as we established in *Ginzburg v. United States*, where the purveyor's sole emphasis is on the sexually provocative aspects of his publications, a court could accept his evaluation at its face value."[30] *Memoirs v. Massachusetts* was strictly a matter of determining the obscenity of a book, not circumstances of production, sale, and publicity.

Justice Douglas, too, revisited old territory. The First Amendment does not permit the censorship of expression "not brigaded with illegal action," Douglas said. (In his strong dissent, with Black, in *Roth-Alberts*, he had written: "Freedom of expression can be suppressed if, and to the extent that, it is so closely brigaded with illegal action as to be an inseparable part of it.") Elaborating more than was his custom, Douglas went on to instruct:

> Every time an obscenity case is to be argued here, my office is flooded with letters and postal cards urging me to protect the community or the Nation by striking down the publication. The messages are often identical even down to commas and semicolons. The inference is irresistible that they were all copied from a school or church blackboard. The drives are incessant and the pressures are great. Happily we do not bow to them. I mention them only to emphasize the lack of popular understanding of our constitutional system. Publications and utterances were made immune from majoritarian control by the First Amendment, applicable to the States by reason of the Fourteenth. No exceptions were made, not even for obscenity. The Court's contrary conclusion in *Roth*, where obscenity was found to be "outside" the First Amendment, is without justification.[31]

56

Here, Douglas is unusually concerned, much more verbal than usual, so much so that the final paragraphs of his separate concurrence are worth repeating for what light they shed on the *social* aspects of obscenity as voiced by a legal expert:

> The censor is always quick to justify his function in terms that are protective of society. But the First Amendment, written in terms that are absolute, deprives the States of any power to pass on the value, the propriety, or the morality of a particular expression. Perhaps the most frequently assigned justification for censorship is the belief that erotica produce antisocial sexual conduct. But that relationship has yet to be proven. Indeed, if one were to make judgments on the basis of speculation, one might guess that literature of the most pornographic would, in many cases provide a substitute—not a stimulus—for antisocial sexual conduct. As I read the First Amendment, judges cannot gear the literary diet of an entire nation to whatever tepid stuff is incapable of triggering the most demented mind. The First Amendment demands more than a horrible example or two of the perpetrator of a crime of sexual violence, in whose pocket is found a pornographic book, before it allows the Nation to be saddled with a regime of censorship. Whatever may be the reach of the power to regulate *conduct* . . . the First Amendment leaves no power to government over *expression of ideas*.[32]

Justice Clark, in an equally detailed and troubled opinion, but in dissent, said he had stomached such cases for almost ten years and that "though I am not known to be a purist— or a shrinking violet—this book is too much even for me." He went on, describing in detail what precisely he disliked Cleland describing in detail:

> It is nothing more than a series of minutely and vividly described sexual episodes. In each of the sexual scenes the exposed bodies of the participants are described in minute and individual detail. The pubic hair is often used for a background to the most vivid and precise descriptions of the response, condition, size, shape, and color of the sexual

organs before, during and after orgasms. There are some short transitory passages between the various sexual episodes, but for the most part they only set the scene and identify the participants for the next orgy, or make smutty reference and comparison to past episodes. There can be no doubt that the whole purpose of the book is to arouse the prurient interest.[33]

When Clark circulated draft copies of his dissent among the justices, Justice Douglas responded on 15 March 1966 with a memorandum: "In view of Brother Clark's passion for detail, why don't we all chip in and buy him a copy of *My Life & Loves*, by Frank Harris, published by Grove Press, Inc." When Brennan delivered his opinion on 21 March, it had only the concurrences of Warren and Fortas. The plurality believed, however, that Brennan's three-part test would likely be followed by the lower courts since Black, Douglas, and Stewart indicated in their separate concurrences that they would go at least that far in limiting First Amendment protection.[34]

Clark, meanwhile, accused the publisher, G. P. Putnam's Sons, of "preying upon prurient and carnal proclivities for its own pecuniary advantage." Seemingly distraught for almost a decade without much outcry, as he put it, the justice challenged Douglas's assertions on antisocial behavior:

Psychological and physiological studies clearly indicate that many persons become sexually aroused from reading obscene material. While erotic stimulation caused by pornography may be legally insignificant in itself, there are medical experts who believe that such stimulation frequently manifests itself in criminal sexual behavior or other antisocial conduct. A number of sociologists think that this material may have adverse effects upon individual mental health, with potential disruptive consequences for the community.[35]

Justice Harlan continued to hold fast to his position, that the Fourteenth Amendment required of a state only that it apply obscenity criteria rationally to the accepted notion of

58

obscenity. He believed the Massachusetts courts had conformed to that requirement in the *Memoirs* case. On the issues of social value and offensiveness, Harlan deferred to his brethren, adding, however, that the state's decision in this case did not exceed constitutional limits.

Attorney Rembar described Harlan's consistency as procensorship for state government and anticensorship for federal government. But this assessment is simplistic, for, as we have seen, Justice Harlan supported states' rights because he believed that authorities at that level were closer to knowing the desires of the people and, further, that the people themselves were their own best authority on matters of governance. An amorphous federal government, on the other hand, remote from the people and the people out of touch with it, was not to be trusted. More to the point on what became apparent several years later, in Harlan's 1971 opinion in *Cohen v. California*, a speech-action case, was a jurist in strong support of First Amendment values.

Justice White, also in dissent, said that if a state insisted on treating *Fanny Hill* as obscene and forbidding its sale, the First Amendment did not prevent it from doing so. "Censure stems from a legislative act, and legislatures are constitutionally free to embrace such books whenever they wish to do so. It is not the Constitution that imposes the ban."[36]

Community standards and social value, in one form or another, dominated the debate in the cases discussed. But, rather than reach some agreement on every aspect of *Roth-Alberts*, the justices sought more and more to make the crime fit the punishment. Brennan had introduced the prurient interest requirement in *Roth-Alberts* in order to position obscenity outside the realm of constitutional protection. In *Jacobellis* and *Memoirs v. Massachusetts*, he sought a national standard and renewal of "utterly without redeeming social value." And, finally, as we shall see, he returned to the drawing board in *Ginzburg* and *Mishkin* to create "deviant" prurience to fit the newly invented crime of pandering. Justice Harlan, who contended that the Court's majority had rewritten the federal statute in order to convict Ralph Ginzburg, accused his colleagues of "judicial improvisation" when they started proscribing variable and contextual obscenity. Harlan feared that Brennan's new "panderer test" and Warren's "conduct of the defendant test" risked elimination of nonobscene material as well from First Amendment protection.

IV

Variable Obscenity

Sex is a fact of life. Though I do not suggest any way to solve the problems that may arise from sex or discussions about sex, of one thing I am confident, and that is that federal censorship is not the answer to these problems.

—Hugo L. Black,
Ginzburg v. United States

RALPH GINZBURG'S legal troubles started in 1962, when U.S. Representative Kathryn E. Granahan of Pennsylvania alerted the post office to a slick and expensive new quarterly "devoted to the joy of love and sex." It was called *Eros*, and Ginzburg was its New York publisher. But the department was reluctant to prosecute because of its recent setback in the *Lady Chatterley's Lover* case. A year later, however, Postmaster General J. Edward Day instructed the Justice Department to bring criminal charges against Ginzburg for mailing copies of obscene matter and ads telling where customers could buy such matter. Ginzburg was in violation of the Comstock Act.

Federal district court judge Ralph C. Body, sitting without a jury in Philadelphia, convicted Ginzburg and three of his corporations on all twenty-eight counts of violating the Comstock Act. He was sentenced to five years in prison and fines amounting to $28,000. The matter involved included

Eros, an expensive hardcover magazine; *Liaison*, a biweekly newsletter; and a short book purporting to be a true account of the author's experiences, *The Housewife's Handbook on Selective Promiscuity*.

Eros had sought mailing privileges from the postmasters of Intercourse and Blue Ball in Pennsylvania, which suggested to the court that the basis of appeal was salacious. Turned down, Ginzburg obtained mailing privileges from Middlesex, New Jersey. In addition, as the Court noted, Ginzburg's circulars stressed the sexual candor of the publications and boasted that the publishers would take full advantage of what they regarded as an unrestricted license allowed by law in the expression of sex and sexual matters.

Ginzburg's conviction was upheld by the Third Circuit Court of Appeals. His appeal to the U.S. Supreme Court was supported by the American Civil Liberties Union, the Authors' League of America, and a number of distinguished citizens. They urged the Court to abandon its test of obscenity in *Roth-Alberts-Memoirs* and declare First Amendment protection for Ginzburg unless the questionable material created a "clear and present danger" of antisocial behavior.[1]

The Court's opinions were handed down in reverse order from the way they were argued: first came *Memoirs*, then *Ginzburg*, finally *Mishkin*. Justices Clark and White voted for suppression in all three cases. Black, Douglas, and Stewart voted against suppression in all three. Harlan voted for suppression in *Memoirs* and *Mishkin* but against it in *Ginzburg*. Brennan, Warren, and Fortas voted for suppression in *Ginzburg* and *Mishkin* but against it in *Memoirs*. Thus, the tally was six to three to lift the ban on *Memoirs*, six to three to affirm *Mishkin*'s conviction, and five to four to affirm *Ginzburg*'s conviction.

Brennan, who wrote all three of the Court's majority opinions, said in *Ginzburg* that the prosecution had brought charges, as he put it, "in the context of the circumstances of production, sale, and publicity" but admitted that, standing alone, the publications themselves might not have been judged obscene. Nevertheless, "abundant evidence" showed that each of Ginzburg's publications "was orginated or sold

◆ VARIABLE OBSCENITY

as stock in trade of the sordid business of pandering," which the justice defined, as had Warren in *Roth*, as "purveying textual or graphic matter openly advertised to appeal to the erotic interest of [their] customers." Brennan concluded, therefore, that such evidence resolved the "ultimate question of obscenity . . . ambiguity and doubt." Since the publishers of the material "proclaimed its obscenity," the court below had made no error when it accepted the defendants' own evaluation at its face value.[2]

Brennan went on to say that, where the purveyor's sole emphasis is on the sexually provocative aspects of the publications, that fact may be decisive in the determination of obscenity; hence, the *Roth-Alberts* test was applicable. With *Ginzburg*, the Court created a new legal concept. The way publications are marketed is pertinent and in doubtful cases could make the difference. "The context of the circumstances of promotion, sale, and publicity" might be considered "as an aid to determining the question of obscenity." Thus aided, the Court found all three Ginzburg publications obscene.[3]

Justice Black, in a sarcastic dissent on the "confusing welter of opinions and thousands of words written" in the three decisions, argued simply that the federal government was without any constitutional power whatever to put any type of burden on speech and expression of any kind as distinguished from conduct. Moreover, Black found that the grounds for punishing Ginzburg were so vague and meaningless, so capricious and whimsical, as to give a judge or jury unbridled discretion in deciding the fate of a person charged with violating censorship statutes:

> As bad and obnoxious as I believe governmental censorship is in a Nation that has accepted the First Amendment as its basic ideal for freedom, I am compelled to say that censorship that would stamp certain books and literatures as illegal in advance of publication or conviction would in some ways be preferable to the unpredictable book-by-book censorship into which we have now drifted. For myself I would follow the course which I believe is required by the

First Amendment, that is, recognize that sex at least as much as any other aspect of life is so much a part of our society that its discussion should not be made a crime.[4]

Douglas dissented on the grounds that (1) exempting advertising techniques from First Amendment protection was unwarranted, and (2) the First Amendment permitted even offbeat and repulsive ideas. In much the same seriocomic vein as Justice Black, Douglas said:

> Today's condemnation of the use of sex symbols to sell literature engrafts another exception on First Amendment rights that is as unwarranted as the judge-made exception concerning obscenity. This new exception condemns an advertising technique as old as history. The advertisements of our best magazines are chock-full of thighs, ankles, calves, bosoms, eyes, and hair, to draw the potential buyer's attention to lotions, tires, food, liquor, clothing, autos, and even insurance policies. The sexy advertisement neither adds to nor detracts from the quality of the merchandise being offered for sale. And I do not see how it adds to or detracts one whit from the legality of the book being distributed. A book should stand on its own, irrespective of the reasons why it was written or the wiles used in selling it. I cannot imagine any promotional effort that would make chapters 7 and 8 of the Song of Solomon any less or any more worthy of First Amendment protection than does their unostentatious inclusion in the average edition of the Bible.[5]

But it was Harlan and Stewart, traditional advocates of the hard-core category of unprotected obscenity, who were most critical of the majority's "dubious gloss" over existing statutory law and for its "astonishing piece of judicial improvisation." Harlan reiterated what he had posited with Stewart in *Roth*, that under the Comstock Act the federal government was limited to banning from the mails only hard-core pornography. He did not think the Ginzburg publications fell into that narrow nonmailable class.[6]

Harlan called the panderer test a new constitutional doc-

◆ VARIABLE OBSCENITY

trine that was likely to eliminate nonobscene material from First Amendment protection. Such material now must be examined in the light of the defendant's conduct, attitude, and motives. "This seems to me a mere euphemism for allowing punishment of a person who mails otherwise constitutionally protected material just because a jury or a judge may not find him or his business agreeable." He suggested that the *Ulysses* opinions of Judges Woolsey and Augustus Hand in the 1930s "might be rendered nugatory if a mailer of Ulysses is found to be titillating readers with its 'coarse, blasphemous, and obscene' portions, rather than piloting them through the intricacies of Joyce's stream of consciousness." Harlan said he had difficulty seeing how the majority's inquiries were logically directed at the question of whether a particular work was obscene.[7]

Stewart found Ginzburg's publications "vulgar and unedifying," but he averred that, if the First Amendment means anything, it means that a man cannot be sent to prison merely for distributing publications that offend a judge's aesthetic sensibilities, "mine or any other's." Censorship, he said, reflected a society's lack of confidence in itself and was the hallmark of an authoritarian regime. The justice described hard-core pornography beyond his simple *Jacobellis* definition, "I know it when I see it," in a footnote to his opinion that contained language borrowed from a brief prepared by Thurgood Marshall, then solicitor general:

> Such materials include photographs, both still and motion picture, with no pretense of artistic value, graphically depicting acts of sexual intercourse, including various acts of sodomy and sadism, and sometimes involving several participants in scenes of orgy-like character. They also include strips of drawings in comic-book format grossly depicting similar activities in an exaggerated fashion. There are, in addition, pamphlets and booklets, sometimes with photographic illustrations, verbally describing such activities in a bizzare manner with no attempt whatsoever to afford portrayals of character or situation and with no pretense to literary value. All of this material . . . cannot con-

ceivably be characterized as embodying communication of ideas or artistic values inviolate under the First Amendment.[8]

Stewart pointed out the obvious contradiction in the majority's holding, that, while the materials mailed were themselves protected by the Constitution, Ginzburg was found guilty but not charged with commercial exploitation, pandering, and titillation. To affirm his conviction on any of those grounds, Stewart said, is to have denied him due process of law. Even more regrettable to the justice was the Court's assuming power it did not have. The First Amendment protects with an even hand, applying its coverage to Ginzburg with no less completeness and force then to G. P. Puntnam's Sons, publisher of *Fanny Hill*. "In upholding and enforcing the Bill of Rights, this Court has no power to pick or to choose. When we lose sight of that fixed star of constitutional adjudication, we lose our way. For then we forsake a government of law and are left with government by Big Brother."[9]

Surprising was the vote of Justice Fortas, the newest arrival to the Court, who, in joining Brennan and the majority, shifted the balance against Ginzburg. As Arthur Goldberg's replacement in 1965, Abe Fortas might have been expected to follow a more permissive line. Once, as a lawyer, he had filed an *amicus curiae*, friend of the court, brief on behalf of *Playboy* magazine and called the federal obscenity law unconstitutional. But Fortas was swayed by Chief Justice Warren, who had become deeply concerned that panderers were taking advantage of the Court's liberality to get rich on smut. Warren hinted at this concern as early as 1957 in *Roth-Alberts*, when he said, "The conduct of the defendant is the central issue, not the obscenity of a book or picture." Warren believed it was okay for the government, whether state or federal, to punish Roth and Alberts because they were "plainly engaged in the commercial exploitation of the morbid and shameful craving for materials with prurient effect."[10]

Earlier in deliberations over all three of the cases, Brennan had convinced Warren and Fortas to join him in a rever-

66

sal of the decision on *Fanny Hill*. In conference, Fortas had expressed strong concern that an affirmance would give rise to a new wave of "book burning" and tacitly hinged his concurrence in *Ginzburg* and *Mishkin* on a reversal in the *Memoirs* case. Brennan told Warren of Fortas's position and reminded him of his own dissenting opinion in another 1957 decision, *Kingsley Books Inc. v. Brown*, where Warren had said that courts should not judge "the quality of art or literature." To do otherwise, he said, "savors too much of book burning."[11]

Fortas, the only justice not already committed on the issue, lined up silently behind the Warren view. The new justice had divided his vote during the justices' conference on 10 December 1965 among the publications Ginzburg had sold. He found *Liaison* obscene, but *Housewife's Handbook* was not obscene because it had therapeutic value, he thought. He said that he would probably join an opinion holding *Eros* obscene. After the conference, Warren persuaded Fortas to join an opinion affirming Ginzburg's conviction based on a pandering approach. Though this concept had not been discussed at the conference, a decision based on pandering dovetailed nicely with Warren's way of dealing with obscenity. Warren's approach was acceptable to Brennan. Fortas, in making a few acceptable minor suggestions, wanted it made clear that it was Ginzburg's *conduct* in distributing his publications, rather than his character or personal qualities, that was relevant.[12]

When Brennan announced his *Ginzburg* opinion on 21 March 1966, he could report it as the opinion of the Court. For the first time in the decade since *Roth-Alberts*, a majority (Brennan, Warren, Clark, White, and Fortas) was garnered on a full opinion that ruled on the alleged obscenity of material sold by a defendant. Meanwhile, the prison-bound Ralph Ginzburg denounced the Court for its change of heart at the same time reform groups across the country rejoiced and cranked up new antismut drives. Justice Fortas told a news group in Washington that he was "not ready" to express his views on obscenity in an opinion but hinted that future changes could be in store.[13]

In *Mishkin v. New York*, the third, and final, obscenity

decision of the 1965 term, the Court affirmed by six to three a state court conviction for publishing, possessing, and hiring others to prepare books admitted to be sadistic and masochistic. Brennan, writing for five members, rejected the contention that books depicting sexual perversions were not obscene under the standards of *Roth-Alberts* merely because they repel the average reader rather than appeal to his prurient interest. Among the fifty or so Mishkin titles were *Dance with the Dominant Whip* and *Swish Bottom*.[14]

Mishkin warned that when material was designed for a so-called deviant sexual group, it was obscene if it appealed to the prurient interest of members of that group. Thus, books with such appeal may be deemed obscene per se. *Ginzburg* and *Mishkin* established a strange new category, variable obscenity, that may vary with the circumstances of the material and the nature of the audience.

There was little doubt that Edward Mishkin had engaged in pandering. But Brennan decided not to follow the Ginzburg approach because he felt that, even without considering the way the books were sold, they were clearly beyond constitutional protection. Thus, *Roth-Alberts* applied. Brennan had to adjust the prurient interest criterion to the deviant groups reached by Mishkin. He maneuvered the crime to fit the punishment, that is, as the justice so deftly intoned: "We adjust the prurient-appeal requirement to social realities by permitting the appeal of this type of material to be assessed in terms of the sexual interests of its intended and probable recipient group; and since our holding requires that the recipient group be defined with more specificity than in terms of sexually immature persons, it also avoids the inadequacy of the most-susceptible-person facet of the Hicklin test."[15] In other words, when materials were aimed at a deviant group the criterion was met when there was prurient appeal to members of that group even if not to the average person.

This new variation on the pandering approach concerned Fortas, who would rather have relied strictly on *Ginzburg*, saying that Mishkin produced and distributed the publications for the expressed purpose of appealing to his customers' prurient interest. Brennan rejected the Fortas suggestion, but he did add a sentence that used *Ginzburg* to assert that

68

Mishkin's "own evaluation of his material confirms such a finding" of prurient appeal. Fortas approved and joined Brennan's opinion without further adjustments. Clark and Harlan also joined, making six justices who supported the *Mishkin* opinion.[16]

Harlan agreed this time with the majority, as opposed to his strong disagreement in *Ginzburg*, reiterating the view he had expressed in his dissent in *Memoirs*. His *Ginzburg* dissent was based on his traditional harshness over federal government censorship and also because he did not find the publications hard-core pornography. With *Mishkin*, a state case, he was less harsh on government suppression. Black, Douglas, and Stewart dissented on much the same grounds as they had in *Ginzburg*. Black said the Constitution prohibits laws "which in any manner abridge freedom of speech and press—whatever the subjects discussed." Stewart dissented because, as was his recurring position, "however tawdry those books may be, they are not hard-core pornography." Douglas simply applied his *Ginzburg* opinion.[17]

The Brennan-Warren intent theory, as opposed to the Harlan-Stewart content theory, weighed heavily against Ginzburg. At the heart of the decision was the Court's belief that material otherwise not obscene may be "pushed over the line" by the way in which it is advertised, promoted, or disseminated. The peg on which Brennan hung his decision was that redeeming social value may be shown in a courtroom to be mere pretense by the publisher's or seller's prelitigation behavior. If the publisher and seller themselves said the material was obscene, a court can take, in Brennan's words, "their own evaluation at its face value and [declare] the book as a whole obscene despite the other evidence."[18]

A few weeks after the Court's announcement of *Ginzburg*, Justice Fortas started to regret his vote affirming the conviction. "I think I was wrong," he confessed in a private note to Justice Douglas. "Subconsciously," he said, he had been "affected by [Ginzburg's] slimy qualities." And if he "had it to do over again," he would have reversed almost all of the obscenity convictions. "Well, live and learn," he added.[19]

Thurman Arnold, a professor at Yale during Fortas's student days there and later his colleague and law partner, wrote him that the decision to uphold the five-year prison term was "a bit rough," as civil libertarians in general insisted. "Demeaning the Court" was the label *The Nation* used for its editorial condemning the *Ginzburg* decision and saying it was "beyond comprehension." Fred P. Graham, Supreme Court correspondent for the *New York Times*, reported that the Justice Department hinted in its brief that the Court might throw out Ginzburg's conviction without hearing arguments. The *New Republic* called 21 March 1966, "a grim day in the temple of justice." An article in the *Village Voice* said, "In the *Ginzburg* case, the Court for the first time equated sex with obscenity."[20]

Numerous cries of anguish and astonishment, as well as those of joy and gratefulness, greeted *Memoirs, Ginzburg,* and *Mishkin.* The *National Decency Reporter,* which was published by the Citizens for Decent Literature, said, "The final results were a major defeat to the smut industry." Thirteen clergymen of all faiths, including three cardinals, applauded all but *Memoirs* in a joint statement, according to the *New York Times,* and expressed the hope that the Supreme Court would reconsider the social-value theory.[21]

From the other side, twenty prominent intellectuals took a full-page ad in the *New York Times* to protest the decisions. Russell Baker, *Times* correspondent, said, "It is obvious that the Supreme Court is over its head on the smut issue." The *New York Herald Tribune* said that the *Ginzburg* decision had "shrunk the limits of free expression." Michael Harrington, in the same paper, said, "The Court has sacrificed very real First Amendment freedoms." According to the *Chicago Sun-Times,* the Court had "added a new dimension to censorship." The *Oakland Tribune* said the "censors' authority has been broadened by the law of the land." The *Detroit News* said the *Ginzburg* decision "does not augur well for the principle of government by law." However, as Charles Rembar noted, "The *Ginzburg* majority did not create a new concept; it took an old one and gave it sharper definition and a more explicit role than it had played in most earlier cases."[22]

Rembar's overall analysis, written approximately a year

70

after the three decisions, is a more tempered look at the cases and the climate around them:

> The common view of the decisions, from the liberal side, was distorted by two factors. One was the lack of realism about how the law stood before March 1966. If you were in favor of freedom and misinformed about the state of the law, you would naturally feel deprived by the decisions, and inclined to take the bleakest view of their meaning. The other was that many people (myself included) felt there were aspects of Ginzburg's trial that seemed unfair and the five-year jail sentence was grotesque. For the individuals the results were unhappy, and to a part of the public scandalous. But for freedom of expression, March 21, 1966, was a very good day. The pandering rule would send Ginzburg to jail, but its future as an inhibiting force on speech and the press would be negligible. The acceptance of the value test would give writers and publishers a freedom they had never before enjoyed.[23]

Brennan's opinion in *Memoirs v. Massacushetts*, which finally gave the social-value test real legitimacy, spent no time differentiating between *importance* and *value*. It simply substituted the latter for the former, implying nonetheless a significant difference. Brennan had first used "social importance" in *Roth-Alberts*, but the value test was at best only implied. The theory became explicit in *Jacobellis*, although only with the support of two justices, and again Brennan said "importance." In *Memoirs*, the theory became a rule of law, and the word used was *value* instead of *importance*. A book cannot be proscribed unless it is found to be "*utterly*"—the italics were Brennan's—"without redeeming social value." And the fact that Brennan used the word *book* instead of *material*, as he had in *Roth-Alberts* and *Jacobellis*, suggested he may have been looking forward to a distinction in the future among so-called obscene works. Rembar, conjecturing on the ultimate meaning of *Fanny Hill*, said, "So far as writers are concerned, there is no longer a law of obscenity." Publishers and booksellers who pander may not enjoy the same freedom, however.[24]

After the three obscenity decisions, the justices decided

whether to grant *certiorari* in two other cases, *Redrup v. New York* and *Austin v. Kentucky*, and if to hear the appeal in a third, *Gent v. Arkansas*. A majority at the conference on 25 March wanted to dismiss them summarily. Several, however, were troubled by affirming in *Gent*, or dismissing for need of a substantial federal question. Justice White, for instance, believed that the "girlie" magazine in question was not obscene because it was not patently offensive. Prior to the next conference, Fortas circulated a 13 April memorandum that said, "At Conference, I shared the apparently prevailing view that we should not at this time review obscenity cases in addition to those already decided. Further consideration has caused me to have serious misgivings as to my initial approach . . . I no longer believe that we can appropriately rest on our laurels."[25]

The Fortas memo suggested that *Redrup* and *Austin* should be taken to resolve the issue of *scienter*—an awareness of prohibited conduct—necessary for conviction in an obscenity case. And that *Gent* should be reviewed for the sole purpose of deciding that the First Amendment prohibits these types of *in rem*—against the thing as distinguished from against the person—proceedings. Fortas said that he had come to the conclusion that the obscenity exception to the First Amendment should be limited to those engaged in "conscious and purposeful 'pandering' of such material." Five justices voted to grant *certiorari* in *Redrup* and *Austin*, and after extended debate also decided to take *Gent* but limited the appeal to whether the Arkansas obscenity statute was invalid as a prior restraint on expression or because of vagueness. Black, Douglas, and Stewart dissented from the limitations.

The Court's 1967 *per curiam* decision in *Redrup*, a simultaneous consideration of the three state cases, reversed convictions for selling "sexy paperback novels" and "girlie" magazines unobtrusively to willing adults. Though brief and unsigned, *Redrup* has been viewed as the most important obscenity ruling since the 1957 *Roth-Alberts* landmark. Scholars have seen it as "a helpful map of the twisting path trod by the Warren Court" and as an attempt to extricate the

◆ VARIABLE OBSCENITY

Court from "the judicial thicket" created by cases since *Roth-Alberts*.[26]

Robert Redrup, a clerk at a New York City newsstand, was arrested when he sold two paperbacks, *Lust Pool* and *Shame Agent*, to a plainclothes policeman for a total of $1.65. His conviction for violating state criminal law was affirmed on appeal. William Austin, owner and operator of a bookstore and newsstand in Paducah, was convicted for violating Kentucky criminal law after one of his saleswomen sold two magazines, *High Heels* and *Spree*, to a female resident of the town. In the third case, an Arkansas prosecutor brought civil proceedings to declare various magazines obscene and to have certain issues confiscated and destroyed.

At the postargument conferences in October 1966, at least five justices wanted to reverse all three cases, on even more grounds than they used in the 1965 term. Fortas, who was not satisfied with the way *Roth-Alberts* had been applied in *Ginzburg* and *Mishkin*, was assigned the opinions. He believed that both the *Roth-Alberts* test and proof of pandering were necessary for a criminal prosecution. It was believed that if Fortas could not secure a majority for his view he might join Douglas and Black in their absolutist approach. Fortas also was supposed to have uttered, with regard to the *Gent* confiscation case, that "book burning" should not be tolerated.

Fortas prepared draft opinions in *Redrup* and *Austin* that regarded the *scienter* requirement the same as the *mens rea* requirement in criminal law. He said that "vicious will," as the great jurist William Blackstone promulgated, was required. His draft in *Gent* indicated that any civil action restraining obscenity would be invalid, and that without *scienter* the seller or publisher would be "stripped of his right to a jury trial" where *scienter* would be proved. Fortas could not obtain a majority for either draft.[27]

Stewart sent around an opinion arguing that the material was not obscene. Black circulated a short view reaffirming his long espoused position, as did Douglas, who attached an article by the Reverend Howard Moody protesting obscenity regulation. Some of the justices may have been shocked by the cleric's frank language: "The dirtiest word in the English language is not 'fuck' or 'shit' in the mouth of a tragic shaman, but the word 'nigger' from the sneering lips of a Bull Connor."[28]

The three cases had arisen from a recurring conflict between state power to suppress the distribution of books and magazines and the guarantees of the First and Fourteenth Amendments. The Supreme Court concluded that distribution in each case was protected *in personam*, "against the person," or *in rem*, "against the thing." Two justices, probably Black and Douglas, held that a state is utterly without power to suppress, control, or punish the distribution of any writings or pictures on grounds of obscenity. Another justice, probably Stewart, held that a state's power is narrowly limited to a distinct and clearly identifiable class of material—hard-core pornography. Other justices, probably Warren, Fortas, and Brennan, subscribed to the three-part *Roth-Alberts-Memoirs* test, the coalescence definition of obscenity.

Justice White, evidently, did not view the social-value element as an independent factor in judging obscenity. Harlan and Clark, the only justices identified by name, dissented, arguing that the Court had failed to address the specific questions raised by each case. The dispositions, Harlan conjectured, did not reflect well on the processes of the Court. Earlier, in one of several of his own draft opinions, Harlan had suggested what he termed "the middle course," that the defendant be allowed to assert that he dealt in obscene material without knowledge of its obscenity. Under this scheme, the test of *scienter* would vary with the importance of the person prosecuted. For example, Redrup, a mere clerk, would be judged differently from, let's say, Austin, a bookseller who controlled the stock in his stores. Harlan would have required the state to prove that Redrup actually knew that what he sold was obscene, while all that would have to be shown regarding Austin was that he should have regarded the material as subject to regulation.[29]

Thus, after dealing with the various tests and opinions, the Court, whether out of disgust, defeat, or delight, announced, "Whichever of these constitutional views is

74

brought to bear . . . it is clear that the judgments cannot stand." Stewart, who announced the *per curiam* on 8 May 1967, had been the justice who sought, and finally got, agreement on the common ground that all three cases dealt with protected matter. He had pointed out that none involved "a specific and limited state concern for juveniles" or "any suggestion of an assault upon individual privacy by publication in a manner so obtrusive as to make it impossible for an unwilling individual to avoid exposure to it" or any evidence of pandering. It then listed the positions of the justices except Harlan.[30]

The seven-member majority in *Redrup* allowed for a special place in obscenity regulation for Stewart's hard-core yardstick, which meshed well with the more elaborate *Roth-Alberts-Memoirs* criteria. The standard of conduct developed in *Ginzburg* and *Mishkin* was reinforced in *Redrup*. First, the Court suggested that statutes reflecting a "specific and limited state concern for juveniles" might be safe, providing they are not meant to limit what all citizens might read. Second, the Constitution might not protect "an assault upon individual privacy by publication in a manner so obtrusive as to make it impossible for an unwilling individual to avoid exposure to it." And, third, the Court reaffirmed its dislike for pandering. Thus, the good and bad of *Redrup* rested in its internal consistency—the "good" of a book's contents may succumb to the "bad" of a seller's or distributor's conduct. "The stringent definition of 'hard-core pornography' advanced by Justice Stewart could be of little protection for a distribution of material that was seen by the court to be an invasion of privacy, a sale to a minor, or a 'pandering' sale," concluded Dwight Teeter and Don Pember. Despite *Redrup*'s questionable if not ambiguous contribution to the evolution of obscenity law, in little more than a year and a half, the Court used it to reverse some thirty-five state and federal obscenity convictions.[31]

The Supreme Court's busy decade of the 1960s neared a quiet close with two obscenity decisions stemming from three cases that dealt with minors. On 22 April 1968, the justices announced eight to one that a Dallas ordinance designed to classify films as suitable or not for persons under sixteen was unconstitutionally vague. And they upheld six to three a state's power to forbid the sale to minors of materials declared obscene for them but not necessarily obscene for adults.[32]

"The conviction of Ginsberg on the present facts is a serious invasion of freedom," wrote Justice Fortas in dissent in *Ginsberg v. New York.* "To sustain the conviction without inquiry as to whether the material is 'obscene' and without any evidence of pushing or pandering . . . is to give the State a role in the rearing of children which is contrary to our traditions and to our conception of family responsibility."[33] The majority, in an opinion written by Brennan, upheld a state law allowing for separate obscenity standards for persons under seventeen that were far more restrictive than those for adults. Brennan said that the well-being of youth justified the double standard; children's speech rights are not coextensive with adults. Moreover, states have a legitimate interest in controlling obscenity directed at unwilling recipients or juveniles. Fortas's view, his only signed opinion on obscenity, grew to haunt him during Senate hearings in July of that year on his nomination to succeed the retiring Earl Warren as chief justice.

What bothered Fortas most about Brennan's stance in *Ginsberg* was its undefined and unlimited approval of state censorship by denying children free access to books and art to which many parents may have wanted their children to have uninhibited access. "For denial of access to these magazines, without any standard or definition of their allegedly distinguishing characteristics, is also denial of access to great works of art and literature."[34] The justice would have allowed for broad police powers against, in his words, "panderers and pushers." It was Fortas who had influenced Brennan in the *Ginzburg* case to consider the conduct of the salesman rather than the material itself. Chief Justice Warren, as we have seen, also had become annoyed with such marketing behavior.

A Fortas biographer, Laura Kalman, believes that the justice, earnestly and perhaps innocently, tried to resolve the welter of obscenity cases by suggesting a new test, as had other members of the Court before him. A showing of pan-

76

dering alone would not be sufficient, he reasoned. "Instead, just as the prosecution was required to show that a criminal possessed the *mens rea*—specific intent—to commit a crime," Kalman explains, "so it must prove that the seller seller possessed the *mens rea* to purvey obscene materials." Thus, the government could justify prosecution only of those individuals responsible for "conscious and purposeful pandering."[35]

However, Fortas could not persuade a majority of his brethren to go along, even on this equivocal basis. He agreed with Brennan's principle of variable obscenity—what is not obscene for an adult may be obscene for a child—but insisted, in his *Ginsberg* dissent, that the Court must first define obscenity, even that which is variable. "We must know the extent to which literature or pictures may be less offensive than *Roth* requires in order to be 'obscene' for purposes of a statute confined to youth." Arguing that the mere selling of books should not be a hazardous trade, Fortas said that Ginsberg was being prosecuted without even a claim that he deliberately and calculatedly sought to induce children to buy obscene material.[36]

"Variable obscenity" is the connecting link for *Ginzburg*, *Mishkin*, and *Ginsberg*. Frederick Schauer, author of *The Law of Obscenity*, defines it as the principle that says that the obscenity of given material may be determined only in the context of the method of distribution and the intended and actual audience for the material. Schauer contrasts it with "constant obscenity," which requires looking at the material to determine obscenity "regardless of the method or objects of distribution." Schauer's idiom may be textbook legalese but the message is clear: variable obscenity means a two-tier, or double, standard, for defining or describing obscenity. The concept actually had its origin in *Regina v. Hicklin*, which stipulated that the determination of obscenity must be based on an evaluation of "into whose hands a publication of this sort may fall."[37]

The modern concept of variable obscenity was developed in a law journal article by William B. Lockhart and Robert C. McClure. Lockhart, former dean of the University of Minnesota law school, later chaired the President's Commission on

Obscenity and Pornography, which issued its multivolume report in 1970. "Variable obscenity," the authors state, "furnishes a useful analytical tool for dealing with the problem of denying adolescents access to material aimed at a primary audience of sexually mature adults. Variable obscenity focuses attention on the makeup of primary and peripheral audiences in varying circumstances, and provides a reasonably satisfactory means for delineating the obscene in each circumstance." Again, the language is tortured but the message declares that, in Brennan's opinion in *Ginsberg*, "the concept of obscenity or of unprotected matter may vary according to the group to whom the questionable material is directed or from whom it is quarantined."[38] On this view, Lockhart and McClure suggested, "Material is never inherently obscene; instead its obscenity varies with the circumstances of its dissemination."[39]

In an earlier work, Lockhart and McClure had explained the premise underlying the concept. If a work "is so advertised and distributed as to reach those upon whom it is likely to have undesirable effects," then, and only then, is the work obscene. Although the *Mishkin* Court, like its predecessors, did not articulate any effects of pornography, mere espousal of the category triggered suspicions that the Court was moving toward a variable standard based on substantive First Amendment analyses.[40]

Justice Brennan said that two governmental interests justify curbing the availability of "sex material" to "minors under 17." First, basic to the structure of our society is the authority parents claim "in their own household" to direct the rearing of their children. "The legislature could properly conclude that parents and others, teachers for example, who have this primary responsibility for children's well-being are entitled to the support of laws designed to aid discharge of that responsibility," the justice wrote. Second, the government has an independent interest in the well-being of its youth.[41]

Brennan, acknowledging the debate over the role pornography may or may not play in unethical and immoral behavior, excerpted, in a long footnote to his opinion, observations by Dr. Willard M. Gaylin, a psychoanalyst, whose views

78

had appeared in his review of Richard H. Kuh's *Foolish Fig-leaves*, a partisan look at pornography from a prosecutor's point of view. Gaylin elaborated on the so-called harm factor. "Surely we must have a solid answer to this question of harmfulness before we can decide intelligently whether and on what basis we should preserve a legal concept of obscenity." On the specifics of the effects of pornography on youth (Brennan's primary concern in *Ginsberg*), Gaylin emphasized that a child might not be as well prepared as an adult to choose intelligently his or her reading material. It is in this period of growth, Gaylin said, that legalized pornography may conceivably be damaging. Therefore, Brennan concluded that, while there is no lack of studies, the "growing consensus" agrees that a causal link has not been demonstrated but neither has it been disproved. The Court's effort to support parents and shield their children succeeded but not without strong disagreement among the justices.[42]

V

Politics and Pandering

The "juvenile delinquents" I have known are mostly over 50 years of age. If rationality is the measure of the validity of . . . law, then I can see how modern Anthony Comstocks could make out a case for "protecting" many groups in our society, not merely children.

—Justice William O. Douglas, Ginsberg v. New York

JUSTICES Harlan and Stewart agreed with Brennan's *Ginsberg* assessment but chose also to add their separate opinions. Douglas and Black dissented, saying, as they had on numerous occasions, that even obscene material was protected by the First Amendment. Douglas, who was joined by Black, said, tongue in cheek, that he saw no reason to limit legislatures to protecting children alone. He called for a constitutional amendment that would authorize the modern Comstocks to censor literature before publishers, authors, or distributors could be fined or jailed for what they printed or sold. That is how ludicrous the justice believed things had become. Douglas went on in this satirical vein:

> As I read the First Amendment, it was designed to keep the state and the hands of all state officials off the printing presses of America and off the distribution systems for all printed literature. Anthony Comstock wanted it the other

way; he indeed put the police and prosecutor in the middle of the publishing business.[1]

Douglas accused the Court of sitting as the nation's board of censors. And, with all respect, he said he did not know of a lesser-qualified group, first, to know what obscenity is when they see it, and, second, to have any serious judgment on what the deleterious or beneficial impact of a particular publication may be on the minds of either young or old.

Justice Stewart said that a state may determine that, in some precisely delineated areas, "a child—like someone in a captive audience—is not possessed of that full capacity for individual choice which is the presupposition of First Amendment guarantees." He compared variable obscenity to variable societal rights in general. "It is only upon such a premise . . . that a State may deprive children of other rights—the right to marry, for example, or the right to vote— deprivations that would be constitutionally intolerable for adults."[2]

Harlan concurred in *Ginsberg v. New York* with his dissent from *Interstate Circuit v. Dallas*, which the Court announced the same day, 12 April 1968.

Justice Thurgood Marshall wrote for six members in the eight-to-one "void for vagueness" ruling on a Dallas ordinance designed to classify films as suitable or not for persons under sixteen. A film was unsuitable if it portrayed "sexual promiscuity" so as to "create the impression on young persons that such conduct is profitable, desirable, acceptable, respectable, praiseworthy or commonly accepted," or if "its calculated or dominant effect on young persons is substantially to arouse sexual desire."[3]

Marshall further noted that vagueness and its "attendant evils" are not rendered less objectionable because the regulation of expression is one of classification rather than direct suppression. Such vague laws, if allowed to spread, could inhibit filmmakers, distributors, and exhibitors. Local exhibitors, who cannot afford to risk losing the youthful audience when a film may be of marginal interest to adults, may contract to show only the totally inane, Marshall said. "The vast wasteland that some have described in reference to another medium might be verdant paradise in comparison." Paradoxically, *Ginsberg* and *Interstate* do not permit suppression of brutality or violence, since they are outside the concept of prurient interest.

Harlan declared that the cases ushered the Court into a new phase of the intractable obscenity problem: May a state prevent the dissemination of obscene or other obnoxious material to juveniles on standards less stringent than those which would govern distribution to adults? Harlan, always the scholar, tried to see beyond the immediate problem of the overbroad Dallas ordinance. He said that in all except rare instances, no substantial free-speech interest was at stake, given Harlan's belief that the states had the right to control obscenity. "From the standpoint of the Court itself the current approach has required us to spend an inordinate amount of time in the absurd business of perusing and viewing the miserable stuff that pours into the Court, mostly in state cases, all to no better end than second-guessing state judges."[4]

Various ways of controlling the distribution of motion pictures have been around for a long time, but in 1968 Hollywood itself adopted a rating system, led by the Motion Picture Association of America, whose new president, Jack Valenti, had recently left a position at the White House. Films in the G category would be family movies; the others would be M, for mature audiences; R, restricted to persons sixteen or older unless accompanied by a parent or guardian; and X, no one under sixteen admitted under any circumstances.

By the late 1960s, X-rated films had increased to where the latest surpassed the one before it in sexual explicitness. Even the movie ads, as William Manchester noted in his sweeping history of the time, were something to put beyond the reach of children. *I Am Curious (Yellow)* was thought shocking when it appeared, with nudity and coitus, but newer productions quickly made it obsolescent. Ads for *The Minx* said it "makes *Curious Yellow* look pale." *The Fox* depicted lesbians kissing passionately and a naked woman masturbating in front of a full-length mirror. A beast had intercourse with a woman in *Rosemary's Baby*.

82

Bob and Carol and Ted and Alice was a comedy about wife swapping. *Blow-Up* provided a daring glimpse of a young woman's pubic hair. The ultimate, or so it seemed at the time, was *Deep Throat*, a smashing hit about cunnilingus and fellatio. In the end, the heroine took a man down to the hilt of his penis, displaying a talent the *New Yorker* magazine compared to that of a sword swallower. The action was photographed at close range, and when the man reached orgasm, so did the woman, with technicolor revealing her full body blush.[5]

Justice Harlan took the opportunity of his dissent in *Interstate* (which doubled as his assent in *Ginsberg*) "to take stock of where we are at present in this constitutional field," to review the uncertain history of the Court's dealings with obscenity, and this in the same year, 1968, that Justice Fortas was to suffer the consequences of that history. "The subject of obscenity has produced a variety of views among the members of the Court unmatched in any other course of constitutional adjudication." Two members, Harlan recalled, had steadfastly held that the First and Fourteenth Amendments "render society powerless to protect itself against the dissemination of even the filthiest of materials." This point of view, advocated by Justices Black and Douglas, had never received the support of other justices, past or present, despite "sharp divergence" as to the proper application of the *Roth-Memoirs-Ginzburg* tests. Cass R. Sunstein, a legal scholar, calls the free-speech absolutism advocated by Black and Douglas a theology with no real followers. On his own model, Sunstein argues that most pornographic material lies far from the center of the First Amendment, and hard-core pornography "has little real cognitive content."[6]

Most justices, Brennan chief among them, felt that the various tests permitted suppression of material that fell short of hard-core pornography in equal terms between federal and state authority. Another view, spoken most frequently by Justice Stewart, was that only hard-core material could be censored, whether by federal or state governments. Harlan's view was that only hard-core pornography may be suppressed by the federal government, "whereas under the Fourteenth Amendment States are permitted wider authority to deal with obnoxious matter than might be justifiable under a strict application of the *Roth-Memoirs-Ginzburg* rules."[7]

Harlan pointed out that differences were also apparent on how the appellate process should work in reviewing obscenity determinations. One position was, and is, that the Court should simply examine whether the lower courts have made a genuine effort to apply the obscenity tests and that their determinations be accepted much as are any findings of fact. Another view, explained the justice, entailed a constitutional judgment for which the Supreme Court had ultimate responsibility to decide for itself the obscenity of the challenged matter.

"The upshot of all this divergence in viewpoint is that anyone who undertakes to examine the Court's decisions since *Roth* [1957] which have held particular material obscene or not obscene would find himself in utter bewilderment," Harlan, the chronicler, opined. His solution: limit federal control to the "miserable stuff" that all would recognize as hard-core, and withhold the federal judicial hand from interfering with state decisions except where action is clearly the product of "prudish overzealousness."[8]

In the juvenile field, Harlan thought that the Constitution was still more tolerant of state policy and its applications. "If current doctrinaire views as to the reach of the First Amendment into state affairs are thought to stand in the way of such a functional approach, I would revert to basic constitutional concepts that until recent times have been recognized and respected as the fundamental genius of our federal system, namely the acceptance of wide state autonomy in local affairs." Harlan said that the language of the Dallas ordinance was no more ambiguous or vague than the language the Court itself has offered. "Yet it should be repeated that the *Interstate Circuit* cases, unlike *Roth* and *Alberts*, involve merely the classification, not the criminal prosecution, of objectionable material."[9]

Granted, New York had been careful in limiting its statute to minors, but the method of regulation raised additional problems. While the Court had previously upheld criminal obscenity laws, *Ginsberg* was the first time the justices had approved of a statute directed at the bookseller rather than

84

the publisher. Applying criminal sanctions to the individual bookseller, where periodicals and a variable standard of obscenity are involved, presents special threats to the First Amendment. The adult standard is difficult for even courts to apply with any precision, as Harlan pointed out in his perceptive *Interstate* opinion. Now, with *Ginsberg*, the added words to be displayed, "of or for minors," complicated the problem for the shopkeeper. Therefore, the result may be to restrict sales to minors of "girlie" magazines and similar material, if the bookseller were to opt out of that part of the business, and in the process restrict the availability of such publications to adults. Thus, material not ostensibly covered by the statute may be barred—in violation of the Constitution.

Justice Fortas's pandering criterion provided a way out of the dilemma. If a state wanted to regulate obscenity for minors, it might consider a pandering requirement in statutes that imply variable obscenity. Pandering itself creates some definitional problems, however, but those difficulties are far less troublesome than having to determine what is obscene under the law in the first place. Because the Court in *Ginsberg* chose not to describe the standard for judging "harmful to minors," the pandering route was a reasonable way out. Such avoidance of the fundamental duty to define obscenity for purposes of censorship of material available to youths is exactly what irked Justice Fortas.

"The Court [reasoned], we need not look at the magazines and determine whether they may be excluded from the ambit of the First Amendment as 'obscene,' " Fortas said. "If [the] statute were confined to the punishment of pushers or panderers of vulgar literature I would not be so concerned by the Court's failure to circumscribe state power by defining its limits in terms of the meaning of 'obscenity' in this field." The state's police powers, the justice said, protected parents and their children from the "public aggression" of panderers and pushers. "But it does not follow that the State may convict a passive luncheonette operator of a crime because a sixteen-year-old boy maliciously and designedly picks up and pays for two girlie magazines which are presumably *not* obscene."[10]

Fortas was a precise legal technician much like Harlan, but unlike his learned brother, he had great difficulty balancing private aspirations against public responsibilities. Fortas enjoyed a special intimacy with Harlan, "one of my dearest friends, although we usually are on the opposite sides of issues here." Both men had been corporate attorneys and both owned summer houses near each other in Westport, Connecticut. Harlan's daughter, a pianist, became one of Fortas's chamber music companions during vacations. Of Harlan, "a man who knew judging," Fortas once remarked, "We need reminding now and then of that super-self-restraint view—so long as it doesn't too often prevail."[11]

Perhaps had Fortas taken to heart in his personal life some of his friend's judicial self-restraint, he might have avoided having to defend against some of the improprieties that certain members of the U.S. Senate found disturbing. During the nomination ordeal for chief justice, when Fortas tried to defend himself to his brethren, Harlan sent a friendly letter that raised a probing question: "To be sure we *are* citizens as well as judges, but am I wrong in believing that the former privilege is burdened by the need for detachment, in appearance as well as in fact?"[12]

The year 1968 has been called "the year everything went wrong." William Manchester, the historian, described it so, referring to the fast-breaking events around the world—Prague, Hanoi, Saigon, Paris, Chicago—which lay beyond even President Lyndon Johnson's reach. Clark Clifford, then Secretary of Defense and close personal adviser to the president, recollected years later how moody and difficult Johnson had become, directing his anger at almost anyone around him. "Perhaps most painful, in personal terms, was the setback the President suffered when the nomination of his close friend, Abe Fortas, to be Chief Justice of the United States had to be withdrawn," Clifford wrote. "Johnson well understood that this disaster reflected his declining political strength in what was once his backyard—the United States Senate." But the episode was just as humiliating for Fortas, whose equivocation over variable obscenity turned into an invariable nightmare.[13]

During the Senate confirmation hearings in July 1968,

Fortas became the scapegoat for the activism and liberalism of the Warren Court. He was prepared to respond to accusations regarding his close friendship with the president and even his political dealings in general. But he was not prepared to deal with the obscenity issue to the degree some members of Congress pursued it. First of all, Republican senators wanted to deny Johnson any appointments to the Court, especially the naming of a new chief justice, since the president had become a lame duck after his surprise announcement in March that he would not seek reelection. They wanted the next president to do that because they were confident he would be a Republican who would nominate a conservative to the Court.

Second, conservatives of both parties desired to focus on Fortas's judicial record and his support of the Warren Court's liberal jurisprudence. Virginia's Senator Harry F. Byrd, among them, contended, "The Warren Court has usurped authority to which it is not entitled and is not serving the best interests of our nation. Mr. Fortas appears to have embraced the Warren philosophy, which philosophy I strongly oppose." Senator James O. Eastland, chairman of the Judiciary Committee both in 1965, when Fortas was named associate justice, and in 1968, asserted, "The main thrust of Justice Fortas' philosophy as expressed in his opinions is to tear down those ideas, ideals, and institutions that have made this country great."[14]

For the first couple of days, Sam Ervin of North Carolina and Robert P. Griffin of Michigan, who were among the more vocal members of the thirteen-member Senate Judiciary Committee, peppered Fortas with questions on what they considered to be the administration's partisan approach to its lame-duck appointments. Specifically, Senator Griffin charged that Fortas had been "participating on a regular, undisclosed basis on decisions of the executive branch while serving on the Bench" and had thus violated the doctrine of "separation of powers." Griffin alluded to undisputed though anonymously reported items in an article by Fred Graham of the *New York Times* that appeared in the paper's Sunday magazine.[15]

Graham reported that Fortas had been consulted by the

president on major policy questions such as Vietnam, steel price increases, transportation strikes, and certain executive and judicial appointments. Fortas had drafted Johnson's statement on the Detroit riots in late 1967. Other presidential speeches and messages to Congress on civil rights and criminal justice reform were said to have been written by Justice Fortas.[16]

Everett Dirksen of Illinois, Senate minority leader, called the cronyism charge and the lame-duck argument "frivolous." "You do not go out looking for an enemy to put him on the Court," he said, and he remarked that Presidents Lincoln, Truman, and Kennedy had appointed friends. In rebuking Senator Griffin, Dirksen said, "It's about time we be a little more circumspect about the kind of language we use." Even when the Judiciary Committee decided to hold hearings—the first time for any nominee to the position of chief justice—Fortas seemed safe. The initial witness, Attorney General Ramsey Clark, pointed out that there was ample precedent for the president to keep Warren on the Court until Fortas's confirmation. Many lesser judges, he noted, were chosen while their predecessors remained in office.[17]

Besides seeking to elevate his friend, President Johnson also wanted to name Homer Thornberry, a judge on the U.S. Fifth Circuit Court of Appeals, to the Supreme Court seat soon to be vacated by Fortas. Thornberry was an old Texas friend with whom he had served many years in Congress. Johnson persisted in this dual appointment, much to the dismay of some of his personal advisers, including Clark Clifford, his Secretary of Defense. Clifford, a longtime "outsider-insider" in the Oval Office, recalled in his memoirs the advice he gave to the President: "I regret to say this, but I do not think you can sell the package to the Congress. The Republicans are convinced they are going to elect the next President. They would probably accept Abe on his own. But if his nomination is tied up with Homer Thornberry's, I am afraid that they will find some way to sidetrack it." Clifford told his boss that the Republicans would oppose Thornberry simply on the grounds that Johnson was trying to pack the court with friends at a very late date in the political calendar.

◆ POLITICS AND PANDERING

Clifford said the Republicans would try to stall both appointments until after their national convention in November. But, with or without Thornberry on Johnson's Supreme Court ticket, the conservatives did more than sidetrack the Fortas nomination. They derailed it.[18]

Southern Dixiecrats in general and Strom Thurmond of South Carolina in particular were restive about Fortas, because of his reputation as a judicial activist, and about the Warren Court generally, for its stance on civil rights matters. The Court had regularly endorsed racial progress, human rights, and dignity in the field of criminal law. Most southern senators disapproved of the Court's extending the rights of black Americans and disparaged the Court's softness on criminals. Committee chairman Eastland of Mississippi could only promise his friend, the president, that he would not hold the nominations in committee indefinitely.

Eastland warned Johnson at the outset, however, that the Fortas nomination could not be confirmed. He said he "had never seen so much feeling against a man as against Fortas." Senator Ervin told the White House that "considering what the Supreme Court has done to the Constitution, I'll have to read Fortas' decisions before I can decide." John McClellan of Arkansas considered Fortas "an SOB" and eagerly anticipated fighting his nomination on the Senate floor. Robert Byrd of West Virginia initially promised to do "everything in my power" to oppose that "leftist" member of the Court, but later modified his position somewhat. Russell Long of Louisiana called Fortas " 'one of the dirty five' who sides with the criminal." Thus, the stage was perfectly set for Senator Thurmond's moralizing and bullyragging.[19]

Schackman v. California, a one-sentence opinion announced by the Court in the term just before the Senate confirmation hearings, symbolized the smut problem for Thurmond. He had convinced Chairman Eastland to allow for the testimony of expert witnesses, one of whom, James J. Clancy, was an attorney who represented Citizens for Decent Literature (CDL). The group was dedicated to "pressing for enforcement of the obscenity laws—laws which the history of our Government has proven essential to the development of good family living." The CDL got permission to voice its concern about the nominee for chief justice to the Judiciary Committee.[20]

Bruce Allen Murphy, historian, interpreted the new wrinkle this way: "The movement of the committee from high drama to low farce, and from the great constitutional debate over the matters of separation of powers and judicial ethics to the gutter of stag films and pornographic materials, was a sign of how far Strom Thurmond was willing to go to win this fight." *Life* magazine would say later that the South Carolina senator had combined a "left to the groin with a right to the more general Southern and conservative hatred of the whole Warren Court." Reporters joked that the "witch hunt" had simply become a "bitch hunt."[21]

Clancy testified that CDL had analyzed fifty-two obscenity decisions over the previous two years and had concluded that in all but three Justice Fortas had provided the deciding fifth vote for reversing the lower court's finding that the material was obscene. What he conveniently failed to explain was that in only one of these cases—*Ginsberg v. New York*—had the justice gone beyond voting to write an opinion actually explaining his views. As a result of Fortas's voting, Clancy said the nation's movie houses and newsstands had been engulfed with pornography. "The smut industry takes its direction from the High Court's decisions," he charged, "advancing a giant step forward each time that the United States Supreme Court hands down a decision adverse to the people's interest." To believe Clancy was to hold Justice Fortas personally responsible for book racks filled with such classics as *Sex Life of a Cop, Orgy Club, Lust School, Lust Web, Lust Pool, Lust Job*, and, of course, *Lust Hungry* and such cinematic wonders as *Erotic Touch of Hot Skin, Rent a Girl*, and those too hot for words—*O-7, O-12*, and *D-15*.[22]

It was the *Schackman* decision, one of the "analyzed" CDL cases, that Clancy found particularly annoying. The film *O-7*, a copy which Clancy brought for committee review, along with some photos from pornographic magazines, had been found obscene by the lower courts. *Schackman*, to be sure, was one of about thirty-five cases that the Court reversed, without opinion and usually without hearing arguments. Since 1967, the decisions had nearly always cited the Court's *Redrup* decision as the basis for reversal. Here is a partial description of the striptease films at issue in *Schackman*:

> These pictures have often clearly displayed and focused upon pubic hair and male sex organs (although not in a state of excitation) and upon occasion they have focused directly upon female genitalia. Among the films which the Court has found not to be "obscene" under the *Roth* standard have been films showing entirely nude women, films showing nude or partially nude women engaging in gyrations, simulated intercourse and simulated oral intercourse and emphasizing and displaying pubic and rectal areas, films showing two partially nude women simulating lesbian activity, and films showing heterosexual activity between a man and a woman (but not revealing genital areas during such activity).[23]

Clancy, who was convinced that pornography bred violence, declared before the committee that Fortas's actions in cases like *Schackman* had caused "a release of the greatest deluge of hard-core pornography ever witnessed by any nation—and this at a time when statistics indicate a pronounced breakdown in public morals and general movement toward sexual degeneracy throughout the Nation."

Senator Thurmond had not seen the film *O-7*, but Clancy's description was enough for him to declare it "obscene and filthy and obnoxious to any right-thinking person." So, in an obvious but nonetheless strategic move to introduce evidence against Fortas's nomination, the senator arranged for his colleagues and the press to see the film. Senator Frank Lausche of Ohio denounced what he had witnessed as "a scandalization of the womanhood of the United States and of the world. If the nominee were my brother, I would not vote for him."[24]

Thurmond, on one occasion, brandished a "girlie" magazine and asked: "Should the Senate confirm a man for Chief Justice of the United States who has reversed the decisions in obscenity cases and allowed such material as this to be sold on the newsstands of this city and other cities of this nation?" However questionable the tactics used by the senator and his allies, it was a clear indication of how little control the White House now had over the course of the fight. Besides the charge of cronyism leading to a possible conflict between two branches of government and the growing bitterness over the Warren Court, the committee now had to deal with the Court's obscenity decisions as well.[25]

It is interesting to note that not all 1967 decisions stemming from *Redrup* were reversals. In one case, *Landau v. Fording*, the Court affirmed a determination of obscenity without opinion. Involved was the film *Un chant d'Amour*, written and directed by Jean Genet, which depicted male masturbation and suggested male homosexual oral-genital sex. In *Grove Press v. Maryland*, an equally divided Court affirmed an obscenity determination regarding the film *I Am Curious (Yellow)*. Clancy's interpretation of *Schackman*, moreover, was incorrect, as Fortas himself pointed out in response to a published attack by the newspaper columnist James J. Kilpatrick. After seeing one of the films, Kilpatrick argued in his column that the Senate should save itself the trouble of debating the twin confirmations and simply show the film on the Senate floor.[26]

"The majority's brusque order of June 12, 1967, is part of a pattern that runs through the fabric of constitutional law as tailored by Mr. Justice Fortas," Kilpatrick wrote.

> This was his idea of protected speech. Does the Senate agree? That's the size of the parliamentary proposition: Boil the issue down to this lip-licking slut, writhing carnally on a sofa, while a close-up camera dwells lasciviously on her genitals. Free speech? Free press? Is this what the Constitution means? The Constitution is, we may remember, what five judges say it is, no less, no more. So remembering, will the Senate advise and consent?[27]

Apparently, this was more than Fortas could bear, for he decided to strike back and reveal the true reasons for the Court's decision in the *Schackman* case. He did this in a letter of 23 August 1968 intended for the *Washington Star*, which had carried Kilpatrick's "unjust, unfair and intemperate assault" on the Court (on 13 August), over the name of

92

his friend Edward Bennett Williams, the famous trial lawyer. But, since Williams could not normally have known of such inside Court information, the letter referred to a memorandum by Senator Philip Hart of Michigan explaining to his colleagues on the Judiciary Committee the rationale behind *Schackman.*

Senator Hart's memo noted that obscenity had played no part in the decision; rather, the conviction was overruled because of improper police procedure. The police had seized the film without a valid search warrant. All of this Kilpatrick might have understood, Fortas said, if he had taken the time to read Senator Hart's memo in the record of the Judiciary Committee. But the memo, Fortas learned shortly after shipping his letter to Williams, had never been introduced into the record. So Fortas had to delete that part of the missive that appeared over Williams's name, thus gutting its substance and noting simply that "no interference can properly be drawn" from the one-sentence reversal "that all members of that majority are 'soft' on obscenity."

A subsequent letter, also drafted by Justice Fortas and signed by several prominent law school deans, appeared in the *Washington Post* two weeks later on 11 September, too late, however, to repair damage already done. Ironically, Fortas, neither completely liberal nor completely conservative (not without fair comparison to his friend John Marshall Harlan), knew but could not reveal his real philosophy on the subject of pornography because of the confidential nature of the Court's private conferences and its unpublished working papers. Privately, he called obscenity a "cess-pool problem," but he also thought that the country was about to experience another wave of "book burning." That's how he was able to convince Justice Brennan, in *Memoirs, Ginzburg,* and *Mishkin,* to look at the conduct of the salesman as well as the content of the material.

By the 1968 term, Fortas had been on the Supreme Court long enough to provide at least the outline of a judicial philosophy. He thought of himself as in the tradition of Louis Brandeis, but with his own brand of "sociological jurisprudence." In this sense, Fortas was much less philosophical than Brandeis and preferred to take into account the practical, real-world consequences of his decisions. His was a mixed bag, conservative on business law and press law, liberal on criminal justice, voting representation, and most individual rights cases.[28]

What all this background suggests is that Fortas actually made it easier, not harder, to convict pornographers accused of marketing obscenity. But, clearly, he was the scapegoat for a prior political agenda. "The veil of secrecy that Fortas had drawn over the Court's work at the hearings," writes Laura Kalman, "meant that he could not tell the Citizens for Decent Literature or the Senate that the Court's decision in *Schackman* had nothing to do with obscenity." Neither could he explain that he was largely responsible for the Court's action in *Ginzburg*, or that he eventually regretted his vote in that case. Even the rebuttal newspaper letters, written to characterize his position as "middle of the road," foundered. "Neither the Senate Judiciary Committee members nor others in Congress ever acquired any more concrete information than Clancy had provided. To them, Fortas stood for obscenity."[29]

Senator Thurmond, meanwhile, simply would not let up when the Judiciary Committee resumed hearings in September. First, Thurmond persuaded Dean B. J. Tennery of the Washington College of Law, American University, to explain to the committee Fortas's role in a seminar at the law school for which he was paid handsomely. What made the arrangement particularly damaging was that the justice had been paid from a fund set up by his former partner, Paul Porter, solely for that purpose and collected from prominent businessmen. Dean Tennery said that Justice Fortas had received $15,000 for nine weeks of teaching, but it was to have included the preparation of a syllabus and other materials to be turned over to the university for publication.

Tennery compared Fortas compensation to that of a popular folksinger, who had received $10,000 for a single performance on the campus. All seemed fishy to the committee, however, what with a former partner appearing to have created a moneymaking scheme for his friend. Senator Thurmond suggested that the substantial business interests of the contributors might at some future date find the men in litigation before the Supreme Court.

The appearance of the law school dean was only the first of a Thurmond double feature on 13 September. "Everyone could see from the loaded film projector in the middle of the hearing room that afternoon that it was show time again in the United States Senate," wrote historian Bruce Allen Murphy.[30] The obscenity issue would not go away, nor was Senator Thurmond about to let it.

After Dean Tennery had testified, Thurmond called to the stand the Los Angeles policeman who had been the arresting officer in the *Schackman* case. Sergeant Donald Shaidell, of the department's Antiobscenity Division, was invited to comment on Fortas's contribution to the proliferation of smut in America. Shaidell brought with him two pornographic films and 150 pornographic magazines for the committee to review. He said that the Supreme Court's action in *Schackman* had opened the floodgates in Los Angeles and that such decisions were making it impossible for the authorities to control the torrent of pornography.

"It is pretty apparent," Senator McClellan said at the end of the day, "that the smut factories and the filth merchants are having a field day under the present lack of law enforcement." Senator Hart, on the other hand, was sickened by these efforts to brand Justice Fortas as a smut peddler, efforts as "obscene and distasteful as the movies themselves," he quipped.[31]

On the evening of 1 October 1968, after it became apparent during the day that Senate Majority Leader Mike Mansfield could not muster the required two-thirds majority for closure of floor debate, Justice Fortas asked President Johnson to withdraw his nomination. Two days later, Thornberry requested the same, and on 10 October, the president announced that he would not nominate anyone else for chief justice. For the present, he said, Earl Warren would stay in office.

When Senator Thurmond got the word of Fortas's withdrawal, he gloated, "In my judgment, this is the wisest decision Justice Fortas has made since he became a member of the Supreme Court. I suggest Mr. Fortas now go a step further and resign from the Court for the sake of good government." The senator was to realize his second wish less than a year later, after it became known that Fortas faced more charges of financial impropriety, pursued by the Nixon White House relentlessly toward garnering the justice's resignation. Fortas resigned in a letter to Chief Justice Warren on 13 May 1969. "The Court's prestige prompts my resignation which, I hope, by terminating the public controversy, will permit the Court to proceed with its work without harassment of debate concerning one of its members."[32]

Clark Clifford, among others in Washington, was saddened at Fortas's downfall. "As intellectually fit for the Supreme Court and the Chief Justiceship as any man in this century, he had been destroyed through a combination of President Johnson's overreach, his own bad judgment, and the Nixon administration's attacks." He was also the victim, but not always unwittingly, of a classic political struggle between conservatism and liberalism, Dixiecrats and Democrats, and, as it turned out by the summer of 1968, between Lyndon Johnson and his old cronies in the Senate. It was, in many ways, a no-win situation. Yet, in the end, it was also the resurging issue of pornography that gave people a basis for voting against the nominee with a clear conscience and a profound (they thought) purpose.[33]

Despite Justice Fortas's problems and the zealousness of certain members of Congress, it would be a number of years before the Supreme Court would undertake any serious remodeling of *Roth-Alberts* and the elaborative and refining decisions that followed it. There was good reason to believe that the Court would never regress to the dark days of routine censorship. This belief, or feeling, was strengthened by a 1969 case in which the Court said that it was permissible for individuals to view or read obscene matter—even obscenity so *declared* by law—in the privacy of their homes.

On 7 April 1969, a rare unanimous Court held that the First and Fourteenth Amendments prohibited making private possession of obscene material a crime. In *Stanley v. Georgia*, the justices qualified the sweeping principle of *Roth-Alberts* on obscenity being not within the First Amendment protection of speech and press. The justices said that the Constitution forbade a state to impose a criminal penalty merely for the knowing private possession of obscene material. Like *Ginsberg*, this case turned as much on a right of privacy as it did on freedom of speech.[34] Consenting adults could have whatever they wanted; nonconsenting adults and children could be protected; and knowing what obscenity is could be avoided.

Perhaps the biggest news at the turn of the decade was the long-awaited report of the President's Commission on Obscenity and Pornography, which had been authorized by Congress in October 1967 and whose members were appointed by Lyndon Johnson in January 1968. President Nixon received the Commission's *Report* on 30 September 1970. The Commission stated that "empirical research . . . has found no reliable evidence to date that exposure to explicit sexual materials plays a significant role in the causation of delinquent or criminal behavior among youth and adults." It went on to say that "established patterns of sexual behavior were found to be very stable and not altered substantially by exposure to erotica." Greater latitude can safely be given to adults, the *Report* said, in deciding for themselves what they will or will not read and view. And, most unsettling to many observers, the Commission recommended that "federal, state, and local legislation should not seek to interfere with the rights of adults who wish to do so to read, obtain, or view explicit sexual material." They urged that such laws be repealed.[35]

The *Report* observed, after looking at federal and state antiobscenity laws, that *obscene* was generally not defined at all in them, and when it appeared to be, the definition merely picked up the language of the *Roth-Alberts* decision. The Commission, in fact, criticized the 1957 landmark for the inadequacy of its three criteria—prurient interest, patent offensiveness, and absence of social value: "It is impossible for a publisher, distributor, retailer or exhibitor to know in advance whether he will be charged with a criminal offense for distributing a particular work, since his understanding of the three tests and their application to his work may differ from that of the police, prosecutor, court or jury."[36]

The Commission's work received mixed reviews, including an overwhelming vote of displeasure in the Senate, sixty to five, and President Nixon's rejection of its conclusions and recommendations, calling them "morally bankrupt." "So long as I am in the White House," he promised, "there will be no relaxation of the national effort to control and eliminate smut from our national life." He was well aware, he said, of the importance of protecting free speech, but "pornography is to freedom of expression what anarchy is to liberty; as free men willingly restrain a measure of their freedom to prevent anarchy, so must we draw the line against pornography to protect freedom of expression."[37]

Included in the *Report*'s several volumes are 150 pages of dissents from the majority's findings, some complaining about the Commission's procedures, others directed at its conclusions. Commissioners Morton A. Hill and Winfrey C. Link submitted a minority report that made the plausible objection that the absence of a demonstrable bond between pornography and crime did not support the inference that pornography was harmless. They specifically objected to the adoption by courts and legislatures of the "utterly without social value" criterion.

For the President and members of Congress to be so adamant at this juncture, and quite vociferous at times, and for the Commission's minority report to get as much public attention, and approval, as the majority's, suggests that the obscenity problem was alive and well at the start of a new decade with two personnel changes on the Supreme Court. Warren E. Burger replaced Earl Warren as chief justice in 1969, and Harry Blackmun was appointed Abe Fortas's replacement on 14 April 1970.

◆ POLITICS AND PANDERING

VI

Social Importance

It is neither realistic nor constitutionally sound to read the First Amendment as requiring that the people of Maine or Mississippi accept the public depiction of conduct found tolerable in Las Vegas or New York City.

—Chief Justice
Warren E. Burger,
Miller v. California

CHIEF JUSTICE Burger, who was appointed by President Nixon in 1969 to replace Earl Warren, went on, in *Miller v. California*, to explain his position: "People in different States vary in their tastes and attitudes, and this diversity is not to be strangled by the absolutism of imposed uniformity."[1]

The new conservative majority thus redefined the community standards that had evolved from *Roth-Alberts* in 1957 through *Jacobellis* in 1964 to *Memoirs* in 1966. That standard stipulated that obscenity must be determined on the basis of a "national" average person and that the primary test for measuring obscene material was whether it was "utterly without redeeming social value." The Burger Court justices said a national standard was unascertainable and purely hypothetical. They were silent, unfortunately, on why state or local standards would be any more ascertainable than a national standard. Also, the *Miller* majority rejected the broad social-value test and substituted a more specific requirement, "does not have serious literary, artistic, political or scientific value."

Between 1969 and 1972, President Nixon filled four vacancies on the Court, opportunities he used to move the body in the direction of conservatism, or, in the phrase he preferred, "strict constructionism." The period from 1962 to 1969, which saw Thurgood Marshall, Arthur Goldberg, and Abe Fortas added to the Court, was probably the most liberal in the Court's history. That started to change with Burger's appointment as chief justice, but not immediately.

After failing to get Senate approval for Clement Haynsworth and G. Harrold Carswell in 1969 and 1970, Nixon succeeded with two moderates, Harry Blackmun for Fortas, who had resigned under a conflict-of-interest cloud, and Lewis F. Powell Jr., a former American Bar Association president, for Black, who had retired in ill health after thirty-four years on the Court. William H. Rehnquist, whose conservatism surpassed even Burger's, was named in 1972 to replace Harlan, who stepped down after sixteen years.

In Chief Justice Burger's first brush with obscenity on the Court, the justices upheld the constitutionality of the so-called Anti-Pandering Act, known also as the Pandering Advertisement Act, which prohibits pandering advertisements in the mails. Under the act, a person who receives matter he or she believes to be "erotically arousing or sexually provocative" can instruct the post office to order the sender to drop their name from its mailing list. Also permitted is the elimination of the names of children under nineteen who live at the addressee's home.[2]

Burger said that "the mailer's right to communicate is circumscribed only by an affirmative act of the addressee giving notice that he wishes no further mailings from that mailer." In other words, the responsibility to stop such mailings is left up to the citizen. *Rowan v. U.S. Post Office Department*, as much a matter of privacy, the right "to be left alone," asserted the revitalization of the concept that "a man's home is his castle" into which "not even the king may enter" and rejected the argument that "a vendor has a right . . . to send unwanted material into the home of another." No one, Burger said, has a right to press even "good" ideas on an unwill-

◆ SOCIAL IMPORTANCE

ing recipient. "The asserted right of the mailer . . . stops at the outer boundary [the mailbox] of every person's domain."[3]

Permitting individual householders to define obscenity for themselves, Congress's declared objective in enacting such legislation, Burger said, was to protect minors and the privacy of homes from unsolicited advertisements that "recipients found to be offensive because of their lewd and salacious character." An amended version of the original law eliminated the proscribing of a class of advertisements, as defined in the *Ginzburg* pandering case and assured the removal of the government from "any determination of the content and nature of . . . objectionable materials." Nothing in the Constitution, the chief justice added, "compels us to listen to or view any unwanted communication, whatever its merit."

Rowan was related to a privacy concern voiced the year before in *Stanley v. Georgia*, when the Court said that the First Amendment prohibited criminal punishment for the private possession of obscene materials. In *Rowan*, Burger enunciated the converse proposition: Congress may protect citizens from being forced to confront undesired reading matter in their homes. As in other decisions where the law seems to follow the crime, the Court's reading of Title III allowed for the addressee to censor material that is protected by the Constitution from government interference.

The Anti-Pandering Act had been challenged by fourteen book publishers, distributors, and mailing-list brokers in the Los Angeles area, including some who specialized in mail-order sales of erotic material and sexual paraphernalia. They complained that it cost $5 to remove each name from a list. Post office officials admitted that a few persons had stopped "junk mail" postings to their homes by objecting that they were aroused by catalogues that contained pictures of girdles and bed sheets.

Soon after his appointment, Chief Justice Burger expressed his unease with the way the Warren Court had handled the problem of obscenity. His basic disagreement concerned the Court's lack of deference to state regulation and state court decisions. In *Cain v. Kentucky*, for example, Burger dissented from the *per curiam* reversal of that state's decision to ban the public showings of the film, *I, A Woman*. In his view, the Court "should not inflexibly deny to each of the States the power to adopt and enforce its own standards as to obscenity and pornographic materials." He expressed a similar view in *Walker v. Ohio*, another reversal of a state court's finding of obscenity. Burger declared that he could find no justification for the Court's "assuming the role of a supreme and unreviewable board of censorship for the 50 States, subjectively judging each piece of material brought before it without regard to the findings or conclusions of other courts, state or federal."[4]

Burger's position was not new to the Court. Justice Harlan had consistently advocated that local traditions, varying moral standards, and disparate conditions across the country necessitate the establishment of state standards for defining obscenity. This viewpoint gained the support of a third justice, when Blackmun, the second Nixon appointee, announced in *Hoyt v. Minnesota* that he found himself "generally in accord" with the Burger-Harlan position. "I am not persuaded that the First and Fourteenth Amendments necessarily prescribe a national and uniform measure—rather than one capable of some flexibility and resting on concepts of reasonableness—of what each of our several States constitutionally may do to regulate obscene products within its borders."[5]

The three justices were particularly concerned about the majority's continued use of the summary *per curiam* method to overrule lower courts which, in their view, had conscientiously tried to apply the Supreme Court standards. "I cannot agree that the Minnesota trial court and those six justices [on the state supreme court] were so obviously misguided in their holding that they are to be summarily reversed on the authority of *Redrup*."[6]

More support for the Court's new position of deference to state obscenity policy emerged in several other *per curiam* decisions, two of which were resolved by a divided Court. The justices affirmed findings of obscenity regarding the showing of the film, *I Am Curious (Yellow)*, and the displaying of a sculptor's representation of the American flag as a phallus.

◆ SOCIAL IMPORTANCE

In *Grove Press v. Maryland State Board of Censors*, the finding of obscenity rested on a determination that the film appealed to prurient interest, that it described sex beyond the limits of candor, and that it was without any redeeming social value. In *Radich v. New York*, the defendant had been convicted of violating a New York flag desecration law when, as a protest against the Vietnam conflict, he created a sculpture which depicted the flag enwrapping a phallic symbol, as a human body hanging from a noose, and as a gun caisson.

The new approach, as instigated by Chief Justice Burger, was not meant to apply to lower courts that supported freedom of expression against governmental restraint. Permissiveness, as articulated in *Stanley v. Georgia* on behalf of consenting adults who had acquired obscene material, was to be dealt with severely by the emerging Burger Court. Those justices who followed Burger's lead together managed to stop any further development of the Warren Court's liberal policy.

A concern for privacy seemed not to have interfered, for example, with the Court's 1971 decisions, *United States v. Reidel* and *United States v. Thirty-Seven Photographs*. Justice White, writing for six brethren, refused to extend the protection granted privately held obscene matter to the commercial distribution of obscenity. In *Reidel*, the Court held that Congress may prohibit the commercial distribution of pornography even to willing adults. In *Thirty-Seven Photographs*, the Court ruled that obscene material imported for commercial use may be seized by customs officials. White said that the proper precedent was *Roth-Alberts*, not *Stanley*, where the Court had sustained a conviction for the indiscriminate mailing of pornography under the same federal law at issue in *Reidel*. White noted that obscenity "is not within the area of constitutionally protected speech or press." While the majority acknowledged that *Stanley* had identified a "right to receive" sexual material, the justices maintained that such a right "is not so broad as to immunize the dealing in obscenity in which Reidel engaged here—dealings which *Roth* held unprotected by the First Amendment."[7]

Norman Reidel, owner of Normax Press in Fontana, California, had been indicted on three counts of violating the federal statute against mailing obscene material. One copy of *The True Facts about Imported Pornography* had been mailed to a postal inspector who was over the age of twenty-one and who had responded to a newspaper advertisement. Two other copies were seized during a search of Reidel's business. The district court ruled that Reidel's ads restricted his products to adults, who, under *Stanley*, had the right to possess them. But the Supreme Court reversed.

Milton Luros, the claimant in *Thirty-Seven Photographs*, returned from Europe with a number of pictures he intended to publish in a new hardcover edition of the *Kama Sutra*, a famous book of erotica candidly describing various and numerous sex-act positions. Customs agents seized the photos as obscene and the local U.S. attorney started proceedings for forfeiture of the material. Luros, who maintained that the pictures were not obscene, got a three-judge panel to declare the federal statute unconstitutional and ordered the photos returned. They said the law was too broad and that *Stanley* required some freedom for distributors as well as private owners. However, the Supreme Court again reversed, holding unprotected the commercial importation of obscene matter.

In the *Stanley* decision of 1969, the Court appeared to back away from its strictly definitional approach to obscenity and positioned the problem within traditional First Amendment doctrine. Not all obscene matter was to be excluded from protection; privately owned material, for example, was held beyond the reach of law. Prohibition on private possession, said Justice Marshall, interfered with an individual's First Amendment "right to read or observe what he pleases—the right to satisfy his intellectual and emotional needs in the privacy of his own home." Marshall emphasized that labeling material obscene was insufficient justification for invading the domicile.[8]

What *Stanley* left unclear was whether Robert Stanley's privacy right stemmed from a right to receive obscene material—as some felt the Court implied—or from a right to be free of state intrusion in his home once he had somehow managed to acquire the material. Though the opinion went on to indicate that the *Roth-Alberts* decision had not been disturbed, the ruling had the potential for invalidating more

◆ SOCIAL IMPORTANCE

obscenity laws than just those directed at private possession. Because of the vagueness of *Stanley's* right to receive, it was reasonable for Norman Reidel and Milton Luros to plead a right to publish and distribute their products. Justice White, however, saw no paradox, no contradiction, and no right.

While Stanley's defense was freedom of thought and mind in the private home, Luros was accorded no such protection because, as the Court said, "a port of entry is not a traveler's home." Luros's right to be let alone neither prevented a search of his luggage nor the seizure of unprotected materials discovered during the search. Justice White said, "Whatever the scope of the right to receive obscenity adumbrated in Stanley, that right . . . does not extend to one who is seeking . . . to distribute obscene materials to the public . . . nor to import obscene materials from abroad, whether for private use of public distribution."[9]

Justice Black, in a strong dissent that Douglas joined, said the Court had created a puzzle in the law by safeguarding the private possession of salacious material but not the means of obtaining it. "The mere act of importation for private use can hardly be more offensive to others than is private perusal in one's home," Black wrote. "The right to read and view any literature and pictures at home is hollow indeed if it does not include a right to carry that material privately in one's luggage when entering the country." Black accused his brethren of reasoning "silently" that a prohibition against the importation of obscene materials for private use was permissible as a way of preventing "ultimate commercial distribution of obscenity." He warned that because intention is difficult to prove, all importation of obscene materials may be outlawed without offending the First Amendment.[10]

Justice Marshall, the author of *Stanley*, dissented in *Thirty-Seven Photographs* with the observation that "it is disingenuous to contend that Stanley's conviction was reversed because his home, rather than his person or luggage, was the locus of the search." This point risks being overstated, but it remains difficult nonetheless to understand why a person who has the right to own and peruse a set of pornographic pictures in his home is not permitted to carry them in his suitcase across the border. Justice White obviously relied on the idea that privacy interests are of lower value at the border than at the doorway.

The *Redrup* and *Stanley* decisions of 1967 and 1969, respectively, were heralded by scholars and defense lawyers as an effort by the Supreme Court to stabilize the intractable obscenity problem. The Court could have at least brought a bit more order to that troubled area of law, but instead it set the kettle bubbling again by reviving and reaffirming the *Roth-Alberts* determination—obscenity is not within the area of constitutionally protected speech or press.

Redrup was used to overturn a number of obscenity convictions in the years immediately following its announcement. "Redrupping" became the password for the reversals. It was also seen as a whittling away of the 1957 *Roth-Alberts* declaration. Two years later, in 1969, the implications of *Redrup* were applied in *Stanley* in an effort, it seemed, to provide some protection for sexually explicit material.

Liberalism was not on a roll at the Supreme Court, as *Reidel* and *Thirty-Seven Photographs* showed. Such may not even have been hoped for, as the final words of Justice Marshall's opinion in *Stanley* suggested: "*Roth* and the cases following that decision are not impaired by today's holding. As we have said, the States retain broad power to regulate obscenity; that power simply does not extend to mere possession by the individual in the privacy of his own home."[11]

Thus, as this brief assessment of the Burger Court's early days implies, *Stanley* did not establish a secure right for consenting adults to enjoy pornography in the privacy of their homes. Nor did the decision weaken prohibition on the sale, importation, and interstate transport of obscene materials. Bob Woodward and Scott Armstrong, the writers, speak plainly of the paradox: "If there was a constitutional right to possess obscene material in one's home, then there was a right to buy it. If there was a right to buy it, there was a right to sell it. If there was a right to sell it, there was a right to distribute it. If there was a right to distribute it, then there must be a constitutional right to write, photograph or film it."[12] Logically, the privacy factor, which turns out to have been more technical device than legal deliverance, would have so blurred the distinction between obscene and not ob-

106

scene as to have made efforts at trying to define obscenity largely irrelevant. There would be no need to define obscenity as long as people had the right to see and read what they wished.

Justice Brennan, author of the *Roth-Alberts* definition, faced a dilemma with *Stanley* and finally dealt with his reluctance to concur by avoiding the definitional issue all together. He joined Potter Stewart and Byron White on the ground that because Stanley's films were seized in violation of the Fourth and Fourteenth Amendments, they were inadmissible as evidence at his trial. Brennan would soon abandon the definitional approach that he had worked so hard to create as a solution to the intractable problem.

During the Warren Court years, 1957 through 1969, Brennan wrote no less than seven majority opinions and only one concurring and one dissenting opinion. During the 1970s, the Burger era, he wrote only two obscenity decisions for the majority and a single concurrence but issued eleven personal dissents and joined Douglas and Marshall in other dissents.

Meanwhile, the newly formed Burger Court in its 1972 term, as if in rehearsal for the major obscenity cases it would confront later, dismissed two cases *per curiam* and a third, on nude entertainment, by six to three in an opinion by Justice Rehnquist, *California v. LaRue*, announced on 5 December.

Rehnquist held that nude dancing in bars may be proscribed, even though the activity may not be obscene and within the limits of the constitutional protection of expression. He said that the state regulations came to the Court, "not in the context of censoring a dramatic performance in a theater, but rather in a context of licensing bars and nightclubs to sell liquor by the drink." He explained that the regulations prohibited bars and nightclubs from displaying, either in the form of movies or live performances that "partake more of gross sexuality than of communication." First and Fourteenth Amendment protection would have been forthcoming had these otherwise "bacchanalian revelries" been the constitutional equivalent of a "performance by a scantily clad ballet troupe in a theater."[13]

The Court said that it was not irrational for California to

decide that "certain sexual performances and the dispensation of liquor by the drink" should not occur simultaneously on licensed premises. The "rationality standard," similar to the variable obscenity principle, a question of context rather than content, was applicable because of what the Twenty-First Amendment requires. Rehnquist noted that the Twenty-First was as applicable as the First and Fourteenth, saying that the state must be allowed wide latitude in order to carry out its broad authority, under the amendment, to control intoxicating liquors.

The Supreme Court had behaved portentously. During its next term, it indicated fervently that more discretion should also be afforded local authorities in the regulation of obscene material. In *Paris Adult Theatre I v. Slaton*, companion to *Miller v. California*, the Court said:

> The sum of experience, including that of the past two decades, affords an ample basis for legislatures to conclude that a sensitive, key relationship of human existence, central to family life, community welfare, and the development of human personality, can be debased and distorted by crass commercial exploitation of sex. Nothing in the Constitution prohibits a State from reaching such a conclusion and acting on it legislatively simply because there is no conclusive evidence or empirical data.[14]

Public displays of allegedly obscene matter was the issue in *Rabe v. Washington*, which a *per curiam* Court in an anonymous opinion by Justice Douglas announced on 20 March 1972. An outdoor theater owner had been convicted of showing an obscene film with knowledge of its contents. *Carmen Baby*, a loose contemporary adaptation of Bizet's opera, had been declared obscene at trial, though the "sexually frank" scenes did not go so far as to portray "sexual consummation." The female lead's body could be seen from outside the theater fence by neighborhood children.

In affirming Rabe's conviction, however, Washington state's high court did not hold that the film was obscene under the *Roth-Alberts-Memoirs* test. Thus, the court concluded that if it were to apply "the strict rules of *Roth*," the

◆ SOCIAL IMPORTANCE

film probably would pass the definitional test if the viewing audience consisted only of consenting adults. Because the film had "redeeming social value" it was not, by itself, obscene under *Roth*. But the court nonetheless upheld the conviction, saying that in "the context of its exhibition," *Carmen Baby* was obscene.[15]

Justice Douglas argued that the movie would not have been called obscene if shown indoors, and since the statute said nothing about location, it was too vague to have given the theater manager fair notice. Rabe's conviction, Douglas said, had been affirmed under a law with a meaning quite different from the one he was charged with violating. If the law in question had been "narrowly drawn" to require that certain films not be exhibited to unwilling viewers and children, it would have been constitutional, Chief Justice Burger added in a separate opinion. Douglas took some consolation that at least Burger was thinking about the difference between public and private exhibition, which, clearly, would have to be a factor in any extension of the *Stanley* privacy doctrine.

Douglas was further encouraged by *Kois v. Wisconsin*, the second *per curiam* ruling and the first obscenity case decided with the participation of all four Nixon appointees, announced 26 June 1972. A radical underground newspaper in Madison had been forced out of business and its publisher harassed by a two-year prison sentence and a $2,000 fine for publishing obscene pictures and a "sex poem." Justice Rehnquist said that the issue of *Kaleidoscope* containing the pictures was not obscene because the photos were "rationally related" to an article that itself was clearly protected by the Fourteenth Amendment. Rehnquist, drawing upon the contention, found in *Roth-Alberts*, that "the portrayal of sex . . . in art, literature and scientific works, is not itself sufficient reason to deny . . . constitutional protection." He said that a court must, of necessity, look at the context of the material as well as its content. Cautiously, the justice then granted the poem "some of the earmarks of an attempt at serious art." Also, while "contemporary community standards" must leave room for some latitude of judgment, and while there is an undeniably subjective element in the obscenity test, Rehnquist said that the dominance of the theme is a question of constitutional fact.[16]

Kois, if nothing else, was an early indicator of future policy. Seriousness of purpose replaced "utterly without redeeming social value" one year later, when, in *Miller v. California*, the Burger Court reformulated the *Roth-Alberts-Memoirs* test. Burger also announced that the practice of issuing unelaborated *per curiam* decisions, used consistently since *Redrup*, had come to an end, and that the *Miller* Court would "attempt to provide positive guidance to federal and state courts."[17]

On 21 June 1973, sixteen years after the historic *Roth-Alberts* decisions, Chief Justice Burger announced that a majority of the justices had reached agreement on a new and comprehensive approach to the obscenity problem. The new policy was set down in five cases, each decided by five-to-four votes, and it included three key elements: rejection of the permissive standards and rationales of prior Courts; establishment of a freedom-restricting test for determining obscenity; and continuation of an attitude of deference toward state efforts as regulation. Specifically, the four Nixon appointees, joined by Justice White, agreed to reaffirm obscenity's exclusion from First Amendment protection, to discard the permissive *Memoirs* test, to accept public morality as a legitimate governmental interest, to extend coverage of the obscenity test to nonillustrated sexual books, and to limit further the "right to receive" concept by denying protection to sexual material disseminated solely to consenting adults.[18]

This rejection of past policy and the establishment of a new approach was announced in *Miller v. California*. Burger encouraged lower courts to be more flexible in applying local, not national, standards. He also had trouble with "utterly without redeeming social value" and, instead, preferred that works should have "literary, artistic, political, and social value" to avoid being found obscene. To deal with the most "egregious abuse" by local prosecutors and judges, the chief justice proposed in a draft of the *Miller* opinion that the Court continue to review obscenity laws individually and

◆ SOCIAL IMPORTANCE

Redrup them, that is, make the defendant's conduct the central issue in most cases. "Even accepting that the 'Redrup technique' compounds uncertainty, I prefer it to a new, uncharted swamp," Burger said. "In the long run this Court cannot act as an efficient Super Censor, and the sooner we leave the problem to the states the better off we and the public will be."[19]

This is precisely what Justice Robert Jackson had foreseen as early as 1948, when, during oral argument in the case involving Edmund Wilson's novel, *Memoirs of Hecate County*, he asked counsel for the publishers, Doubleday and Company: "Does your argument mean that we would have to take every obscenity case and decide the constitutional issues on the merits of the literary work? It seems to me that would mean that we would become the High Court of Obscenity." Some critics of the Court's recurring ambivalence might say that the gloomy Jackson prophecy, reiterated by Burger in the *Miller* case, has been fulfilled.[20]

Justice Brennan, meanwhile, decided to counter Burger with a draft opinion of his own, and he also decided to risk writing it as a majority view, admitting that he had been wrong in 1957, with *Roth-Alberts*, and wrong in later attempts to define obscenity. He said he was wrong in *Stanley* not to extend privacy to include privately owned pornography. While believing that private possession should be legal, Brennan based his *Stanley* view on the ground that seizure of the films violated the Fourth and Fourteenth Amendments and were inadmissible as evidence. He was willing to retain some definition of obscenity for public places in order to protect children and unwarned adults. But that was about as far as he was willing to go.

Brennan circulated his draft on 13 June, to which Burger responded immediately. Then, on 19 June, Burger sent around a note that appeared to summarize the stalemate. "In the present posture of the [obscenity] cases neither Justice Brennan nor I can make specific recommendations as to the disposition of the cases." At the justices' 22 June conference, they agreed with Brennan to take three additional cases, all dealing with consenting adults who had sought out pornography, instead of just those cases that involved unwilling viewers. The justices also decided to argue them early in the next term, beginning October 1972, and hold over the three cases before them, for a total of eight.[21]

Several of the decisions announced on 21 and 25 June 1973, were among the most publicized and most controversial of the term. Also decided the same term were the landmark abortion holdings, *Roe v. Wade* and *Doe v. Wade*, which were equally disturbing for the justices and, to this day, at least as controversial as obscenity. Like the abortion cases, as well as the school desegregation decisions before them, the obscenity decisions, as usual, raised about as many questions as they answered.

All of the obscenity decisions revised the seven-year-old test for obscenity reported in the *Memoirs of a Woman of Pleasure* case, renouncing the Brennan rule that material must be "utterly without redeeming social value" before it can be called obscene and abandoning the search for uniform national community standards of what appeals to the prurient interest in favor of state standards of candor and offensiveness. But the Court still relied heavily on *Roth-Alberts*, which upheld a conviction for violation of a federal statute on the mailing of "obscene, lewd, lascivious or filthy" material. To this day, in fact, obscene matter, once defined (no easy job), receives no legal protection whatsoever. The trick, as well as the problem, is in the defining process.

Meanwhile, the decisions announced on 21 June upheld by five to four a California statute prohibiting the mailing of unsolicited sexually explicit material. The Court also affirmed a ruling by the Georgia Supreme Court that two films shown in an adult-only theater were hard-core pornography not entitled to protection. Next, the justices upheld the conviction of the proprietor of an adult bookstore for selling a plain-cover, unillustrated book that described sexual conduct. In its fourth case, the Court endorsed the right of Congress to prohibit the importation of obscene matter for private personal use. Finally, the Burger majority overruled a federal court that had declared unconstitutional a law prohibiting the transport of obscene matter in interstate commerce. Chief Justice Burger wrote each decision, remanding all in light of the new obscenity policy outlined in *Miller v.*

◆ SOCIAL IMPORTANCE

California, the lead decision. Justice Douglas dissented alone, and Brennan joined Stewart and Marshall.[22]

Marvin Miller had been convicted under a California law after he had conducted a mass-mailing campaign advertising illustrated books and films for adults. A restaurant owner in Newport Beach and his mother complained to police after they had received one of Miller's brochures, which depicted men and women in a variety of sexual activities where genitals were often prominent. The young restaurateur had opened his mail in front of his mother; together they reported the embarrassing incident. Miller's conviction was affirmed by the state superior court and appealed directly to the Supreme Court. Although the justices were sympathetic to the California determination, they nevertheless found the conviction improper because a wrong standard for determining obscenity had been applied.

Thus, for the first time in sixteen years—since *Roth-Alberts* in 1957—five justices managed to agree on a definition. Chief Justice Burger's determination to reach consensus was helped along by the Warren Court's failure to muster five votes for a single definition. This lack of agreement presented Burger with an opportunity to leave his mark in an area of the law on which the Court had been wavering for so long.

Burger explained that *Miller* had been tried on the basis of the three-pronged *Memoirs* test, which "has been abandoned as unworkable by its author [Brennan in dissent], and no Member of the Court today supports the *Memoirs* formulation." He then presented the new guidelines: (a) whether "the average person, applying contemporary *community standards*" would find that the work, taken as a whole, appeals to the *prurient interest*; (b) whether the work depicts or describes, in a *patently offensive* way, sexual conduct specifically defined by the applicable state law; and (c) whether the work, taken as a whole, lacks *serious* literary, artistic, political, or scientific *value*.[23]

Burger added that, while the Court was severely critical of the liberal *Memoirs* test, it kept the basic framework of *Roth-Alberts* before dropping the "*utterly* without redeeming social value" prong, which had never commanded the adherence of more than three justices at one time. Burger said that in *Roth-Alberts* obscenity was presumed to be without social value, while the *Memoirs* test required proof of worthlessness. His *Miller* majority also kept the concept of social value but changed it slightly to "serious value."

Thus, the *Miller* theory, a "giant step backward," according to historian Margaret A. Blanchard, began with the *Roth-Alberts-Memoirs* premise that obscenity was unprotected speech because it was utterly without redeeming importance and wound up redefining obscenity in such a way as to jeopardize works with some social value. *Miller* also insisted on balance, if not coalescence, among the three prongs, but they could be applied separately. A patently offensive and prurient work could still be brought within the protection of the First Amendment if one of the specified serious values was present. *Roth-Alberts-Memoirs* required coalescence of all the criteria.[24]

Burger emphasized that it was not the Court's function to propose regulatory schemes for the states, though he did offer "a few plain examples" of what a state statute might define as "patently offensive" material: (a) representations or descriptions of ultimate sexual acts, normal or perverted, actual or simulated; and (b) representations or descriptions of masturbation, excretory functions, and lewd exhibitions of the genitals. "Sex and nudity may not be exploited without limit by films or pictures exhibited or sold in places of public accommodation any more than live sex and nudity can be exhibited or sold without limit in such public places," Burger wrote. At a minimum, prurient, patently offensive depictions or descriptions must have serious literary, artistic, political, or scientific value to merit First Amendment coverage. It must, in short, have serious value, or worth, to society.[25]

Although the chief justice said that the new test was applicable only to hard-core pornography, his description of patently offensive sexual conduct covered the kinds of activities that were given protection by the Warren Court. More revealing is Burger's explanation of how the new *Miller* test would function with respect to questionable material, e.g., medical books for the education of physicians and related

114

personnel would be "saved" because of their serious scientific value. Borderline matter, however, if it does not meet the minimum, and unspecified, threshold of prurience and patent offensiveness, could be viewed as obscene.

On the matter of "contemporary community standards," Burger admitted the national nature of the Constitution, that First Amendment limitations on the states do not vary from town to town. But, he insisted, this did not mean that there were, "or should or can be," fixed, uniform national standards of precisely what appeals to prurient interest or is patently offensive. "When triers of fact are asked to decide whether 'the average person, applying contemporary community standards' would consider certain materials 'prurient,' it would be unrealistic to require that the answer be based on some abstract formulation," Burger wrote. To require a state to structure obscenity proceedings around evidence of a national community standard would be an exercise in futility. Burger said that jurors, as representatives of the average person, could apply local standards when evaluating obscene matter.[26]

Of the dissenting justices, Douglas attached his views to *Miller*, but Brennan, joined by Stewart and Marshall, saved his lengthy voice for the companion case, *Paris Adult Theatre v. Slaton*. Brennan's opinion is discussed at length in the next chapter.

Douglas argued, as he and Justice Black had together for many years, that there was no constitutional prohibition against obscenity and no exception from the First Amendment for obscenity. "The Court is at large because we deal with tastes and standards of literature," Douglas said. "What shocks me may be sustenance for my neighbor. What causes one person to boil up in rage over one pamphlet or movie may reflect only his neurosis, not shared by others. We deal here with a regime of censorship which, if adopted, should be done by constitutional amendment after full debate by the people."[27]

The new test, Douglas thought, "would make it possible to ban any paper or any journal or magazine in some benighted place." He said that the idea that the First Amendment permitted government to ban publications that are offensive to some people puts an ominous gloss on freedom of the press. "The First Amendment was not fashioned as a vehicle for dispensing tranquilizers to the people. Its prime function was to keep debate open to 'offensive' as well as to 'staid' people. We deal with highly emotional, not rational, questions. To many the Song of Solomon is obscene."

There is at best a plus-minus aspect to the Burger Court's passionate reasoning during the 1972 term. On the plus side, a local jury having to determine obscenity on the basis of its assessment of prurience and offensiveness reserves for judges the more manageable role of determining whether sex is the dominant theme of a work and if the jury considered the work as a whole. On the minus side, such power in the hands of laypersons who would resolve sensitive questions of fact *and* law, and judges who would be confined pretty much to questions of law, has the potential of chilling speech generally.

Justice Harlan, in his *Jacobellis* dissent, suggested the inevitable ad hoc nature of standards. "In truth the matter in the last analysis depends on how particular challenged material happens to strike the minds of jurors or judges and ultimately those of a majority of the members of this Court."[28] The greater reliance on juries and lesser control by judges might lead to increased unpredictability and capriciousness. The Burger Court, in attempting to reduce the ambivalence created by *Roth-Alberts-Memoirs*, contributed to even greater uncertainty in *Miller* and progeny by being precise in law and whimsical in fact-finding. This becomes more apparent in Justice Brennan's confessional dissent in *Paris Adult Theatre*.

VII

Consenting Exposure

No other aspect of the First Amendment has, in recent years, demanded so substantial a commitment of our time, generated such disharmony of views, and remained so resistant to the formulation of stable and manageable standards.

—Justice William J. Brennan Jr.,

Paris Adult Theatre I v. Slaton

SO BEGAN Justice Brennan's famous dissent in *Paris Adult Theatre I v. Slaton*, the second of five obscenity decisions announced on 21 June 1973, and which also served as his dissent in the first, *Miller v. California*. "I am convinced that the approach initiated sixteen years ago in *Roth v. United States*, and culminating in the Court's decision today, cannot bring stability to this area of the law without jeopardizing fundamental First Amendment values, and I have concluded that the time has come to make a significant departure from that approach." Thus, Brennan joined Justices Clark and Harlan before him in disgust and frustration over, in Harlan's view, the intractable problem.[1]

Tom C. Clark, whose 1949 appointment to the Court President Truman later called "my biggest mistake," used his dissent in the *Fanny Hill* case to vent his feelings: "I have 'stomached' past cases for almost ten years without much outcry." This is discussed in chapter 3, but here *Memoirs v. Massachusetts* is recalled to illustrate again the growing frustration among the justices. Clark's outcry, though not of the same conciliatory nature nor from the same ideological perspective as Brennan's, was a more-than-mild measure of his contempt for "lascivious scenes organized solely to arouse prurient interest and produce sustained erotic tension."[2]

To support his growing intolerance, Clark tied the question of "anti-social effect" to the more limited question of social value and found evidence to support a disturbing (to him) relationship between sexual arousal and the reading of obscene material. Unfortunately, Justice Clark had retired before the publication in 1970 of the *Report of the [President's] Commission on Obscenity and Pornography*, which concluded that empirical research "designed to clarify the question" had found no evidence that exposure to explicit sexual materials caused delinquent or criminal behavior among youth or adults.[3]

Justice Harlan, on the other hand, had moved more in the direction of Brennan. "The upshot of all this divergence in viewpoint is that anyone who undertakes to examine the Court's decisions since *Roth* which have held particular material obscene or not obscene would find himself in utter bewilderment," Harlan said. For the justice, bewilderment could have been resolved with clearer, but perhaps not more liberal, judicial guidelines—better law, in other words. Reiterating the viewpoint he had expressed in earlier opinions, Harlan said he would limit federal control to hard-core pornography and allow greater state control free of the "federal judicial hand," except where local action is the product of "prudish overzealousness." His carefully crafted protection for speech in *Cohen v. California* still stands as a strong endorsement of First Amendment values. How Clark and Harlan would have reacted to the Burger Court's *Miller*-inspired rulings is anyone's guess, but one suspects their sympathies—at least Harlan's—would have been with Justice Brennan.[4]

This chapter's analysis of the effect privacy has had on Supreme Court obscenity decisions begins with *Paris Adult*

◆ CONSENTING EXPOSURE

Theatre I v. Slaton for two essential reasons. First, *Paris Theatre* is tied to the most recent landmark ruling on the subject, *Miller v. California*, handed down the same day. And, second, the analysis begins with *Paris Theatre* because of Chief Justice Burger's great reliance on privacy in the five-to-four decision. Although the Court's earlier *Redrup* decisions hinted at privacy, in none of the three *Redrup* cases was there any suggestion of an assault upon personal privacy so obtrusive as to make it impossible for unwilling individuals to avoid exposure. So long as one could escape a privacy invasion, no invasion could take place.

In *Stanley v. Georgia*, decided in 1969, two years after *Redrup v. New York*, the Court said that the private possession of obscene material at home was protected. Actually, an earlier decision had set the stage. In *Redmond v. United States*, a *per curiam* ruling, the justices reversed the conviction of a husband and wife who had been convicted for "having mailed undeveloped films of each other posing in the nude . . . for developing, and having received through the mails the developed negatives and a print of each." The Court noted that the prosecutor had violated the policy of the Justice Department not to prosecute private correspondence for obscenity except in aggravated circumstances.[5]

The legal right to privacy, as opposed to the moral right to solitude and seclusion, has found its way into society's attempt to manage, if not control, popular pornography. As with the myriad of other zones of privacy determined by the courts, including the legal right to an abortion, society has looked to this juridical route as yet another way out of its moral dilemma over obscenity.

The *Roe* and *Doe* decisions of 1973, the year also of *Miller v. California*, legalized abortion, but they also changed the Supreme Court's image by fostering renewed attacks on judicial activism. The rulings legalized abortion, but they did not legitimize the policies thus promulgated. Similarly, the Court's many obscenity decisions, even the seeming landmarks, appeared to add to the confusion over how to regulate "trash" while protecting "serious literary, artistic, political, or scientific" speech.

Privacy as a concept has always been a factor in obscenity

litigation, seldom critical or central but in the background nonetheless, for the reason suggested more recently by Justice Antonin Scalia: "Many accomplished people . . . have found literature in Dada and art in the replication of a soup can." Despite the Court's uneven efforts over the years to define obscenity, let alone deal with it constitutionally, it has tried to allow private taste to rule the day whenever feasible. In *Pope v. Illinois*, where the Court held that community standards were not appropriate for judging the value of a work, Justice Scalia went so far as to argue that the "objective" or "reasonable man" test of *Miller* needed to be reconsidered, since it was impossible to come to an objective assessment of literary or artistic value. "Just as there is no use arguing about taste, there is no use litigating about it," Scalia said.[6]

Meanwhile, in the *Paris Theatre* case, two Atlanta movie houses had asserted that state regulations of access by consenting adults to obscene material violated the constitutionally protected right of privacy enjoyed by their customers. In question were the films *Magic Mirror* and *It All Comes Out in the End*, which depicted conduct characterized by Georgia's high court as "hard core pornography" leaving "little to the imagination." Chief Justice Burger responded that it was "unavailing" to compare a theater, open only to the public for a fee, with the private home of *Stanley* and the marital bedroom of *Griswold*.

Burger said that on numerous occasions the Court had refused to hold that commercial ventures, such as a motion picture house, were private for the purpose of civil rights litigation and statutes. He quoted from an article, "On Pornography II," by Professor Alexander Bickel, who wrote that a man may be entitled to read an obscene book in his room but not if he demands the right to obtain such material in the market because that right affects "the world about the rest of us, and . . . impinge[s] on other privacies."[7]

With *Griswold v. Connecticut*, the Court had made its clearest statement at the time, as well as its most sweeping to date, of the constitutional foundations of, in the words of one law professor, "a yearning for privacy." The decision invalidated a state law forbidding the dissemination of

◆ CONSENTING EXPOSURE

birth control information as a violation of a right to marital privacy. Justice Douglas, delivering the opinion of the seven-member majority, said that any important liberty not safe-guarded by the Bill of Rights can be found in the penumbra, or shadow, of a specific guarantee. "Various guarantees create zones of privacy," he said.[8]

Justice Harlan concurred but did not join the Douglas opinion. For Harlan, the penumbra approach, while sufficient to strike down the Connecticut statute, did not go far enough, and he found that the Court's "incorporation" doctrine could be used later to restrict the Fourteenth Amendment due process clause. Differing dramatically with Douglas, the justice said that the decision need not depend on "radiations" from the Bill of Rights. "The Due Process Clause . . . stands . . . on its own bottom."

Harlan's position was dramatic because, while it recognized the personal nature of marriage, it implied that confusion would probably follow when the courts, like the shepherd boy who cried wolf once too often, were confronted with genuine infringement. As usual, Harlan's view was as portentous as it was profound; but, again, the judge's judge, as he was known, was not around to support Brennan's *Paris Theatre* dissent nor to attack Burger's narrower view of privacy.[9]

When Burger, like a Pirandello character in search of an authority, learned of the Bickel article, "On Pornography II," he circulated it among his colleagues. Most fetching was the professor's ability to agree with the *Stanley* decision—that willing viewers should be left alone to watch what they wanted in the privacy of their homes—but disagree with the notion that home privacy should be extended to other zones. For if it were, he reasoned, there would be an increased risk of invading the privacy of others. Burger especially liked Bickel's final statement: "We should protect his privacy. But if he demands a right to obtain the books and pictures he wants in the market, and to foregather in public places—discrete, if you will, but accessible to all—with others who share his tastes, then to grant him his right is to affect the world about the rest of us, and to impinge on other privacies."[10]

The new cases, *Paris Theatre* among them, had been argued in mid-October, and those left from the 1971 term reargued in early November. Burton Marks, a flamboyant criminal lawyer, lectured the justices on the realities of pornography. "We are back again before this court . . . to discuss . . . the continuing saga of life in the pits, or what goes on in the lower courts, because we don't know what, actually, this Court is saying with respect to the pornographer." He said that his clients were business people who did not want to violate the law. "Maybe they're in a dirty business that you don't like, but, nevertheless, they are in business."[11]

During the next weekly conference, Chief Justice Burger made it clear that he had decided to reject the *Stanley* privacy argument, and he already had Rehnquist's support. Brennan, on the other hand, reiterated his desire to extend privacy, provided that children and unwilling adults could be protected. He had Stewart and Marshall on his side. Douglas, Brennan knew, would never join any opinion that preserved any definition of obscenity, but he figured he would at least concur with his dissent. White, Powell, and Blackmun—two Nixon appointees and an increasingly conservative Kennedy appointee—were inclined to be more restrictive than Brennan, yet they had problems with Burger's view, too.

Burger had dismissed other right-to-privacy decisions. For example, he noted that in *Palko v. Connecticut* and *Roe v. Wade*, the Court had held the Fourteenth Amendment to protect "only personal rights that can be deemed 'fundamental' or 'implicit in the concept of ordered liberty.' " The privacy right encompasses and protects, he said, the intimacies of the home, the family, marriage, motherhood, procreation, and child rearing. But, if obscene material unprotected by the First Amendment carried with it a penumbra of constitutionally protected privacy, Burger believed that the Court would have found it necessary to decide *Stanley* on the narrow basis of the "privacy of the home," which he interpreted as hardly more than reaffirming that "a man's home is his castle." The Court, moreover, had on other occasions refused to equate home privacy with a zone of privacy that follows a distributor or consumer of obscene matter wherever he goes. "The

◆ CONSENTING EXPOSURE

idea of a privacy right and a place of public accomodation are, in this context, mutually exclusive," Burger wrote.[12]

The right to privacy, as first enunciated in an 1890 essay by Samuel D. Warren and his young partner Louis D. Brandeis, is not as expansive as "to be let alone," the coinage of Judge Thomas Cooley in his famous 1879 treatise on tort law. Milton R. Konvitz, in the meantime, has drawn a more-than-subtle distinction between the phrases. Right to privacy is at once more general and more restrictive, suggesting what has been withdrawn from public view—the marital bedroom or a respectable married woman's past immoral life. It implies secrecy and darkness, elements of the private life that are detrimental to public welfare.

Privacy, said Konvitz, may also be essential to acts performed in public view, such as membership in an organization or worshipping in a church or synagogue. A person may be asserting her or his right to privacy when they dress in an unorthodox way or when they loaf in a public park. "A person may claim the right to be let alone when he acts publicly or when he acts privately," according to Konvitz. Judge Cooley's right implies the kind of space a person may carry anywhere, into the bedroom or into the street. But, the *Paris Theatre* majority, persuaded more by Burger's argument, firmly endorsed, as they had in specific privacy decisions over the years, the more restrictive Warren and Brandeis right to privacy over the broader right to be let alone.[13]

Paris Theatre affirmed that the privacy of pornography enjoys only negative status. If a right to privacy exists, it exists for the unconsenting majority, not for those who wish access to obscene material. The Court's "right to know" doctrine, recognized explicitly in *Lamont v. Postmaster General* has never been applied to pornography. In that case, the justices unanimously held that the First Amendment protected those who wanted to receive information and ideas as well as those who wanted to communicate with others. Justice Brennan, in a separate concurrence in *Lamont*, joined by Goldberg, said: "I think the right to receive publications is . . . a fundamental right. It would be a barren marketplace of ideas that had only sellers and no buyers."[14]

It was in a 1943 case, *Martin v. City of Struthers*, that the Court first decreed that the First Amendment "necessarily protects the right to receive" information. Douglas said in *Griswold* that the right to know was within the penumbra of the First Amendment: "The right of freedom of speech and press includes not only the right to utter or to print, but the right to distribute, the right to receive, the right to read." Freedom of speech and press, however, did not include the right to receive obscene matter, according to Burger.[15]

"Private use" as an integral part of personal privacy has been the cause of acrimony among the justices at least since the *Griswold* decision created the concept of zones of privacy but provided little substantive help for defining a protected zone. Justices Douglas and Black had little trouble, as one might expect. If *Stanley* was a major breakthrough in private possession, then *Thirty-Seven Photographs*, two years later in 1971, was a major setback.

Milton Luros, whose photos for private, though commercial, use were seized as obscene, had no *Stanley* protection because, as the Court said, "a port of entry is not a traveler's home." Decisions after *Stanley*, including if not culminating in *Paris Theatre*, led to the interpretation of the Court's decisions as protecting obscenity only to the extent that no communication between people, at least people outside the home, was involved. Black and Douglas quipped in dissent in *Thirty-Seven Photographs* that *Stanley* may only protect a person who "writes salacious books in his attic, prints them in his basement, and reads them in his living room."[16]

Because human behavior formed much of the basis of Burger's *Paris Theatre* decision, it is once again useful to return briefly to Chief Justice Warren's troubled concurrence in *Roth-Alberts* of 1957, where he had questioned the wisdom of using such broad language. In a passage that has since come to symbolize a double bind for the Supreme Court as well as for pornographers and buyers of obscene materials (what Attorney Burton Marks no doubt had in mind in his oral presentation to the justices), Warren wrote:

> The conduct of the defendant is the central issue, not the obscenity of a book or picture. The nature of the mate-

rials is, of course, relevant as an attribute of the defendant's conduct, but the materials are thus placed in context from which they draw color and character. A wholly different result might be reached in a different setting.[17]

Warren said in *Roth* that it was proper for state and federal governments to punish individuals who were "plainly engaged in the commercial exploitation of the morbid and shameful craving for materials with prurient effect." This presents a double bind because of the implied dilemma it presents to pornographers and their clients, both of whom were to be judged, according to Warren, by the "morbid and shameful conduct," not for the obscenity of their wares. Subsequent rulings, as discussed earlier, have tended to focus on behavior, a privacy issue not taken into account by the majority in *Roth-Alberts. Ginzburg* in 1966 was the first case to criticize openly and directly pandering or "the business of purveying textual or graphic matter openly advertised to appeal to the erotic interest of customers." The Court said, "The question of obscenity may include consideration of the setting in which the publications were presented as an aid to determine the question of obscenity."[18]

Chief Justice Burger declared in *Paris Theatre* that the Court categorically disapproved the theory, adopted by the Georgia trial judge, that obscene, pornographic films acquired constitutional immunity from state regulations simply because they were exhibited for consenting adults only. "In an unbroken series of cases extending over a long stretch of this Court's history," Burger wrote, "it has been accepted as a postulate that 'the primary requirements of decency may be enforced against obscene publications.' " There is, in particular, a legitimate state interest in "stemming the tide of commercialized obscenity, even assuming it is feasible to enforce effective safeguards against exposure to juveniles." Professor Bickel also said, in the same article that influenced the chief justice, "Even supposing that each of us can, if he wishes, effectively avert the eye and stop the ear (which, in truth, we cannot), what is commonly read and seen and heard and done intrudes upon us all, want it or not."[19]

Burger also drew upon the *Report of the Commission on*

Obscenity and Pornography, especially the so-called "Hill-Link Minority Report." In language strikingly similar to that used by Lord Chief Justice Cockburn in the nineteenth century *Hicklin* case, Burger argued that government has a legitimate interest not only in protecting the collective community but also in protecting "the weak, the uninformed, the unsuspecting, and the gullible from the exercise of their own volition." Besides having a "corrupting and debasing" impact on an individual's personality, the chief justice maintained that government may act on the assumption that exposure to obscene materials may have a tendency to produce antisocial behavior.[20]

This resurrection of the "bad tendency" test, which had been used by the courts in the 1920s to punish subversive activity without having to demonstrate causality, was the Burger Court's response to the empirical studies conducted by the President's Commission. One of the objectives of this body, created by Congress during the Johnson administration, was "to study the effect of obscenity and pornography upon the public . . . and its relationship to crime and other antisocial behavior."[21] But its findings were not in keeping with the Court's—at least not Burger's—stated position.

Relying on survey research and aggregate data, the Commission found no evidence that exposure to obscene material caused immoral or antisocial behavior. "Erotic stimuli appears to have little or no effect upon already established attitudinal commitments regarding either sexuality or sexual morality. The overall picture is almost completely a tableau of no significant change." Nor did the Commission find that such materials operate as a "significant determinative factor in causing crime and delinquency." Yet, in an effort not to overstate its position, the Commission noted that, while it felt certain about "no conclusive" relationships, "it is obviously not possible, and never would be possible, to state that never on any occasion, under any conditions, did any erotic material ever contribute in any way to the likelihood of any individual committing a sex crime."[22]

Rejecting the Commission's major conclusion and findings, at the same time drawing upon the Commission's minority report, Burger said, "It is conceivable that an 'adult'

◆ CONSENTING EXPOSURE

theater can—if it really insists—prevent the exposure of its obscene wares to juveniles. An 'adult' bookstore . . . cannot realistically make this claim." Burger said that the "Hill-Link Minority Report" emphasized that, although most pornography may be bought by adults, the heavy users and most highly exposed people were adolescents. "The legitimate interest in preventing exposure of juveniles to obscene materials cannot be fully served by simply barring [them] from the immediate physical premises of 'adult' bookstores, where there is a flourishing 'outside business' in these materials."[23] Defiantly, Burger said that, despite the lack of conclusive proof linking obscenity to behavior, legislatures could "quite reasonably determine that such a connection does or might exist." He said that lawmakers could base public policy on the "morally neutral judgment" that the commercial exhibition of obscene material might have "a tendency to injure the community as a whole, to endanger the public safety, or to jeopardize . . . the States' 'right . . . to maintain a decent society.' "[24] More poignantly, and sarcastically, Burger wrote, pulling all stops:

> The sum of experience, including that of the past two decades, affords an ample basis for legislatures to conclude that a sensitive, key relationship of human existence, central to family life, community welfare, and the development of human personality, can be debased and distorted by crass commercial exploitation of sex. Nothing in the Constitution prohibits a State from reaching such a conclusion and acting on it legislatively simply because there is no conclusive evidence or empirical data.[25]

After years of experimentation and debate, Justice Brennan confessed in *Paris Theatre* that none of the formulas, including the new one espoused in *Miller v. California*, could reduce the vagueness to a tolerable level that would strike an acceptable balance between the First and Fourteenth Amendments and legislative interest in regulating the spread of certain sexually oriented material.

"I put 16 years into that damn obscenity thing," Justice Brennan told Nat Hentoff, the writer:

I tried and I tried, and I waffled back and forth, and I finally gave up. If you can't define it, you can't prosecute people for it. And that's why, in the *Paris Adult Theatre* decision, I finally abandoned the whole effort. I reached the conclusion that every criminal obscenity statute—and most obscenity laws are criminal—was necessarily unconstitutional, because it was impossible, from the statute, to define obscenity. Accordingly, anybody charged with violating the statute would not have known that his conduct was a violation of the law. He wouldn't know whether the material was obscene until the court told him.[26]

In his dissent, Brennan said that the essence of the problem was the Court's inability to provide sensitive tools for separating obscenity from other sexually oriented but constitutionally protected speech so that efforts to suppress one do not spill over into the suppression of the other. He said that even such concepts as "prurient interest," "serious literary value," and "patent offensiveness" are indefinite and their meaning varies, depending on the experience, outlook, and idiosyncrasies of the person defining them. "Although we have assumed that obscenity does exist and that we 'know it when [we] see it,' we are manifestly unable to describe it in advance except by reference to concepts so elusive that they fail to distinguish clearly between protected and unprotected speech."[27]

Brennan discussed the problems of fair notice, chilling protected speech, and the stresses imposed on state and federal judiciary machinery. A vague law, he said, failed to provide adequate notice to the people engaged in the type of conduct that the law could be thought to proscribe. To help this problem, the Court had felt in the past that any definition must be drawn as narrowly as possible so as to minimize interference with protected expression. "The problem is . . . that one cannot say with certainty that material is obscene until at least five members of this Court, applying inevitably obscure standards, have pronounced it so." He alluded to the stress factor, cause of the tension among state and federal courts, then turned to the need for a significant

◆ CONSENTING EXPOSURE

change in the Court's direction and the limited alternatives open to the justices.[28]

Brennan said that the *Miller* restatement was only different academically from the *Roth-Alberts-Memoirs* test and was likely to permit far more sweeping suppression, including material deserving of protection. He said First Amendment protections had never before been limited to expressions of serious literary or political value. "Whether it will be easier to prove that material lacks 'serious' value than to prove it lacks any value at all remains to be seen."[29]

The justice said that too many statutes were predicated on unprovable, although strongly held, assumptions about human nature and behavior, morality, sex, and religion. So, in concluding a long and sometimes painful journey, Brennan believed that, in the absence of distribution to juveniles or obtrusive exposure to unconsenting adults, the Constitution prohibited suppression on the basis of the content of allegedly obscene matter. States may continue to regulate distribution but not ban total access.

Justices Stewart and Marshall joined Brennan's dissent. Douglas, who wrote a separate dissent, applauded "Brother Brennan . . . for seeking a new path through the thicket" and for forsaking the lower road, which Douglas believed the Court had followed in this field. "Art and literature reflect tastes," he wrote, "and tastes, like musical appreciation, are hardly reducible to precise definitions." He continued:

> Matters of taste, like matters of belief, turn on the idiosyncrasies of individuals. They are too personal to define and too emotional and vague to apply, as witness the prison term for Ralph Ginzburg, not for what he printed but for the sexy manner in which he advertised his creations.
>
> "Obscenity" at most is the expression of offensive ideas. One of the most offensive experiences in my life was a visit to a nation where bookstalls were filled only with books on mathematics and books on religion. But in a life that has been short, I have yet to be trapped into seeing or reading something that would offend me. I never supposed that government was permitted to sit in judgment on one's

tastes or beliefs—save as they involved action within the read of the police power of government. Our society—unlike most in the world—presupposes that freedom and liberty are in a frame of reference that makes the individual, not government, the keeper of his tastes, beliefs, and ideas. That is the philosophy of the First Amendment; and it is the article of faith that sets us apart from most nations in the world.[30]

Douglas liked what Brennan had written, but he might even have questioned "unconsenting" as too much of a restriction. Consenting or unconsenting, willing or unwilling, this was a matter of personal choice to Douglas, not reliance on some nebulous external force.

The obscenity decisions of 1973, *Miller v. California* et al., quickly impacted the lower courts, though by no means did the revised guidelines solve the puzzle of pornography or reduce the erratic and unpredictable jury convictions. The four obscenity dissenters—Brennan, Douglas, Marshall, and Stewart—continued to believe the Court could reverse such convictions. But despite their strong four-vote dissent, they did not insist that each case be granted review. Brennan's strategy was to hold off pushing to take a case until a fifth vote seemed likely. Brennan, with Stewart a close ally, thought Justice Powell was most susceptible to being won over. Through Stewart, Brennan would send exhibits of what he thought were outrageous convictions, but each time Powell was reluctant to second-guess a local jury. Then appeared *Jenkins v. Georgia*, a clear misapplication of the *Miller* standard. It seemed a sure bet to Justice Brennan.[31]

A movie-house operator in Albany, Georgia, had been convicted and fined $750 for showing the critically acclaimed R-rated film *Carnal Knowledge*. The jury had ruled the film obscene, per the Supreme Court's advice in *Miller v. California*, which stated that "triers of facts," usually juries, could determine community standards of decency. And because the Albany jury found that *Carnal Knowledge* had violated those standards, the state high court upheld the conviction. While the film had scenes of partial nudity, it contained no

◆ CONSENTING EXPOSURE

explicit sexual scenes and found its way on many "Ten Best" lists for 1971. Mike Nichols, the highly regarded director of Broadway plays and Hollywood films, was director and Ann-Margret had been nominated for an Oscar.

The Supreme Court unanimously reversed the ruling in an opinion written by Justice Rehnquist, at 47 the youngest justice, who said that the Georgia courts obviously misunderstood the *Miller v. California* decision. The jury had the right to determine community standards, the first prong of *Miller*, but only those descriptions or depictions of sexual conduct that are patently offensive, the second prong, can be censored, regardless of local standards. Therefore, under *Miller*, a jury is limited to what it can find obscene to hardcore pornography, and that juries do not have "unbridled discretion" to decide what is patently offensive.

Carnal Knowledge was not hard-core, according to Rehnquist, because the camera did not focus on the bodies of the actors during scenes of "ultimate sexual acts" nor were the actors' genitals exhibited during those scenes. In fact, during the justices' special viewing of the film, Justice Marshall complained, "I thought we were going to see a dirty movie." Justice White added, "The only thing obscene about this movie is that it is obscenely boring." Chief Justice Burger left early but not before telling his clerks that the camera work and lighting had been well done. Rehnquist liked the music. Thus, at conference all nine justices were prepared to say that the film was not obscene and to reverse the conviction. Rehnquist, who became the hundredth justice of the Supreme Court when he replaced Justice Harlan in December 1971, was given the assignment of explaining why the film was not obscene and why, in a companion case, *The Illustrated Presidential Report of the Commission on Obscenity and Pornography* was.[32]

Miller had stipulated that the jury could use a local community standard in order to give meaning to prurient interest and patent offensiveness, but, as *Jenkins* demonstrated, these elements remained debatable. Interestingly, *Miller*'s third part, "serious value," was not a factor in *Jenkins*, probably because the original conviction had occurred under the more lenient *Roth-Alberts-Memoirs* standard of "utterly without redeeming value." This accidental (or deliberate) avoidance of the third part suggests a reluctance on the part of the Court to go beyond its own jurisdictional borders in search of critical acclaim for serious works. After all, serious value would seem to be not only a check on the first two parts of the *Miller* test but a more relevant factor in determining obscenity.[33]

Jenkins was a state prosecution under *Miller v. California*. In *Hamling v. United States*, announced the same day, 24 June 1974, the justices upheld the federal conviction of the mailer of an obscene brochure advertising what was purported to be an illustrated edition of the 1970 *Report of the Commission on Obscenity and Pornography*. William L. Hamling and three coworkers had been convicted by a jury on twelve counts of mailing and conspiring to mail the obscene brochure to approximately 55,000 people around the country. The photos in the brochure were identified by the appellate court and their descriptions reiterated by Justice Rehnquist:

> The folder opens to a full page splash of pictures portraying heterosexual and homosexual intercourse, sodomy and a variety of deviate sexual acts. Specifically, a group picture of nine persons, one male engaged in masturbation, a female masturbating two males, two couples engaged in intercourse in reverse fashion while one female participant engages in fellatio of a male; a second group picture of six persons, two males masturbating, two fellatrices practicing the act, each bearing a clear depiction of ejaculated seminal fluid on their faces; two persons with the female engaged in the act of fellatio and the male in female masturbation by hand; two separate pictures of males engaged in cunnilinction; a film strip of six frames depicting lesbian love scenes including a cunnilinguist in action and female masturbation with another's hand and a vibrator, and two frames, one depicting a woman mouthing the penis of a horse, and a second poising the same for entrance into her vagina.[34]

The reverse side of the brochure contained a fascimile of the *Report's* cover and an order form for the *Illustrated Report*. It also contained a message thanking President Nixon for commissioning this "monumental work of research and investigation" and urging its purchase by libraries "seriously concerned with full intellectual freedom and adult selection." The major difference between the actual report and the illustrated one was that the latter included illustrations "as examples of the type of subject matter discussed and the type of material shown to persons who were part of the research projects for the Commission as the basis for its *Report*."[35]

"A juror," said Justice Rehnquist, "is entitled to draw on his own knowledge of the views of the average person [not the most prudish or the most tolerant] in the community or vicinage from which he comes for making the required determination, just as he is entitled to draw on his knowledge of the propensities of a 'reasonable' person in other areas of the law. Our holding in *Miller* that California could constitutionally proscribe obscenity in terms of a 'statewide' standard did not mean that any such precise geographic area is required as a matter of constitutional law."[36]

Expert testimony, Rehnquist added, was irrelevant in defining obscenity or community standards, and there was no need for federal laws to look to national standards of decency, even though the *Hamling* trial judge had instructed the jury largely in terms of national criteria. "The *Miller* cases, important as they were in enunciating a constitutional test for obscenity, were intended neither as legislative drafting handbooks nor as manuals of jury instructions."[37] Thus, an important aspect of the *Hamling* case is that the application of a national community standard was not sufficient cause for error. The Court also said that jurors were not required to pay any attention to experts who testify, that they themselves are, in effect, the experts.

Justice Douglas, in dissent, said, "If officials may constitutionally report on obscenity, I see nothing in the First Amendment that allows us to bar the use of a glossary factually to illustrate what the report discusses." Brennan, joined by Stewart and Marshall, argued, as he had in dissent in *Paris Theatre*, that absent distribution to juveniles or obtrusive exposure to unconsenting adults, the First and Fourteenth Amendments prohibit suppressing sexually oriented material on the basis of their allegedly obscene contents. He said community or local standards would force self-censorship by national distributors.

VIII

Content Restriction

WITH THIS and subsequent decisions, Justice Stevens, whom President Ford had nominated to replace William O. Douglas in 1975, became the Court's chief advocate for the content-based sliding-scale theory of First Amendment values. "Even though we recognize that the First Amendment will not tolerate the total suppression of erotic materials that have some arguably artistic value, it is manifest that society's interest in protecting this type of expression is of a wholly different, and lesser, magnitude than the interest in untrammeled political debate that inspired Voltaire's immortal comment."[1] Earlier in the opinion, Stevens had alluded to Voltaire's famous response to the notion that the violent overthrow of tyranny might be legitimate: "I disapprove of what you say but I will defend to the death your right to say it."[2] This remark, Stevens said, had served to characterize the Court's "zealous adherence" to the principle that the government may not tell its citizens what they may or may not say. Such broad statements of principle, however, are sometimes qualified by actual Court adjudications, the justice pointed out.

Historically, a cardinal rule of First Amendment jurisprudence has been that the government cannot regulate speech on the basis of content. Such has long been an operating assumption of the courts when deciding freedom of speech cases. Ordinarily, the Supreme Court has said, the constitutional guarantee of freedom of speech means, as Justice Marshall reiterated in 1972, that "government may not grant the use of a forum to people whose views it finds acceptable, but deny use to those wishing to express less favored or more controversial views." Government has no power, Marshall said, to restrict expression because of its message, its ideas, its subject matter, or its content.[3]

One of the Court's earliest and certainly most famous validations of content regulations may be found in *Schenck v. United States* of 1919, where Justice Oliver Wendell Holmes promulgated his controversial "clear and present danger" test:

> The character of every act depends upon the circumstances in which it is done. The most stringent protection of free speech would not protect a man in falsely shouting fire in a theater, and causing a panic. It does not even protect a man from an injunction against uttering words that may have the effect of force. The question in every case is whether the words used are used in such circumstances and are of such a nature as to create a clear and present danger that they will bring about the substantive evils that Congress has a right to prevent. It is a question of proximity and degree.[4]

Schneider v. Irvington, decided in 1939, endorsed the belief that freedom of speech was a fundamental personal right of liberty. The Court said that, while the ordinances being challenged in four cities were primarily if not solely aimed at regulating litter, not speech, the real effect might be an abridgment of speech. Government animus or lack of enthusiasm for particular points of view as expressed in leaflets,

136

for example, could be the impetus for the enactment of laws that profess only an interest in public safety.

"Mere legislative preferences or beliefs respecting matters of public convenience may well support regulation directed at other personal activities, but be insufficient to justify . . . the exercise of rights so vital to the maintenance of democratic institutions," Justice Owen Roberts wrote for the Court. "And so, as cases arise, the delicate and difficult task falls upon the courts to weigh the circumstances and to appraise the substantiality of the reasons advanced in support of the regulation of the free enjoyment of rights."[5]

In spite of the absolutist appearance of *Schneider*, the Court allowed for what has since become known as the time, place, and manner approach to regulating speech. It said that legislatures may enact regulations "in the interest of public safety, health, welfare or convenience" so long as they do not abridge individual liberties secured by the Constitution "to those who wish to speak, write, print or circulate information or opinion."[6]

Professor Steven H. Shiffrin claims significance for the *Schneider* decision because the Court, while appearing indifferent to the devious motives and bureaucratic attitudes of government, focused on the need to protect the liberty of free speech from unjustified regulation wholly apart from why the government wanted to regulate in the first place. However, Shiffrin admits that the claim that government can bear no animus toward any particular point of view is itself overbroad. While there is, in the Court's words, an "equality of status in the field of ideas," some types of speech, such as the obscene and the libelous, lack value for protection.[7]

In *United States v. O'Brien*, a 1968 decision, which upheld a conviction for draft-card burning, the Court further endorsed time, place, and manner restrictions. It said that the government can regulate the conduct aspects of symbolic speech if the regulation is (1) content neutral, (2) serves significant government interest, (3) is narrowly tailored, and (4) leaves open alternative channels of communication. Professor John Hart Ely observed that *O'Brien* requires that laws restricting speech not outrun the interests they are designed to serve. Another First Amendment scholar, Frederick

Schauer, put it still another way: "Determination that a restriction on communication is only incidental to a state regulatory purpose unrelated to communicative impact is . . . one path to nonprotection."[8]

Meanwhile, in *Young v. American Mini Theatres* in 1976, the Supreme Court upheld for the first time the *general* regulation of otherwise protected speech on the basis of content. It had previously upheld specific content-based restrictions on some speech directed at minors and on speech aimed at unconsenting adults. The fact that a type of speech was entitled to some protection did not mean that speech was totally immune from regulation.

Justice Stevens, writing for the five-to-four Court, acknowledged the strong constitutional principle against content-based regulation. However, he maintained that the principle had already been qualified in previous decisions, and he cited two reasons why it did not forbid absolutely the passage of an ordinance like the one in Detroit. First, he said the ordinance did not violate the government's "paramount obligation of neutrality," since it did not regulate particular speech on the basis of government approval or disapproval of a point of view. Second, Stevens said that society's interest in sexually explicit "adult" expression is "of a wholly different, and lesser, magnitude than the interest in untrammeled political debate."[9]

The justice reasoned that "few of us would march our sons and daughters off to war to preserve the citizen's right to see 'Specified Sexual Activities' exhibited in the theaters of our choice." This was in reference to Detroit's theater classification system, which characterized an adult establishment by its emphasis on matter depicting, describing, or relating to "Specified Sexual Activities" or "Specified Anatomical Areas." The Court noted that Detroit had a factual basis for believing that its scheme would serve the city's interest in trying to preserve the "quality of urban life." Since the ordinance left a sufficient number of sites for adult theaters to accommodate all patrons, it did not "greatly restrict" access. It was, therefore, in Stevens's view, constitutional.[10]

American Mini Theatres Inc. had sought a certificate of occupancy for a theater devoted to adult films. The city, in

◆ CONTENT RESTRICTION

denying the certificate, cited its Anti–Skid Row Ordinance prohibiting new adult theaters in close proximity to certain other land uses in order to avoid neighborhood deterioration. Mini Theatres challenged the constitutionality of the law in federal court, which granted summary judgment on the basis of the city's "rational attempt" to preserve its neighborhoods. The Sixth Circuit reversed, however, finding that the ordinance was an impermissible content regulation. The Supreme Court reinstated the judgment for Detroit.

Justice Stevens drew upon the Court's recent First Amendment decisions on libel and commercial speech, areas where decisions to protect or not protect often depend on the content of the speech. "The line between permissible advocacy and impermissible incitation to crime or violence depends, not merely on the setting in which the speech occurs, but also on exactly what the speaker had to say," Stevens said. "Even within the area of protected speech, a difference in content may require a different governmental response."[11]

In the landmark *New York Times v. Sullivan* decision of 1964, the Court recognized that the First Amendment placed certain content restrictions on the states' power to enforce their libel laws. The Court held that a public official may not recover damages from a critic of her or his official conduct without proof of actual malice. Stevens wrote in *American Mini Theatres*: "Implicit in the opinion [*New York Times v. Sullivan*] is the assumption that if the content of the newspaper article had been different—that is, if its subject matter had not been a public official—a lesser standard of proof would have been adequate."[12]

Stevens emphasized, however, that while the content of a story must be examined to decide whether it involves a public figure or a public issue (an issue determined by rulings after *Times v. Sullivan*), "the Court's application of the relevant rule may not depend on its favorable or unfavorable appraisal of that figure or that issue." Absolute government neutrality, as prescribed by *O'Brien*, must be maintained.[13]

Stevens recalled that in commercial speech decisions the Court made it clear that the content of a particular advertisement may determine the extent of First Amendment protection. A public transit system may accept some advertisements and reject others. A state statute may permit highway billboards to advertise businesses located in the neighborhood but not elsewhere, and regulatory commissions may prohibit businesses from making statements which, though literally true, are potentially deceptive. "The measure of constitutional protection to be afforded commercial speech will surely be governed largely by the content of the communication," Justice Stevens said.

Closer to the heart of the Detroit zoning decision, Stevens referred to opinions that dealt with the suppression of sexually oriented materials on the basis of their "obscene character." The Court upheld in *Ginsberg v. New York*, for example, a conviction for selling to a minor magazines that were not obscene if shown to adults. But, while the First Amendment does not foreclose such a prohibition, the justice said that it was equally clear that any such ban must "rest squarely" on an appraisal of the content of material otherwise within a protected area. "Such a line may be drawn on the basis of content without violating the government's paramount obligation of neutrality in its regulation of protected communication."[14]

"The regulation of the places where sexually explicit films may be exhibited is unaffected by whatever social, political, or philosophical message a film may be intended to communicate," Justice Stevens wrote. "Whether a motion picture ridicules or characterizes one point of view or another, the effect of the ordinance is exactly the same."[15]

Justice Powell agreed with Stevens but rejected the contention that sexually explicit materials should be treated differently under First Amendment principles from other forms of protected expression. To Powell, the Anti–Skid Row Ordinance was more an example of "innovative land-use regulation," implicating First Amendment concerns only incidentally and to a limited extent. Focusing on the citywide distribution of adult materials, Powell determined that the ordinance neither limited film creators' freedom of expression nor threatened movie patrons' freedom to receive this form of expression. Detroit's intention, he said, was not to regulate or suppress adult expression as an end in itself, but only to control the "secondary effects" of such expression on

◆ CONTENT RESTRICTION

neighborhoods. Powell applied the four-part *O'Brien* test and concluded that an "incidental" interference was constitutional.

The dissenters in *American Mini Theatres* were the usual ones, Brennan, Stewart, Marshall, plus Blackmun, who believed that many aspects of the city's ordinance were vague. Stewart found the ordinance's content-based distinction unconstitutional as a way of selectively controlling offensive speech. He accused the majority of a "drastic departure" from established principles, and he characterized the Court's value judgments as "wholly alien to the First Amendment," especially in light of the Court having in *Roth v. United States* considered sex "one of the vital problems of human interest and public concern." As for Voltaire's "immortal comment," it now stands on its head, snapped Stewart.[16]

What is especially noteworthy about the decision is that five justices, led by Stevens, justified their support of content-based regulation on the theory that sexually explicit speech has lesser value than other speech. Also, with the *American Mini Theatres* case, Justice Stevens introduced his sliding-scale approach to First Amendment jurisprudence.

In 1975, almost a year to the day *prior* to the Detroit zoning decision, the Court had invalidated an ordinance prohibiting nudity on drive-in movie screens visible from public places outside the theater area. Justice Powell, who wrote for the Court in *Erznoznik v. City of Jacksonville*, held that equal protection principles are violated by a distinction between classes of speech unless there are "clear reasons" for the distinction. He said, for instance, that the Jacksonville ordinance discriminated among movies solely on the basis of their content, "however innocent or even educational" the nudity. Powell also adopted the view of Justice Harlan, who had said in *Cohen v. California* that an audience is not captive if its members may "avert . . . their eyes." Powell thus concluded that the limited privacy interest of persons on the public streets near the drive-in did not justify the censorship of otherwise protected speech on the basis of its content.[17]

Justice Douglas agreed and said that a "pure" movie is apt to be just as distracting to drivers as an "impure" one and to be just as intrusive upon the privacy of an unwilling but captive audience. "Any ordinance which regulates movies on the basis of content, whether by an obscenity standard or by some other criterion, impermissibly intrudes upon the free speech rights guaranteed by the First and Fourteenth Amendments."[18]

Chief Justice Burger and Justice Rehnquist disagreed and said that the Jacksonville ordinance regulated only "unique public exhibitions of nudity." Passersby could see the films but not hear them, and the same films were being shown in indoor theaters in the city. "It would be absurd to suggest that [the ordinance] operates to suppress the expression of ideas," the dissenters argued. Burger and Rehnquist asserted that the First Amendment interest in the case was "trivial at best."[19]

A year later, with John Paul Stevens in place of Douglas, Justice Powell reaffirmed his view of Jacksonville's nuisance ordinance and compared it to Detroit's comprehensive zoning law. The Jacksonville ordinance was overbroad because it proscribed the showing of any nudity and overinclusive because scenes other than the nude ones might also affect traffic. While the Jacksonville ordinance was a "misconceived" attempt to regulate the content of expression, Detroit's by comparison affected expression only incidentally, Powell believed. But he issued a warning: "Courts must be alert to the possibility of direct rather than incidental effect of zoning on expression, and especially to the possibility of using the power to zone as a pretext for suppressing expression."[20]

There is great reluctance on the Court to support complete acceptance of either Stevens's or Powell's rationales for upholding content-based regulation. In fact, there was general acceptance of *Erznoznik* by the *American Mini Theatre* majority. One interpretation of the Detroit zoning decision is to see it as the Court's willingness to accept some degree of speech restriction, perhaps using Stevens's sliding scale, in the interest of a demonstrated greater need to protect the city's neighborhoods. Continued use of the scale, moreover, would suggest the Court's desire to do away with the all-or-nothing approach to speech protection. This has been true with the traditionally unprotected categories of libelous and commercial speech, where the Court has been more flexible

142

and inclined to weigh the nature (if not always the content) and the amount of government interest in regulation against the burden imposed by the regulatory process.

The broad power of zoning was established as early as 1926, when in *Village of Euclid v. Ambler Realty Co.*, municipalities were given the power to further the public health, safety, morals, and welfare by restricting the permissible uses of land. Since that decision, zoning has become a powerful tool for controlling and shaping both urban and suburban life. Alfred C. Yen asserts that zoning regulations have helped improve modern life in more ways than simply controlling the location of obnoxious land uses. They preserve historical landmarks, encourage development, and control disorderly growth. But as Yen found in his review of zoning laws affecting entertainment, a community's right to provide for its social welfare often conflicts with an adult entertainer's freedom of expression. While tension between zoning power and the First Amendment was the focus of the *American Mini Theatre* case, the Supreme Court justices ruled narrowly that Detroit's dispersal of adult establishments served the substantial interest in attempting to preserve the quality of urban life.[21]

The next important obscenity case to bear Justice Stevens's imprimatur was *Smith v. United States*, announced on 23 May 1977, and the second of four obscenity decisions during the 1976 term. Stevens dissented in all, arguing on behalf of uniform community standards, more precise adherence to "social significance," and greater specificity in dealing with the "inherent vagueness of the obscenity concept."[22]

Jerry Lee Smith had been convicted of posting obscene matter from Des Moines to addresses in Mount Ayr and Guthrie Center, Iowa, at the request of postal inspectors masquerading as customers. The mailings consisted of a magazine, *Intrigue*, depicting nude males and females engaged in masturbation, fellatio, cunnilingus, and intercourse, and two films, *Lovelace* and *Terrorized Virgin*, also showing these activities. But the only Iowa law in force at the time banning the distribution of obscene material applied just to children under eighteen. Smith was found guilty of violating the old federal Comstock Act, which makes unmailable "every obscene, lewd, lascivious, indecent, filthy or vile article, matter, thing, device, or substance" and makes it a felony to deposit that material in the mails.[23]

Justice Blackmun, writing for the Court, relied largely on the basic guidelines laid down by *Miller v. California*. He said that jurors could determine prurient interest and patent offensiveness but should confine the latter to hard-core types of conduct as described in *Miller*. In that decision, the majority gave "plain examples" of what a state could regulate— patently offensive representations or descriptions of ultimate sex acts, masturbation, excretory functions, and "lewd exhibition of the genitals." Blackmun said the jury could rely on its own knowledge of community standards and that state legislative determinations of standards were not binding or conclusive. Noting the close analogy between "contemporary community standards" and "reasonableness," the justice then observed:

> It would be just as inappropriate for a legislature to attempt to freeze a jury to one definition of reasonableness as it would be for a legislature to try to define the contemporary community standard of appeal to prurient interest or patent offensiveness, if it were even possible for such a definition to be formulated.[24]

Justice Stevens, in dissent, took issue with the Court's "offensiveness" touchstone, as he called it, and questioned the suitability of criminal prosecution as the mechanism for regulating the distribution of erotic material. He said that "a federal statute defining a criminal offense should prescribe a uniform standard applicable throughout the country." This proposition was so obvious that it had not been questioned during the first ninety years of enforcement of the Comstock Act under which Smith was prosecuted, Stevens asserted. "In my judgment, the line between communications which 'offend' and those which do not is too blurred to identify criminal conduct. It is also too blurred to delimit the protections of the First Amendment."[25]

Stevens believed that a standard dependent on variable local attitudes was defective when used to define a federal crime. Such flexibility was desirable, however, as part of a

144

civil rule designed to protect the individual's right to select the kind of environment in which he wanted to live. It is wrong to say that local communities are any less diverse than the nation as a whole. Nor are their geographic boundaries more easily drawn. Moreover, the derivation of the relevant community standard "for each of our countless communities is necessarily dependent on the perceptions of the individuals who happen to compose the jury in a given case."[26]

It was Justice Harlan who, in 1959, first raised the problem of community standards, whether they would be national or local. With Justice Frankfurter, Harlan put this controversial part of the original *Roth-Alberts* test at the center of the obscenity issue. In 1962, Harlan maintained that patent offensiveness and prurient interest must be demonstrated to declare a work obscene, and he called for a national standard of decency. Two years after that, Justice Brennan seized upon Harlan's language as support for a national approach to the definition of obscenity. A presumed national standard remained in effect until 1973, when Chief Justice Burger intoned, in *Miller*, "People in different States vary in their tastes and attitudes, and this diversity is not to be strangled by the absolutism of imposed uniformity." To which Stevens replied, in *Smith*, that in a culturally diverse state such as California the standard for judging obscenity was assumed to be more readily ascertainable than a national one. As obscenity is by no means a neutral subject, so it is impossible for jurors to be evenhanded and consistent, Stevens pointed out.[27]

Stevens's dissent in *Smith* gave him the opportunity to explain and elaborate on *Young v. American Mini Theatres* of the previous term. That decision, he said, rejected the premise that all protected communications are equally immune from governmental restraint, whereas those outside the protected zone are utterly without social value and, hence, deserving of no protection. "As long as the government does not totally suppress protected speech and is faithful to its paramount obligation of complete neutrality with respect to the point of view expressed in a protected communication, I see no reason why regulation of certain types of communication may not take into account obvious differences in subject matter." It seemed to Stevens silly to assume that no regulation of sexual material is permissible unless the same could be applied to political comment.[28]

On the other hand, Justice Stevens expressed wariness of the average citizen's understanding of an amorphous community standard and of judges' appraisals of serious artistic merit. "If First Amendment protection is properly denied to materials that are 'patently offensive' to the average citizen," he said, "I question whether the element of erotic appeal is of critical importance." The average person may find some portrayals of violence, disease, or intimate bodily functions (such as the birth of a child) equally repulsive, Stevens said. It is comic to suggest that one of the examples of an "unprotected representation" identified by the Court—excretory functions—would have any erotic appeal to the average person. For Stevens, Jerry Lee Smith's behavior in Iowa did not even constitute a nuisance, let alone grounds for criminal prosecution.[29]

In another obscenity case during the 1976 term, *Splawn v. California*, the Court upheld the conviction of a California man for selling two reels of obscene film. Roy Splawn objected to the trial judge's instruction that permitted jurors to say that the films had some social significance but nevertheless find him guilty because they were advertised and sold as "sexually provocative." Justice Rehnquist, for the Court, cited both *Hamling* and *Ginzburg* in ruling that pandering to prurient interests is a factor in determining whether material is obscene.[30]

Brennan, Stewart, and Marshall wrote short dissents. Brennan said that the law under which Splawn was convicted was overbroad. Stewart said the statute was invalid on its face. They also joined Justice Stevens in a longer dissent. "Truthful statements which are neither misleading nor offensive are protected by the First Amendment even though for a commercial purpose," Stevens said. "If they [the films] were not otherwise obscene, I cannot understand how these films lost their protected status by being truthfully described. Under any sensible regulatory scheme, truthful de-

146

scription of subject matter that is pleasing to some and offensive to others ought to be encouraged, not punished."[31]

Stevens found it ironic that, in upholding obscenity laws, the Court had stressed the state's legitimate interest, as it said in *Miller*, "in prohibiting dissemination or exhibition . . . when the mode of dissemination carries with it a significant danger of offending the sensibilities of unwilling recipients or of exposure to juveniles." Pungently, he added: "To ban advertising of a book or film is to suppress the book or film itself."[32]

In the final obscenity decision in 1977, *Ward v. Illinois*, the Court upheld Illinois's obscenity statute. Stevens, again in strong dissent, saw the ruling as an abandonment of one of the cornerstones of the *Miller* test—the requirement of specificity. Even though the state court made it clear that the statute covered all of the *Miller* examples of obscene material, the court nevertheless had not stated that the law was limited to those examples or to any other specified category.

Wesley Ward, operator of an adult book store in Peoria, had been convicted after he sold two books on sadomasochism. All of his issues were rejected by the Court: (1) the vagueness of the statute because it gave no notice that such material was prohibited specifically; (2) sadomasochistic materials were not included in the *Miller* examples; (3) the materials were not obscene under the three-part *Miller* test; and (4) the statute did not conform to the *Miller* requirement that particular depictions of sexual conduct must be specified in the applicable state law.

Justice White, for the Court majority, said that the first issue was wholly without merit because sadomasochistic materials had been held to violate the Illinois statute long before *Miller v. California* of 1973. On the second issue, White said that the *Miller* examples were just that, examples, and the list was not meant to be exhaustive. The Court dismissed the third issue by noting that it was foreclosed by *Mishkin v. New York* of 1966, where convictions were upheld for the publication of a large number of books dealing with many forms of sexual activity, including sadomasochism, fetishism, and homosexuality. As for Ward's fourth issue,

White said that Illinois had complied with *Miller* when the state high court had interpreted the law to incorporate the tripartite standard of *Memoirs* and the *Miller* guidelines.

Brennan, joined by Stewart, again noted that the statute was overbroad and unconstitutional on its face, as well as on the grounds stated by Stevens, who accused Illinois of having paid only "lip service" to the requirement of specificity in Miller. Professor Frederick Schauer used the lip service description in his analysis:

> The specificity requirement and the proper substantive test for obscenity are separate and independent. The presence of the latter does not eliminate the need for the former. It is therefore obvious that merely using the word "obscene" or its equivalent, without the benefit of any statutory or judicial definition, is insufficient, although other courts have done little more than pay lip service to the specificity requirement in *Miller*.[33]

Another part of the *Miller* test had come under review earlier in the 1976 term in *Marks v. United States*, where Justice Stevens concurred that the *Miller* standard could not apply to a case that arose before that decision.[34] Under the *Memoirs* test, the law when Stanley Marks was convicted of transporting obscene materials in interstate commerce, the standard was whether the material was "utterly without redeeming social value." Marks argued, correctly, that *Miller v. California* cast a much wider net than *Memoirs v. Massachusetts*. The Court said that to apply *Miller* retroactively violated the due process clause of the Fifth Amendment, "much as retroactive application of a new statute to penalize conduct innocent when performed would violate the Constitution's ban on *ex post facto* laws."[35]

Stevens, who dissented in remanding the *Marks* case for a new trial, said that his "brief experience" on the Court had persuaded him that "grossly disparate treatment of similar offenders is a characteristic of the criminal enforcement of obscenity law." He asserted that the constitutional standards for determining obscenity were "so intolerably vague that evenhanded enforcement of the law is a virtual impossibility." Alluding to the landmark privacy decision, *Stanley v.*

◆ CONTENT RESTRICTION

Georgia, he said that the statute was predicated on the "somewhat illogical premise that a person may be prosecuted criminally for providing another with material he has a constitutional right to possess." He took umbrage, too, of law that regulates expression and implicates First Amendment values. "However distasteful these materials are to some of us, they are nevertheless a form of communication and entertainment acceptable to a substantial segment of society; otherwise, they would have no value in the marketplace."[36]

In its 1977 term, the Supreme Court ruled on three obscenity cases, two positing "community standards" problems and the third involving the broadcasting of "indecent but not obscene" words.[37]

In the first, *Ballew v. Georgia*, the justices said that Claude Davis Ballew, manager of the Paris Adult Theatre in Atlanta, had been deprived of his right to a proper jury trial. Obscenity itself was not the major issue, as it had been in the 1973 case involving the same theater. Ballew attacked the Georgia procedure of allowing misdemeanors to be tried by a five-person jury, saying that in an obscenity trial such a peer review was not adequate to assess the standards of the community. The Supreme Court said that a state criminal trial of a nonpetty offense before a jury of less than six persons had in fact deprived Ballew of a proper trial as guaranteed by the Sixth and Fourteenth Amendments.

In *Pinkus v. United States*, the Court held that the instructions to the jury had been in error. When considering community standards, "children are not to be included . . . as part of the 'community,' " explained Chief Justice Burger. On the other hand, it was permissible to instruct the jury to take into account the impact of the material on "sensitive" or "insensitive" persons so long as they were looked at as part of the "community as a whole." Burger added that the jury was permitted to consider the appeal of material to the prurient interest of "deviant" groups and the degree to which William Pinkus had pandered his material through the mail.[38]

Justice Stevens noted that he would have voted to reverse the conviction if the Court had been prepared to reexamine this whole area of the law. "But my views are not now the law," Stevens said. Because the chief justice had written an opinion faithful to the cases on which it relied, Stevens said he had joined the Court's opinion and cast a less-than-enthusiastic fifth vote. Beyond the content-based sliding scale for obscenity cases, the justice found wanting the recurring community standards debate.

Justice Brennan, joined by Stewart and Marshall, concurred in the judgment but said that the statute was "clearly overbroad and unconstitutional." Powell, dissenting, believed that, while the jury instruction as to children should not have been given in a federal prosecution, the error in this case was harmless.

Meanwhile, in the broadcasting case, George Carlin, the satirist, lost out to John Paul Stevens, the jurist, who again successfully applied his content-based sliding scale theory, but this time, unlike with *Smith v. United States*, the nuisance factor prevailed as well. In *FCC v. Pacifica Foundation*, the Court upheld the authority of the Federal Communications Commission to discipline a radio station for broadcasting indecent language that was not obscene. While the FCC has used its statutory powers to regulate the content of radio broadcasts on several occasions by penalizing stations for broadcasting "vulgar" speech, the *Pacifica* case was the first time that the Supreme Court reviewed the extent of the government's power to prohibit certain radio speech because of its patently offensive content.[39]

Pacifica Foundation operates a number of nonprofit, educational radio stations around the country, the two principal ones in San Francisco and New York. In the early afternoon of 30 October 1973, the New York station, WBAI(FM), broadcast a recorded twelve-minute monologue by comedian George Carlin as part of a special discussion on contemporary attitudes toward language. In his "Filthy Words" monologue, Carlin repeatedly used seven words that he quipped could never be said on the public airwaves. Just prior to airing the skit, the program's host advised listeners that the record contained "sensitive language which might be regarded as offensive to some." It was also clear that Carlin meant

◆ CONTENT RESTRICTION

to satirize society's "childish" attitudes toward the taboo words.[40]

Five weeks later, the FCC received a complaint about the program from a listener who had heard the broadcast while driving with his fifteen-year-old son. Although WBAI had warned its listeners before the skit, the listener said in his letter that "any child could have been turning the dial, and tuned into that garbage." In response to this single complaint, the FCC issued a memorandum opinion, noting that the seven words "depict sexual and excretory activities and organs in a manner patently offensive by contemporary community standards for the broadcast medium." The words were deemed "indecent" and therefore prohibited by the federal obscenity law. Section 1464 of the act imposes criminal penalties for the broadcast of "any obscene, indecent, or profane language by means of radio communications." The FCC also grounded its action in another statute that requires the commission to "encourage the larger and more effective use of radio in the public interest." The commission declined, however, to impose formal sanctions on the station.[41]

Although the commission recognized that the language Carlin used was not obscene, it ruled that when children are in the audience, the speech's literary, artistic, political, or scientific value cannot save it. The FCC's opinion stated that during late evening a different standard "might conceivably be used," in which case it would consider the redeeming value of the speech. In a second clarifying memo, the commission said it did not intend to impose an absolute prohibition on the broadcast of indecent language; rather, it desired to channel that speech to a time when children are less likely to be in the audience. A divided three-judge panel of the U.S. Court of Appeals for the District of Columbia Circuit reversed the FCC's order. Chief Judge David Bazelon, for one, concluded that unless the Supreme Court was prepared to recognize indecency as a new category of unprotected speech, the commission's order was overbroad and vague. The commission, in its appeal to the Supreme Court, raised both statutory and constitutional claims regarding the extent of the FCC's authority, whether its order violated its censorship power, especially over offensive language that the Court had never categorized as beyond the scope of First Amendment protection.

Justice Stevens, writing for the five-to-four plurality Court, rejected Pacifica's claim that *indecent* means no more than *obscene* in Section 1464 of the obscenity law and that the FCC, therefore, can proscribe only obscene speech. He argued that "the plain language" of the statute displays the words "obscene, indecent, or profane" as disjunctive, each with a separate meaning. Stevens determined that "prurient appeal is an element of the obscene, but the normal definition of 'indecent' merely refers to nonconformance with accepted standards of morality." Though conceding that the Court had previously construed *indecent* in similar statutes to mean *obscene*, he reasoned that both the history of Section 1464 and the type of medium to which it was addressed (broadcast as opposed to print) warranted a different construction in its case. Thus, Stevens concluded that the FCC, in keeping with its statutory authority, might regulate the broadcast of indecent though not obscene speech.[42]

Justice Stevens said that a higher degree of government intervention was both allowable and desirable in the regulation of radio speech than in the regulation of, for example, newspapers or the mails. "Patently offensive, indecent material presented over the airwaves confronts the citizen, not only in public, but also in the privacy of the home, where the individual's right to be left alone plainly outweighs the First Amendment rights of an intruder," Stevens wrote. While admitting the possibility that broadcasters might start censoring themselves, Stevens, here writing for himself, Chief Justice Burger, and Justice Rehnquist, contended that the FCC's order would "have its primary effect on the form, rather than the content, of serious communication . . . [because] few, if any, thoughts . . . cannot be expressed by . . . less offensive language." Partly because Stevens felt that patently offensive references to excretory and sexual organs are at the "periphery of First Amendment concern" and partly because he saw the regulation as a response to a specific context, he concluded that the FCC's action was not overly broad.[43]

◆ CONTENT RESTRICTION

Asking whether the Constitution forbids *any* abridgment of the right to broadcast nonobscene speech on radio, Stevens cited instances of permissible content-based regulation, where both the content and the context of speech were crucial elements of First Amendment analysis. Obscenity, libel, and fighting words are all content-based exceptions to constitutional protection, Stevens stressed. Further, the justice found that, while "some uses of even the most offensive words are unquestionably protected," protection may vary according to context. Thus, the "vulgar," "offensive," and "shocking" *content* of Carlin's monologue, together with the *context* of an early afternoon radio broadcast, convinced Justice Stevens that the FCC's order did not offend the First Amendment.[44]

Perhaps more central to Stevens's thinking was his angst over the broadcast media's "uniquely pervasive presence in the lives of all Americans" and their programs being "uniquely accessible to children, even those too young to read." Referring to Justice Harlan's brilliant analysis in *Cohen v. California*, Stevens said that "although Cohen's written message ["Fuck the Draft"] might have been incomprehensible to a first grader, Pacifica's broadcast could have enlarged a child's vocabulary in an instant." And, finally, emphasizing the narrowness of *FCC v. Pacifica Foundation*, Stevens said that the commission's decision rested entirely on a nuisance rationale "under which context is all-important"; or as Justice Sutherland wrote in *Euclid v. Ambler Realty Co.*, "a right thing in the wrong place—like a pig in the parlor instead of the barnyard."[45]

In his concurring opinion, Justice Lewis Powell, joined by Harry Blackmun, disavowed the variable approach to the content-based regulation of speech advocated by Stevens. Powell did not subscribe to the "theory that the Justices . . . are free . . . to decide on the basis of its content which speech protected by the First Amendment is most 'valuable' and hence deserving of the most protection, and which is less 'valuable' and hence deserving of less protection." Judgments on the value of speech must be left to the individual. For Powell, the validity of the FCC's action turned on the "unique characteristics of the broadcast media," which

Stevens had noted, and on that alone he found channeling of indecency by the Commission acceptable.[46]

Justice Stewart, speaking for the four dissenters, himself, Brennan, White, and Marshall, confined his discussion to the language of Section 1464 of the federal obscenity law. Contrary to the FCC's holding, that *indecent* was a broader concept than *obscene*, Stewart thought that *indecent* should properly be read as no more than *obscene*. And, since the Carlin monologue was not obscene, the commission lacked statutory authority to ban it. Justice Brennan agreed that the statutory issue was sufficient, but he considered the privacy interests of unwilling adult listeners diminished because radio is a public forum—indeed, a public forum from which the listener, if offended, can withdraw by simply turning the dial.

Society's interest in protecting children, Justice Brennan said, might merit carefully deflecting indecent broadcasts away from young audiences, but he felt that Stevens and Powell had exaggerated the significance of the interest. Some parents might actually find Carlin's unabashed attitude towards the seven "dirty words" healthy and deem it desirable to expose their children to the manner in which Carlin "defuses the taboo surrounding the words," Brennan averred. Additionally, Brennan found in the majority's analysis a lack of distinction between prohibited and permissible "offensiveness." Taken to its conclusion, the Court's rationales would support "the cleansing of public radio of any 'four-letter words' regardless of context.[47]

Brennan perceived two disturbing aspects of the majority's view of the First Amendment. First, he found misguided the proposition, advanced by Justice Stevens, that regulating indecency would affect the time, place, and manner but not the substance of communication. Such reasoning, he felt, ignored the fact that the emotive impact of speech may be as important as its cognitive message. "A given word may have a unique capacity to capsule an idea, evoke an emotion, or conjure up an image," Brennan said. "Even if an alternative phrasing may communicate a speaker's abstract ideas as effectively as those words he is forbidden to use, it is doubtful

◆ CONTENT RESTRICTION

that the sterilized message will convey the emotion that is an essential part of so many communications."[48]

Second, Brennan accused both Stevens and Powell of judging offensiveness by the standards of their own cultural experiences, experiences different from other Americans who make up many of "the innumerable subcultures that compose this Nation." He disliked the idea of the Court's "attempt to impose *its* notions of propriety on the whole of the American people." His Irish-American bootstrap mentality at near-breaking point, Brennan said that Powell and Stevens displayed "a depressing inability to appreciate that in our land of cultural pluralism, there are many who think, act, and talk differently from the Members of this Court, and who do not share their fragile sensibilities. It is only an acute ethnocentric myopia that enables the Court to approve the censorship of communications solely because of the words they contain." He then quoted from the poetic prose of Justice Oliver Wendell Holmes: "A word is not a crystal, transparent and unchanged, it is the skin of a living thought and may vary greatly in color and content according to the circumstances and the time in which it is used." Insofar as "majoritarian conventions" are seen as the acceptable standards for judging indecency, *Pacifica*, in Brennan's view, was in danger of being "another of the dominant culture's inevitable efforts to force those groups who do not share its mores to conform to its way of thinking, acting, and speaking."[49]

For the second time in two years, the Court refused to embrace completely the notion that the degree of First Amendment protection varies with the social value of the regulated speech. Even Justice Stevens, the chief spokesman for the sliding-scale, or two-level, theory of protection, never urged excluding all indecent broadcast speech from the First Amendment. Indeed, he ended his opinion by emphasizing its narrowness, saying that the particular facts of *Pacifica* were controlling. Stevens borrowed from the space zoning in *American Mini Theatres*, that offensive broadcasts may be channeled into time zones where they are less likely to cause harm. While similar rationales exist in the two decisions, it is important to note that the Detroit case had more compelling reasons for limiting speech and fewer access obstacles for audiences to overcome. As defended by Justice Powell, the Detroit ordinance furthered an important local interest unrelated to the suppression of speech. Its purpose was not to abridge speech or control its content but rather to control crime, protect the city's tax base, and revitalize its neighborhoods.[50]

Justice Stevens's sliding-scale analysis evolved over the three cases, *American Mini Theatres*, *Smith v. United States*, and *Pacifica*. Offensive speech, according to the justice, when balanced against other expressions of higher content value is of peripheral First Amendment worth. The adult books and films in *American Mini Theatres*, like the Carlin monologue, are not excluded from protection but the protection is minimal. Second, Stevens insisted on a more relaxed standard of review to a regulation involving a civil rather than a criminal penality, in effect, urging the decriminalization of obscenity. In dissent in *Smith*, the justice argued that criminal prosecution was an unacceptable method of regulating offensive speech. And, third, it was important to Stevens in *American Mini Theatres* and *Pacifica* that no total suppression of speech was involved. Stevens's position entails both the context and content of speech. Instead of an elaborate scheme of categorization, as devised by the *Miller* Court, the justice recommends a determination based on weighing the speech's social value in context. Unfortunately, the Stevens approach, while less confusing, is more subjective and therefore no less complex in application than the more objective rules approach of *Miller v. California*.

◆ CONTENT RESTRICTION

IX

Expressive Activity

PORNOGRAPHY may be a blight, even a scourge, but censorship has not become the constitutional way for government regulatory agencies, such as the Supreme Court, to fight society's "porn" merchants. Instead, during the 1980s and on into the 1990s, the Court continued mainly to hone the principles it had set down in 1973 in *Miller v. California*, to this day its most recent major obscenity ruling; *Miller* in turn had been a reworking of *Roth-Alberts* of 1957 and *Memoirs* of 1966. For example, in 1981, 1986, and 1991, the justices supported city zoning, as they had in *Young v. American Mini Theatres* in 1976, as a way of regulating but not prohibiting obscene matter.[1] Also, they extended special protection to minors, especially those under sixteen, from being exploited in sex-act and genital-display portrayals. The Court, in 1990, even upheld a ban on the *possession* of materials showing nude minors, so determined were the justices to protect children and punish purveyors.[2]

The Supreme Court opened the 1980s with, among others,

a town zoning case, *Schad v. Borough of Mount Ephraim.* Unlike their support of Detroit's ordinance in *Young v. American Mini Theatres* in 1976, the justices in the *Mount Ephraim* ruling invalidated a zoning law for its overbreadth in proscribing *all* live entertainment, including nude dancing. Justice White, author of the majority opinion, observed:

> Entertainment, as well as political and ideological speech, is protected; motion pictures, programs broadcast by radio and television, and live entertainment, such as musical and dramatic works, fall within the First Amendment guarantee. Nor may an entertainment program be prohibited solely because it displays the nude human figure. "Nudity alone" does not place otherwise protected material outside the mantle of the First Amendment. Furthermore, as the state courts in this case recognized, nude dancing is not without its First Amendment protections from official regulation.[3]

White, reiterating the Court's long-standing commitment to close scrutiny of legislation that "diminishes the exercise of rights so vital to the maintenance of democratic institutions," said that the justices, in upholding Detroit's ordinance and not Mount Ephraim's, made the distinction between *dispersing* entertainment, as in Detroit, and *prohibiting* it all together. "The Court did not imply [in *American Mini Theatres*] that a municipality could ban all adult theaters—much less all live entertainment or all nude dancing—from its commercial districts citywide."[4]

The appellants had operated what Justice White called an "adult bookstore" in Camden County, New Jersey, since 1973, stocking books, magazines, and films, and it had a number of coin-operated booths in which customers could watch adult films. In 1976, the store installed another coin-operated device that permitted the customer to watch a live dancer, usually nude, performing behind a glass panel. The bookstore owners were convicted of violating the local zoning ordinance, which listed a number of permitted uses in the borough, and prohibited "all uses not expressly permitted in this chapter." The state courts found that the ordinance prohibited all live entertainment, including live nude

◆ EXPRESSIVE ACTIVITY

dancing. The state superior court affirmed the guilty verdict and fine, and the New Jersey Supreme Court denied review.

The U.S. Supreme Court rejected the argument that no First Amendment guarantees were implicated because the case involved simply a zoning ordinance. By excluding live entertainment from the borough, Justice White said, the law prohibited a wide range of expression that had long been within the protections of the First and Fourteenth Amendments, and that the First Amendment required there be "sufficient justification for the exclusion of a broad category of protected expression as one of the permitted commercial uses in the Borough."[5]

Justice Blackmun, concurring separately, pointed out that the presumption of validity that attends a local government's exercise of its zoning powers carries little weight when the regulation trenches on First Amendment rights. Blackmun also disapproved of the suggestion that a local community should be free to eliminate a particular form of expression so long as that form is available in nearby communities. "Were I a resident of Mount Ephraim, I would not expect my right to attend the theater or to purchase a novel to be contingent upon the availability of such opportunities in 'nearby' Philadelphia, a community in whose decisions I would have no political voice." As the Court said in 1939, one is not to have the exercise of her or his liberty of expression in appropriate places abridged on the plea that it may be exercised in some other place. Finally, Blackmun warned against, as the Court had in 1949, the "standardization of ideas . . . by . . . dominant political or community groups."[6]

Justice Powell, joined by Stewart, noted that, while he agreed that Mount Ephraim had failed to justify its broad restriction of protected expression, a more carefully drawn ordinance might be valid where all commercial activity was excluded. Justice Stevens concurred in the judgment but did not join the Court's overbroad analysis. He wrote separately, and ironically, asserting that the record was "opaque" and complaining that the Court was left to speculate on the reasons for proceeding against the bookstore. "The record in this case leaves so many relevant questions unanswered that the outcome, in my judgment, depends on the allocation of the burden of persuasion," the justice wrote. And then he waxed poetic and sarcastic:

> Even though the foliage of the First Amendment may cast protective shadows over some forms of nude dancing, its roots were germinated by more serious concerns that are not necessarily implicated by a content-neutral zoning ordinance banning commercial exploitation of live entertainment.
>
> Without more information about this commercial enclave on Black Horse Pike, one cannot know whether the change in appellants' business in 1976 introduced cacophony into a tranquil setting or merely a new refrain in a local replica of Place Pigalle.
>
> While a municipality need not persuade a federal court that its zoning decisions are correct as a matter of policy, when First Amendment interests are implicated, it must at least be able to demonstrate that a uniform policy in fact exists and is applied in a content-neutral fashion. Municipalities may regulate expressive activity—even protected activity—pursuant to narrowly drawn content-neutral standards; however, they may not regulate protected activity when the only standard provided is the unbridled discretion of a municipal official.[7]

Chief Justice Burger and Justice Rehnquist dissented, seeing the case as simply involving the right of a small community to ban an activity "incompatible with a quiet, residential atmosphere." The issue was not whether the borough could ban traditional live entertainment, the dissenters said, but whether it may ban nude dancing used as bait by the bookstore. "When, and if, this ordinance is used to prevent a high school performance of 'The Sound of Music,' for example, the Court can deal with that problem."[8]

The *Mount Ephraim* case was not the first time that the Supreme Court had confronted nude dancing. Justice Stevens mentioned three in which the Court had protected "some forms," *California v. LaRue* in 1972 and *Southeastern Promotions Ltd. v. Conrad* and *Doran v. Salem Inn Inc.*, both in 1975. In *LaRue*, the pacesetter, discussed earlier, the Court,

◆ EXPRESSIVE ACTIVITY

in an opinion written by Rehnquist, allowed for the regulation of live entertainment in bars and nightclubs where liquor was sold, a "rational exercise," it said, of the state's broad authority under the Twenty-First Amendment, even though protected expression was proscribed. However, when "certain *sexual performances*," including nude dancing, are not dispensed with "liquor by the drink" the assumption had been that they may be covered by the First Amendment.[9]

The Court tried to underscore that point three years later in *Doran*, which Justice Rehnquist, writing again for the Court, distinguished from *LaRue*. He noted that the local ordinance not only banned topless dancing in bars but also prohibited any female from appearing in "any public place" with exposed breasts. "Any public place" could include the theater, the town hall, the opera house, as well as a public marketplace, street, or any place of assembly indoors or outdoors. Thus, Rehnquist opined that the ordinance would prohibit the performance of the Ballet Africains and a number of other artistic works of socially redeeming significance.[10] The law could not be allowed to stand.

Although the Court alluded to the possible extension of the First Amendment to nude dancing in *LaRue*, not until *Doran* did there emerge a strong notion that the justices would view this kind of dancing as expression deserving constitutional protection. Subsequent decisions have strengthened this supposition, although, as the justices made clear in *LaRue*, such protection could be counterbalanced by a legitimate state interest. Recently, for example, in *New York State Liquor Authority v. Bellanca*, the Court took the position it had enunciated in *LaRue*, that First Amendment coverage may be overcome by the state's broad powers under the Twenty-First Amendment.

What's interesting is that whenever the Court has dealt with nude dancing its decisions have been either rooted in zoning ordinances, as in *Shad*, or alcoholic beverage regulations, as in *LaRue* and *Bellanca*. Thus, the justices have never addressed *directly* the First Amendment implications of nude dancing. Justice Stevens, dissenting in *Bellanca*, noted: "Although the Court has written several opinions implying that nude or partially nude dancing is a form of expressive activity protected by the First Amendment, the Court has never directly confronted the question."[11]

Such was also the case ten years later, in 1991, when the justices once again avoided the issue in a sharply divided five-to-four ruling that let stand an Indiana statute banning nude dancing in bars and other adults-only establishments. In *Barnes v. Glen Theatre Inc.*, Indiana's public indecency law was challenged by a South Bend bar, an adult bookstore that included live dancing, and three dancers. The law, similar to those in effect in a number of other states, required female performers to wear at least pasties and a G-string. The respondents had lost in federal district court but won in the appeals court, which said that nude dancing was inherently expressive and therefore protected by the First Amendment. The parties agreed that the performances, while erotic, were not obscene, so that Supreme Court precedents allowing for no constitutional protection were not at issue.[12]

The Court's holding, with a plurality opinion by Rehnquist, who became chief justice in 1986, was supported by three separate opinions. Justices Sandra Day O'Connor and Anthony M. Kennedy joined his opinion, while Justices Antonin Scalia and David H. Souter, Brennan's replacement, wrote separate concurring opinions. Only Scalia said there was no First Amendment protection at all for nude dancing. As with its previous decisions, the majority decided to employ a narrow approach rather than draw into question protection for many forms of artistic expression.

Referring to *Doran, LaRue,* and *Schad,* in that order, Chief Justice Rehnquist said: "Nude dancing of the kind sought to be performed here is expressive conduct within the outer perimeters of the First Amendment, though we view it as only marginally so." Rehnquist relied heavily on the 1968 case involving the burning of a draft card on the steps of a Boston courthouse, *United States v. O'Brien.*[13] The Court had rejected David O'Brien's contention that his act was symbolic speech protected by the Constitution, saying that government regulation of expression is legitimate if it meets four requirements: (1) if it is within the government's constitutional power; (2) if it furthers an important government in-

162

terest; (3) if that interest is unrelated to the suppression of free expression; and (4) if the restriction causes minimal intrusion on the First Amendment freedom in question. Rehnquist said the Indiana law met all four parts of the *O'Brien* balancing test.

Souter, who provided the majority with an equivocal fifth vote, said he agreed with much of Rehnquist's analysis but wrote separately to question the public morality rationale on which the chief justice relied. Rehnquist had said that a state's traditional interest in "protecting societal order and morality" was both substantial and not aimed at free expression. "Public indecency statutes such as the one before us reflect moral disapproval of people appearing in the nude among strangers in public places," Rehnquist said.[14]

Souter, on the other hand, said that the law was valid because of "the State's substantial interest in combating the secondary effects of adult entertainment" of the kind involved in the case. He identified those effects as prostitution, sexual assaults, and "other criminal activity." Souter noted that under his approach "it is difficult to see" how a state would be justified in applying a public nudity law to such plays as *Hair* or *Equus* that were performed "somewhere other than an 'adult' theater." Other members of the majority did not address possible applications of the law beyond the confines of the case.[15]

Justice White, in his dissenting opinion for himself, Marshall, Blackmun, and Stevens, said that by banning nude dancing, a state inevitably prohibited the communication of an idea because "the nudity itself is an expressive component of the dance." He said, "It is only because nude dancing performances may generate emotions and feelings of eroticism and sensuality among the spectators that the State seeks to regulate such expressive activity." White said that the essence of communication was the generating of thoughts, ideas, emotions.[16]

For that reason, White said, the Court's precedents dictated that nude dancing not be treated the way draft-card burning was in the *O'Brien* decision but rather as expressive activity entitled to the full First Amendment protection that the justices gave to the act of burning the American flag in

1989.[17] The justice said that the *O'Brien* test was inappropriate because the activity for which he was convicted did not depend on its public nature—it was illegal to burn one's draft card in the privacy of one's home as well as on the courthouse steps. By contrast, Indiana's law was aimed at public nudity. "The purpose of forbidding people from appearing nude in parks, beaches, hot dog stands, and like public places is to protect others from offense," White wrote, and added:

> But that could not possibly be the purpose of preventing nude dancing in theaters and barrooms since the viewers are exclusively consenting adults who pay money to see these dances. The purpose of the proscription in these contexts is to protect the viewers from what the State believes is the harmful message that nude dancing communicates.[18]

Challenging Scalia's suggestion that performance dancing is not inherently expressive activity, Justice White quoted Aristotle, who believed that the purpose of dance was "to represent men's character as well as what they do and suffer," and the French poet Stephane Mallarme, who declared that the dancer "writing with her body . . . suggests things which the written work could express only in several paragraphs of dialogue or descriptive prose."[19] White and Scalia parried in their opinions over whether harm to others is an appropriate constitutional standard. Scalia wrote:

> The purpose of Indiana's nudity law would be violated, I think, if 60,000 fully consenting adults crowded into the Hoosierdome to display their genitals to one another, even if there were not an offended innocent in the crowd. Our society prohibits, and all human societies have prohibited, certain activities not because they harm others but because they are considered . . . immoral.

White replied that the Indiana statute would indeed apply to the sixty thousand in the Hoosierdome, but "those same 60,000 Hoosiers would be perfectly free to drive to their respective homes all across Indiana and, once there, to parade around, cavort, and revel in the nude for hours in front of relatives and friends."[20]

More will be said later on the possible contribution, as

164

well as the obvious frivolousness, of the nude-dancing cases, especially *Barnes v. Glen Theatre Inc.*, to obscenity law. Now it is only important to summarize that the Court has clearly endorsed zoning laws, starting at least with *American Mini Theatres* as a means of controlling pornographic matter. At the same time it has said that some forms of erotic performance are sufficiently expressive to warrant First Amendment protection.

When the justices faced the growing problem of child pornography in 1982, they unanimously upheld a New York state law prohibiting sexual performances by children that were not obscene under the *Miller v. California* definition. The Court carefully enunciated the greater leeway it accorded the states in regulating child pornography and found the value of expression that depicts children engaged in sex acts as *de minimus*, minimal, and far outweighed by the evils of child abuse and exploitation. The justices reaffirmed the *Miller* formulation for obscenity but found it inapplicable to child pornography because its standards did not serve to protect minors shown in pornographic materials. Thus, with *New York v. Ferber*, child pornography—"kiddie porn" in the vernacular—joined the categories of speech that lack protection under the First Amendment, and once again, the Court found speech whose value was outweighed by other considerations.

Traditionally, the controversy over pornography and obscenity has focused on the possible harmful effects of such material on readers, listeners, or viewers. Child pornography posed a totally different problem, though not unrelated to adult pornography. Child pornography was not solely a question of morality or artistic taste or political ideas. The primary concern was not how to protect the community from exposure to sexually explicit materials; rather the concern was how to protect innocent children from sexual abuse. The debate over obscenity laws and censorship has been broadened to include concerns with the physical and psychological abuse of children engaged in the production of materials— the process by which children become "induced" into "pornographic activity," including runaway children and "kiddie porn rings" as well as the commercial and private production and distribution and possession of child pornography materials. On this there is little disagreement: the purpose of child pornography laws is to control the abuse of children.[21]

When the growing problem of child pornography in the United States surfaced in the late 1970s, federal and state governments swiftly made the activity illegal. Between 1977 and 1982, forty-seven states and the federal government enacted laws prohibiting child pornography. Twenty states banned its dissemination regardless of whether the material was obscene. The federal government and fifteen states prohibited such material only if it was obscene as defined by *Miller v. California*. Nobody, however, questioned the criminality of the creation of pornography that involves the sexual exploitation of children.

Congress enacted in 1977 the Protection of Children from Sexual Exploitation Act, which prohibited the production of any sexually explicit material using a child under sixteen. Federal legislators also banned the transportation, shipping, mailing, or receipt of child pornography in interstate commerce "for the purpose of sale or distribution for sale."[22] Private trading of material was unaffected by the act and its provisions only extended to "sexually explicit" material that was judged obscene under *Miller*.

The new law was successful in reducing the commercial nature of child pornography, but it was also instrumental in driving the activity underground. Moreover, the act was seen as not as effective as expected because prosecutors had to prove the materials in question were obscene. Also, much of child pornography was made by child abusers themselves and then either kept or informally circulated to other abusers, therefore not meeting the commercial purposes requirements of the law. From 1978 to 1984 only one person was reported to have been convicted for the commercial production of child pornography. Child pornography had not been eradicated; it thrived underground.

New York v. Ferber provided a more potent weapon. Justice White, writing for six justices, said that the Court could find no value whatsoever in encouraging children to engage in sex and that states could go beyond the limits imposed by *Miller v. California* in regulating pornographic depictions of

◆ EXPRESSIVE ACTIVITY

children. "The prevention of sexual exploitation and abuse of children constitutes a government objective of surpassing importance," he wrote. The value of permitting live performances and photographic reproductions of children engaged in lewd conduct is "exceedingly modest," seldom constituting an important and necessary part of a literary performance or scientific or education work. The justices refused to apply the *Miller* obscenity test, which they said bore no connection to the issue of "whether a child has been physically or psychologically harmed in the production of the work."[23] Thus, the test of whether a work, taken as a whole, appeals to the prurient interest of the average person was deemed irrelevant.

The Court also reasoned that circulation of child pornography would exacerbate the harm and that the elimination of its distribution would effectively control the sexual exploitation of children. "The most expeditious if not the only practical method of law enforcement may be to dry up the market for this material by imposing severe criminal penalties on persons selling, advertising, or otherwise promoting the product." Yet despite the many reasons for banishing the new category, "child pornography," to unprotected status, Justice White insisted that proscribed conduct be adequately defined and that laws be limited to works that *visually* depicted sexual conduct by children below a specified age. The category of "sexual conduct" must also be suitably described.[24] White added that the New York law was not substantially overbroad and that, in any event, it properly reflected a legitimate and compelling state interest.

Justice O'Connor noted separately that New York need not have excepted from its law material with serious literary, scientific, or educational value, for a child photographed while masturbating surely suffers the same psychological harm whether the community labels the photo "edifying" or "tasteless." She cautioned, however, that the statute was quite possibly overbroad in that it banned "depictions that do not actually threaten the harms identified by the Court," such as pictures of adolescent sexuality in medical textbooks and ritualistic cultural events that might appear, for example, in *National Geographic*. But potential overbreadth was not "sufficiently substantial to warrant facial invalidation of New York's statute."[25]

Brennan, with Marshall, said that absent particular harm to children or unconsenting adults, states lacked power to suppress sexually oriented materials. The First Amendment protects depictions of children that have serious literary, artistic, scientific, or medical value. Stevens added that, while he disagreed with the Court on such speech being totally without First Amendment protection, he agreed that generally "marginal speech" does not warrant the extraordinary protection afforded by the First Amendment when the overbreadth doctrine is applied. He drew upon his content-based sliding-scale theory of First Amendment values that he first elaborated on in 1976 in *Young v. American Mini Theatres*. "The question whether a specific act of communication is protected by the First Amendment always requires some consideration of both its content and its context," Stevens wrote.[26] Blackmun concurred without opinion.

Congress, bolstered by the Court's action, amended the 1977 act by enacting the Child Protection Act in 1984 to restrict the distribution of nonobscene child pornography. The new provisions also removed the commercial purpose requirement and eliminated the proof of obscenity from the 1977 law. It also raised the age limit from 16 to 18 But pressure continued for the enactment of harsher measures. When the Attorney General's Commission on Pornography reiterated in 1986 the need for vigorous enforcement of the laws, Congress responded with more revisions, including a prohibition on making, printing, publishing, exchanging, buying, advertising, distributing, displaying, or reproducing visual depictions of child pornography.[27]

In 1985, Congress passed the Computer Pornography and Child Exploitation Act, which was aimed at establishing "criminal penalties for the transmission by computer of obscene matter, or by computer or by other means, of matter pertaining to the sexual exploitation of children, and for other purposes." Senators Strom Thurmond, an old foe of pornography, and Dennis DeConcini cosponsored the Child Protection and Obscenity Enforcement Act, part of the Anti–Drug Abuse Act, in 1988. The bill prohibited the use of children in pornography, the transmission of advertisements "seeking or offering children for use in pornography," and the "distribution of any obscene matter on cable or subscription television whether or not children are involved."[28]

Other areas covered by the 1988 bill included provisions that made it a crime to sell or possess material on federal property and the forfeiture of not only obscene material itself but any mainstream inventory that is purchased with the proceeds of the obscene material. The language of the bill seemed to allow that a bookseller or publisher could be prosecuted for possessing as few as two copies of a publication that might later be determined by any local jury to be obscene.

Onerous record-keeping provisions of the bill included requirements that "at every level of the creative process in film or publishing that each person—the publisher, the printer, the stock house, the photographer, the photo-lab—must identify on a first-hand basis the age of every person depicted in a pose that contains frontal nudity or sexual activity." Fortunately, this provision was found unconstitutional by a federal judge in May 1989, following vigorous protests by a coalition of booksellers, publishers, the American Library Association, and others who feared the censorship of nonobscene materials.[29]

And so it went, the problem of child pornography emerging forcefully in the 1970s and legislators and judges responding with equal force in the 1980s. The extension of child pornography into a child abuse problem has, it seems, caused legislation to be passed that has the potential for encroaching on the First Amendment. Judges have expressed concern, as has the Supreme Court, notably in *New York v. Ferber*. The whole issue of child pornography conflates problems of child abuse, sexual exploitation of children, censorship and privacy, and, of course, the Constitution itself. But, as the justices implied, the prevention of harm to children is of such surpassing importance as to warrant unprecedented measures.

Brockett v. Spokane Arcades Inc. presented the justices with some housekeeping chores of the semantic variety. A Washington state law regarding "moral nuisance" defined *lewd* matter as synonymous with *obscene* matter. The statute's definition of obscene matter followed the *Miller* test but included a definition of *prurient* as "that which incites lasciviousness or lust." The U.S. Court of Appeals for the Ninth Circuit found the entire law unconstitutional, ruling that a definition of *lust* necessarily encompassed "healthy, wholesome human reaction common to millions of well adjusted persons in our society, not shameful or morbid desire." The court therefore found the statute prohibited protected material. The Supreme Court reversed and reaffirmed the definition of "prurient interest" in *Roth-Alberts*.[30]

Justice White, in his opinion for the Court, said that the appeals court was surely aware that *Roth* had indicated that material appealing to the prurient interest was that which had "a tendency to excite lustful thoughts" but did not intend to characterize as obscene material that provoked only normal, healthy sexual desires. White said that by using the phrase "lustful thoughts," the Court was referring to sexual responses "over and beyond those that would be characterized as normal."[31]

While perhaps only a housekeeping case, *Brockett* nonetheless helped to clarify the meaning of "prurient interest." Indirectly, the Court excluded normal, healthy sexual desires—whatever they are—from the *Roth-Alberts* definition. And it reinforced *Miller*'s limiting obscenity to hard-core pornography.

In its 1985–1986 term, the justices revisited zoning as a means of regulating obscenity. In *City of Renton v. Playtime Theatres*, they upheld an adult-use zoning ordinance similar to the Detroit one they had endorsed in 1976 in *American Mini Theatres*. This time, however, the Court's opinion, written by Justice Rehnquist, commanded a clear majority. Only Brennan and Marshall dissented. The majority held that adult-use ordinances should be treated as content-neutral, with time, place, and manner restrictions, provided they are designed primarily to combat the secondary land-use effects of adult businesses and are not related to the suppression of unpopular views.[32]

As Rehnquist framed the test, the ordinance was constitutional if it was narrowly tailored to serve a substantial gov-

◆ EXPRESSIVE ACTIVITY

ernment interest and allowed for reasonable alternative avenues of communication. It is important to note that in addition to the secondary effects rationale, the justice relied on Stevens's language in *American Mini Theatres*, that sexual speech is less valuable than political speech. "Secondary effects" include the prevention of crime, protection of retail trade, maintenance of property values, and, in general, preservation of a town's quality of neighborhoods and commercial districts.[33]

> Cities may regulate adult theaters by dispersing them, as in Detroit, or by effectively concentrating them, as in Renton. The First Amendment requires only that Renton refrain from effectively denying respondents a reasonable opportunity to open and operate an adult theater within the city, and the ordinance before us easily meets this requirement.[34]

In their dissent, Brennan and Marshall questioned the characterization of the ordinance as "content-neutral." They argued that the law's "selective treatment" of movie theaters specializing in "adult motion pictures" strongly suggested that Renton's interest was in discriminating against adult theaters based on the content of the films they exhibit, not in controlling the secondary effects of adult businesses. It should be recalled that Justice Stevens's opinion in *American Mini Theatres* suggested that while adult-use ordinances may be content-based, they should be viewpoint-neutral.[35]

Pope v. Illinois started out as another housekeeping case regarding a trial judge's erroneous instructions but ended up at the Supreme Court as another illustration of the persisting divisions among the justices on the obscenity issue. The six-to-three Court ruled that judges and juries deciding whether sexually explicit material was largely obscene must assess the social value of the material from the standpoint of a "reasonable person" rather than applying community standards. The justices wrote five separate opinions, but in the process they actually narrowed the legal boundaries of what constitutes obscenity.[36]

Justice White, writing for himself, Rehnquist, Powell, O'Connor, and Scalia (Blackmun concurred in part and dissented in part), held that the "serious literary, artistic, political, or scientific value" component of the *Miller* standard was not to be judged by the application of contemporary community standards. Rather, the intellectual value of a given work must be determined by a national standard that asks "whether a reasonable person would find such value in the material, taken as a whole." The state had objected in its brief that the two standards amounted to the same thing in practice. The Court responded that "the risk . . . is that under a 'community standards' instruction a jury member could consider himself bound to follow prevailing local views on value without considering whether a reasonable person would arrive at a different conclusion."[37]

Justice Scalia, who joined the majority opinion but also wrote separately on the "objective" or "reasonable person" test, suggested that it was impossible to come to an objective assessment of (at least) literary or artistic value. "Many accomplished people . . . have found literature in Dada, and art in the replication of a soup can." He continued:

> I think we would be better advised to adopt as a legal maxim what has long been the wisdom of mankind: De gustibus non est disputandum. Just as there is no use arguing about taste, there is no use litigating about it. For the law courts to decide "What is Beauty" is a novelty even by today's standards.[38]

Justice Stevens, in part of his dissenting opinion that was joined by Brennan, Marshall, and Blackmun, argued that the convictions should have been reversed because of the trial judge's error in instructing the jury. They said the majority's decision amounted to a perversion of the Court's "harmless error" doctrine, which has ordinarily been used to avoid reversing criminal convictions whenever a judge makes a relatively inconsequential error in a trial. They believed it would undercut the rights of criminal defendants.

Stevens, Brennan, and Marshall, but not Blackmun, also dissented from White's incorporation of the "reasonable person" standard into the legal definition of obscenity. White, in explaining why the Illinois jury instruction was unconstitutional, said that

◆ EXPRESSIVE ACTIVITY

just as the ideas a work represents need not obtain majority approval to merit protection, neither, insofar as the First Amendment is concerned, does the value of the work vary from community to community based on the degree of local acceptance it has won. . . .

The mere fact that only a minority of a population may believe a work has serious value does not mean the "reasonable person" standard would not be met.[39]

But Stevens said that "the Court announces an obscenity standard that fails to accomplish the goal that the Court ascribes to it." He said there were many cases in which reasonable people would disagree about whether particular materials had value and that "the Court's formulation does not tell the jury how to decide such cases." Neither *Ulysses* nor *Lady Chatterley's Lover* would have literary appeal to the majority of the population, Stevens averred, but it is conceivable that a jury asked to create "a reasonable person" might believe that the majority of the population who find no value in such books are more reasonable than the minority who do. The justice added: "The difficulties inherent in the Court's 'reasonable person' standard reaffirm my conviction that government may not constitutionally criminalize mere possession or sale of obscene literature, absent some connection to minors, or obtrusive display to unconsenting adults."[40]

He called obscenity laws a "trap for the innocent," adding that when the two defendants, Richard Pope and Michael Morrison, accepted jobs as part-time clerks in the adult bookstore, "they could hardly have been expected to examine the stores' entire inventories, and even if they had, they would have had no way of knowing which, if any, of the magazines being sold were legally 'obscene.' "[41]

Justice Stevens's reservations about the implications of *Pope* are compelling indeed. On its face, the decision appears to be minor, essentially a matter of housekeeping, but nonetheless an expansion of the First Amendment. Closer inspection, however, suggests, first, that the standard for determining intellectual value as a national one does little more than state what had been the common understanding.[42] Second, the introduction of a "reasonable person" standard may

Expressive Activity ◆

portend, as Stevens himself warned, a limitation on the protection of fringe or avant-garde material. "The problem with this formulation," he said, "is that it assumes that all reasonable persons would resolve the value inquiry in the same way." Moreover, the reasonable person's judgment may not necessarily coincide with the opinion of members of the population who have a professional interest in preserving access to material in their respective areas of expertise, such as art scholars, scientists, or literary critics. "Certainly a jury could conclude that although those people reasonably find value in the material, the ordinary 'reasonable person' would not."[43]

Yet, as one critic points out, if Justice Stevens's fears are well founded, *Pope* simply will have integrated the third component of the *Miller* standard into the intellectual scheme to which Stevens himself gave voice in *American Mini Theatres*. The two-level, or sliding-scale, approach to the First Amendment, and the morality principle on which it is based, by definition eschews the value skepticism Stevens sanctions in his *Pope* dissent. Misapplied, the Stevens approach could lead to legal determinations of value based on society's ability to enforce through law, as the Supreme Court perceived in *Chaplinsky v. New Hampshire*, "society's interest in order and morality." This interpretation of the First Amendment, writes Steven Gey, "gives the dominant members of society the right to govern such expression in order to enforce their moral code on the society as a whole—which inevitably leads to the suppression of unorthodox and controversial sexually explicit speech."[44]

Another "read" on the *Pope* decision is that the Court majority, as well as the three dissenters, who simply felt that the majority had not made its argument strongly enough, made it explicit that local community tastes were not the criterion for judging value. In so doing, the justices made it much more difficult for local prosecutors to outlaw sexually explicit creative works as obscene. "It expands intellectual freedom, and that's to the good," *The Philadelphia Inquirer* editorialized.[45]

Meanwhile, in an unusual 1988 decision that the Supreme Court requested, *Virginia v. American Booksellers*,

174

the Virginia Supreme Court ruled that sixteen books by James Joyce, John Updike, Judy Blume, and other authors would not be banned under a state statute protecting minors from harmful material. Booksellers feared that the books, several of which have considerable literary merit, could be barred entirely under the law protecting minors from sexually explicit books and films. The Virginia court ruled that none of the sixteen books would be banned under the statute that bars display of harmful materials in such a way that juveniles might "examine and peruse" them. The Virginia court also ruled that store owners do not have to hide harmful materials to keep juveniles from examining them. It is enough, the court said, for booksellers to keep sexually explicit materials in their sight so that juveniles may be stopped if they attempt to peruse them.[46]

Child pornography reappeared on the Supreme Court's agenda in 1989, 1990, and 1992. In *Massachusetts v. Oakes*, the majority, in an opinion by Justice O'Connor, ruled that a state criminal statute prohibiting adults from posing or exhibiting nude minors was overbroad. In *Osborne v. Ohio*, Justice White, for the majority, said that it was within the Constitution for a state to proscribe the possession and viewing of child pornography. Justices Brennan, Marshall, and Stevens dissented in both. In *Jacobson v. United States*, the majority agreed that a Nebraska farmer had been entrapped by federal postal inspectors into purchasing child pornography in violation of the Child Protection Act of 1984.[47]

Under a Massachusetts statute, it is a crime to knowingly permit a child under eighteen "to pose or be exhibited in a state of nudity . . . for purpose of visual representation in any book, magazine, pamphlet, motion picture film, photograph, or picture." In 1984, Douglas Oakes was convicted for having taken about ten color photographs of his partially nude and physically mature fourteen-year-old stepdaughter in a manner said to have been sexually provocative. At the time, the stepdaughter was attending modeling school. A divided Massachusetts Supreme Judicial Court reversed, holding, first, that the speech was protected and, second, that the law was "substantially overbroad." After the U.S. Supreme Court agreed to hear the appeal, the statute was amended so as to make the posing and exhibiting activities illegal only if done with "lascivious intent." Although unable to agree on an opinion, six justices said that remand was necessary to determine whether the amended statute could constitutionally be applied to Oakes. In dissent, Brennan, joined by Marshall and Stevens, said that, despite revisions to the statute, overbreadth still applied as a defense, noting also:

> Many of the world's great artists—Degas, Renoir, Donatello, to name but a few—have worked from models under 18 years of age, and many acclaimed photographs and films have included nude or partially clad minors. The First Amendment rights of models, actors, artists, photographers, and filmmakers are surely not overborne by the . . . interest in protecting minors from the risk of sexual abuse and exploitation, especially in view of the comprehensive set of laws targeted at those evils.[48]

A basic issue in the legal fight against child pornography, as we have seen, is the conflict between preventing child abuse, on the one hand, and protecting First Amendment rights of free speech, on the other. Some twenty states have criminalized the possession of child pornography, enacting legislation that is in apparent conflict with the Supreme Court's 1969 decision in *Stanley v. Georgia* that struck down statutes prohibiting the private possession of obscene material. With the *Osborne* ruling, however, the justices tried to resolve the conflict by saying that Ohio's ban on the possession of child pornography was not inconsistent with the First Amendment.

Ohio's child pornography law prohibited the private possession or viewing of material depicting a nude minor unless the materials had a bona fide "proper purpose" or the parents had consented to their child's depiction in the materials. In 1985, a trial court convicted Clyde Osborne for possessing four sexually explicit photos of a fourteen-year-old boy. After an appeals court upheld his conviction, Osborne went to the state supreme court, arguing that the statute's reference to nudity was unconstitutionally overbroad. In rejecting the claim, Ohio's high court narrowly construed *nudity* to mean "a lewd exhibition" or involving "a graphic

◆ EXPRESSIVE ACTIVITY

focus on the genitals." Osborne also contended that even allowing for such a narrow construction, the trial judge had denied him due process by failing to instruct the jury on the "lewd exhibition of the genitals" definition or on any intent requirement. The Ohio Supreme Court rejected these claims because Osborne had not raised them at trial. The U.S. Supreme Court, in its six-to-three decision, said that the statute was constitutional but overturned Osborne's conviction on the ground that the jury had not been instructed properly.

The right to possess expressive materials in one's home, established by *Stanley*, was substantially reduced, if not severely eroded, by *Osborne*. Moreover, in justifying its decision, the Court vacillated between evaluating child pornography under the two-tier, or sliding-scale, approach and a more novel "low-value speech" theory. In any event, Justice White said, the outcome was not governed by *Stanley*, "a narrow holding," because "the interests underlying child pornography prohibitions far exceed the interests justifying the Georgia law at issue in *Stanley*."[49]

In the Georgia case, the state "sought to proscribe the private possession of obscenity because it was concerned that obscenity would poison the minds of its viewers." But the Court found that "paternalistic" motive impermissible under the First Amendment, Justice White said. By contrast, the purpose of the Ohio law was to "protect the victims of child pornography," and the state "hopes to destroy a market for the exploitative use of children." The justice added that it was "reasonable for the state to conclude that it will decrease the production of child pornography if it penalizes those who possess and view the product, thereby decreasing demand."[50]

White pointed out that in 1982, in *Ferber*, the Court had used much the same rationale in upholding a New York state statute outlawing the distribution of child pornography. Thus, the majority rejected Osborne's use of *Stanley* and the overbreadth argument but reversed the conviction because the trial had not revealed whether the jury had found that Osborne's photographs depicted a lewd exhibition of or graphically focused on the child's genitals.[51]

In a dissenting opinion, Justice Brennan, joined by Marshall, who wrote the *Stanley* decision, and Stevens, agreed on the reversal but disagreed that Osborne should be retried. He said the Ohio law was both overbroad and unconstitutional under *Stanley*. It was overbroad because it prohibited pictures of "simple nudity" that were protected by the First Amendment. The Ohio law was written in a way that he said could permit prosecution of those who own pictures of "teenagers in revealing dresses" or "even of toddlers romping unclothed." Brennan concluded:

> At bottom, the Court today is so disquieted by the possible exploitation of children in the *production* of the pornography that it is willing to tolerate the imposition of criminal penalties for simple *possession*. While I share the majority's concerns, I do not believe that it has struck the proper balance between the First Amendment and the State's interests, especially in the light of the other means available to Ohio to protect children from exploitation and the State's failure to demonstrate a causal link between a ban on possession of child pornography and a decrease in its production.[52]

The justices split five to four in deciding that Keith Jacobson, a Nebraska farmer, had been tricked by postal inspectors into accepting through the mail two copies of a pornographic magazine, *Boys Who Love Boys*. Jacobson was one of more than 160 men arrested in 1987 by inspectors in the U.S. Postal Service's covert investigation, Operation Looking Glass. The inspectors were operating under the Child Protection Act, which outlaws the purchase or acceptance of child pornography, described as a "visual depiction [that] involves the use of a minor engaging in sexually explicit conduct." Within three months of the law's passage, government agents sought repeatedly, through several fictitious mail-order organizations and a bogus pen pal, to encourage Jacobson's "willingness to break the new law by ordering sexually explicit photographs of children through the mail."[53]

Jacobson first came to the attention of government agents in 1984, when, during a raid of an adult bookstore in California, they confiscated the subscription list. Jacobson had ordered from the outlet a magazine that included photographs of naked boys but did not depict any sexual activity. The

◆ EXPRESSIVE ACTIVITY

magazine, *Bare Boys*, was legal when Jacobson bought it, but within months of his purchase, the new law had broadened the definition of pornography to include such a magazine. Over the span of more than two years, the government sent Jacobson a number of sexual solicitations, and, after eight of them, he succumbed. Agents soon arrived at his home and of course found what they were looking for.

A three-judge panel of the U.S. Court of Appeals for the Eighth Circuit threw out, by a two-to-one vote, Jacobson's conviction in January 1990. But the entire court, voting eight to two, reinstated it nine months later. "The Constitution does not require reasonable suspicion of wrongdoing before the government can begin an undercover investigation," the appeals court said. "The postal inspectors did not apply extraordinary pressure on Jacobson. . . . Unlike face-to-face contacts, Jacobson easily could have ignored the contents of the mailings if he was not interested in them." In a dissenting opinion, Judge Donald Lay called the government's conduct "reprehensible." Judge Gerald Heaney, in a separate dissent, said: "Had the government left Jacobson alone, he would have, on the basis of his past life, continued to be a law-abiding man, caring for his parents, farming his land and minding his own business. Now he stands disgraced in his home and his community with no visible gain to the Postal Service in the important fight against the sexual exploitation of children."[54]

The Supreme Court's majority opinion, written skillfully by Justice White, said the government, in its zeal to enforce the law, could not single out an "otherwise law-abiding citizen" and then "induce commission of the crime so that the government may prosecute." Justice O'Connor, who wrote for the dissent, said the Court had expanded the entrapment defense by making it harder to show the required "predisposition" to commit a crime. In the end, however, she deferred to the jurors, "the conscience of the community," she called them, and they had found Jacobson "a willing participant" in the activity and not "an innocent dupe."[55] Joining White were Blackmun, Stevens, Souter, and Clarence Thomas, the newest member of the Court. With O'Connor were Chief Justice Rehnquist, Kennedy, and Scalia.

Restrictions on the types of expressive activity presented and discussed in this chapter—nude dancing and child pornography—are as much the result of morality as they are of concrete harms. Society's taboo on nudity, for example, especially as it applies to public displays, is surely behind our efforts at punishment and is not because of any deep worry over public indecency or the secondary effects of topless bars. Child pornography has a similar history, but with it suppression is more clearly warranted to protect the innocent participant. So, too, with pornography in which an adult is physically injured, as well as pornography exhibited to an unconsenting audience. Note, however, that topless bars are seldom frequented by unwilling patrons.

Richard A. Posner, a judge of the U.S. Court of Appeals for the Seventh Circuit and a senior lecturer at the University of Chicago Law School, provides a learned analysis of the Indiana nude-dancing case. While writing a separate opinion, he joined the circuit court's reversal of the district court's finding that nude dancing was not expressive and protected by the First Amendment. But the Supreme Court, as we saw earlier in *Barnes v. Glen Theatre*, upheld the state law banning nude dancing in bars and other adults-only establishments. It is Posner's analysis that is enlightening, starting with the assertion: "Thirty years ago a striptease that ended in complete nudity would have been thought obscene. No more."[56]

But obscenity was not the core issue in the *Barnes* case. There was no contention that the stripteases of the Kitty Kat Lounge dancers were obscene. The contention, rather, was that the dances were not expressive, so the First Amendment did not protect them; thus there was no obstacle to enforcing the Indiana statute against the dancers and their accomplice, the proprietor of the lounge. "If this reasoning is correct," said Judge Posner, "the arts are in jeopardy." Dance is a medium of expression, of communication. "Erotic dances express erotic emotions, such as sexual excitement and longing." While nudity and disrobing are not *invariably* associated with sex, the goal of the striptease is to enforce the association in the viewer's imagination. That's the "tease" in "striptease." Posner continued:

◆ EXPRESSIVE ACTIVITY

Of course, there would be no female stripteases without a prurient interest in the female body; but that is just to say that there would be no erotic art without Eros. The striptease is the ensemble of the music, the dance, the disrobing, and the nude end state; it is more erotic than any of its components; and what makes it more erotic than the body itself, or the disrobing itself, is, precisely that it is *expressive* of erotic emotion. The State of Indiana may be empowered to regulate or even suppress it, but not on the ground that it is not expression.[57]

Posner is most persuasive when he broadens the concept of democracy to include art as well as political speech. If the purpose and scope of the First Amendment's speech and press clauses are exhausted in the protection of political speech, because freedom of political speech is all that is necessary to preserve our democratic political system, he says that this implies the exclusion from the amendment's protection not only of all art (other than the political) but also of science. "For one can have democracy without science, just as one can have democracy without art." Moreover, the Constitution "does not look down its nose at popular culture even if its framers would have done so." In the end, the "classification games" played by lawyers and judges, such as expression versus nonexpression, ideas versus emotions, art versus entertainment, or speech versus conduct, avoid the real reason for wanting to exclude striptease dancing from the First Amendment. Behind the gnashing is the tendency to think political expression more important than artistic expression because of, in large part, the cultural influences of puritanism, philistinism, and promiscuity, which are "complexly and often incongruously interwoven."[58]

Expressive Activity ◆

X

Syndicated Sex

The First Amendment is a rule of substantive protection, not an artifice of categories. The Court has been consistent in adopting a speech-protective definition of prior restraint when the state attempts to attack future speech in retribution for a speaker's past transgressions. The rights of free speech and press in their broad and legitimate sphere cannot be defeated by the simple expedient of punishing after in lieu of censoring before.

—Justice Anthony M. Kennedy,
Alexander v. United States

PERHAPS the only major change in Supreme Court strategy for dealing with obscenity was its endorsement in 1989 of the Racketeering Influence and Corrupt Organizations Act (RICO) as a way of prosecuting obscenity cases. What may be problematic for First Amendment speech, however, is that RICO, enacted in 1970 to limit the influence of organized crime, particularly on legitimate businesses and labor unions, may chill forms of expression that are controversial or socially unpopular but not necessarily legally obscene. Congress viewed RICO mainly as a tool for attacking the specific problem of infiltration of legitimate business by organized crime syndicates. As such, RICO has hardly been a dramatic success. Few notable RICO prosecutions have dealt directly with this sort of criminal activity.[1]

More specifically, the government can use the RICO law to seize the property of booksellers, videotape dealers, and other purveyors of communicative materials, even if the obscene materials constitute only a fraction of the defendant's inventory. RICO prosecutions can lead to wholesale forfeiture of both business and personal holdings, as well as the other extraordinary sanctions available under RICO, if the businesses are suspected of laundering money for the mob.[2] And all this can occur before a trial takes place.

The Attorney General's Commission on Pornography, which issued its report in 1986, concluded that organized crime exerted enormous influence and control over the obscenity industry. "Though a number of significant producers and distributors are not members of LCN [La Cosa Nostra] families, all major producers and distributors of obscene material are highly organized and carry out illegal activities with a great deal of sophistication," the commission reported. For example, the panel said that the millions of dollars grossed by the film *Deep Throat*, produced for a mere $25,000 by members of the Columbo crime family, were used to build "a vast financial empire" that included drug-smuggling operations in the Caribbean.[3]

Several such examples were cited by the Attorney General's Commission in its effort to link organized crime to obscenity and the pornography trade, noting along the way that the role and influence of the mob had increased substantially since the President's Commission on Obscenity and Pornography issued its report in 1970. That panel reported that, while some people testified that organized crime worked "hand-in-glove" with the distributors of adult materials, "there is at present no concrete evidence to support these statements." But, sixteen years later, the 1986 panel found evidence in numerous reports from law enforcement officials, prosecutors, and legislators to support its conclusions and recommend that citizens create laws and insist on their enforcement.[4]

Federal RICO violations are punishable by a fine, a maximum prison term of twenty years, or both, in addition to the penalties for the underlying crimes making up the RICO offense. But what makes RICO truly revolutionary is the power it gives the courts to order forfeiture of both property involved in and proceeds derived from a RICO violation. In other words, a conviction under RICO carries with it a much harsher penalty than a conviction under a traditional obscenity law. When RICO applies, judges have extraordinary sanctions available to them, and they can also use their equitable powers and a variety of prejudgment remedies, including restraining orders, injunctions, seizures, or "any other action to preserve the availability of property . . . for forfeiture." Congress empowered courts to order a judgment of property forfeiture once a person is convicted of a "pattern of racketeering activity" to prevent the RICO defendant from committing future violations.[5]

Congress enacted RICO in response to its finding that "organized crime activities . . . weaken the stability of the Nation's economic system, harm innocent investors and competing organizations, interfere with free competition, seriously burden interstate and foreign commerce, threaten the domestic security and undermine the general welfare of the Nation and its citizens." Neither the federal act nor the state counterparts were intended to apply solely to members of organized crime. Because Congress could not sufficiently define "organized crime," it made a person's *conduct*, not one's associations or affiliations, the object of RICO's prohibitions. By its terms, RICO applies to "enterprise criminality—patterns of unlawful conduct by, through, or against an enterprise." While the listed offenses may be committed primarily by members of crime syndicates, Congress only claimed that those offenses are characteristic of organized crime.[6]

Prohibited racketeering activities are called "predicate acts" under the federal RICO act and most state statutes and include murder, kidnapping, perjury, gambling, narcotics trafficking, and fraud. In 1984, even before the attorney general's report, Congress became convinced that organized crime was contributing to and profiting from an "explosion in the volume and availability of pornography in our society." Following many state actions, Congress expanded the list of predicate acts under RICO to include violations of both the federal obscenity code and any generic state provi-

◆ SYNDICATED SEX

sion prohibiting "dealing in obscene matter." Senator Jesse Helms of North Carolina proposed such an amendment to the Omnibus Crime Control Act because of the "heavy involvement of organized crime in the pornography trade." Before 1984, the only weapon available to federal prosecutors was the federal obscenity code and, of course, postal regulations.[7]

According to one study, twenty-seven states and Puerto Rico have passed statutes patterned on the federal RICO law since its enactment in 1970. These are generally called "RICO" statutes as well, although the formal titles may vary.[8] In Indiana, for instance, which generated the first Supreme Court case, the law is called, with some slight variation from the original, the Racketeer Influenced and Corrupt Organizations Act. In Minnesota, a state without a RICO law, authorities used the federal statute to garner a conviction in a case that became the Court's second review of the First Amendment implications of RICO as applied to obscenity violations. Before these decisions, however, the Court hinted at RICO concerns in 1986 when it upheld New York's state nuisance statute that allowed for the closure of an adult bookstore used for prostitution and lewdness. "Bookselling in an establishment used for prostitution does not confer First Amendment coverage to defeat a valid statute aimed at penalizing and terminating illegal uses of the premises," intoned Chief Justice Burger, setting the stage for the use of the Court's new weapon.[9]

In *Arcara v. Cloud Books Inc.*, the Court, in a six-to-three decision, held that the First Amendment did not preclude a city from closing down an adult bookstore, pursuant to a New York public health law, where solicitation of prostitution had occurred on the premises. This reversed the New York Court of Appeals, which had found that an order closing a bookstore because of the solicitation of prostitution could operate as an unconstitutional prior restraint on expression. The justices found the health statute unrelated to the suppression of any expression and refused to extend First Amendment protection to the illegal conduct simply because it happened in a bookstore selling material covered by the Constitution.

During the fall of 1982, the Erie County sheriff's department conducted an undercover investigation into reported illicit sex activities at the Village Books and News Store in Kenmore, New York. A deputy said he personally observed patrons masturbating, fondling, and engaged in fellatio, plus instances of prostitute solicitation. After the owners failed in their motion for summary judgment, the New York State Court of Appeals modified the order and granted partial summary judgment. That court agreed that the public health law applied to establishments other than houses of prostitution but reversed on First Amendment grounds. It analogized, or likened, an order closing a bookstore or movie house based on previous distribution of obscene materials to an unconstitutional prior restraint.

Chief Justice Burger, for the majority, applied, as had the New York Court of Appeals, the standards set down in *United States v. O'Brien* for analyzing regulations aimed at nonspeech activity but which have an incidental effect on speech, such as, in that case, the burning of draft cards. However, the New York high court found closure of the bookstore an unconstitutional restraint on the owners' First Amendment rights because it was not essential to the purposes of the law. Even though in *O'Brien* the Court found draft-card burning not ordinarily expressive conduct, Burger said it had some semblance of expression not apparent in this case. "Unlike . . . symbolic draft card burning . . . , the sexual activity carried on in this case manifests absolutely no element of protected expression." He also pointed out that, since every civil and criminal remedy imposes some burden on First Amendment activities, no one would claim that all such liability gives rise to a valid First Amendment claim. "The legislation providing the closure sanction was directed at unlawful conduct having nothing to do with books or other expressive activity. First Amendment values may not be invoked by merely linking the words 'sex' and 'books.' "[10]

Justice O'Connor, with Stevens, argued that the First Amendment standard of review was not applicable, since the government was regulating neither speech nor an incidental nonexpressive effect of speech. Justice Blackmun, with Bren-

◆ SYNDICATED SEX

nan and Marshall, dissented on the ground that when the state impairs First Amendment activity by shutting down a bookstore it must show, at a minimum, that it has chosen the least-restrictive means of pursuing its otherwise legitimate objectives. "An obvious method of eliminating such acts is to arrest the patron committing them." Instead, Blackmun said, the statute imposes absolute liability on the store simply because the activity occurs on the premises.[11]

In at least two ways, RICO laws differ from the statute at issue in *Arcara*. First, the regulation of sexual activity by the public health law was less restrictive of speech, and second, the bookstore was only required to stay closed for one year. The owners were free to sell their books and magazines at another location at any time. Thus, there was little First Amendment infringement in *Arcara*, despite the dissenters persuasive argument to the contrary. The majority of the Court said that sexual activity carried absolutely no element of protected expression. Burger stressed that the health statute did not relate to the right to sell printed materials. He noted that the closure order was not "imposed on the basis of an advance determination that the distribution of particular materials is prohibited—indeed, the imposition of the closure order has nothing to do with any expressive conduct at all." The same could not be said, however, of the application of RICO to the "predicate offense" of "dealing in obscene matter." RICO, through its forfeiture provisions, implicates the right to sell printed materials and, thereby, involves the First Amendment.[12]

Much earlier, in *Marcus v. Search Warrant*, the Supreme Court had endorsed the proposition that, although a governmental unit had broad authority to regulate property used in violation of a law, courts are entitled to circumscribe that authority when it conflicts with the First Amendment. In striking down the procedure for issuing a warrant for the seizure of obscene materials, the Court said that it was no answer to say that obscene books are contraband for purposes of search and seizure. Consequently, the standards governing such searches and seizures must not differ from those used in seizing narcotics, gambling paraphernalia, and other contraband. Drugs and gambling, as well as prostitution in *Arcara*, ordinarily do not involve the sale of books or other expressive material. But a law directed at "dealing in obscene matter" will nearly always touch First Amendment concerns and affect the availability of nonobscene literature and films.[13]

In its first direct encounter with the use of racketeering laws to fight obscenity, the Supreme Court faced a challenge to two such statutes in Indiana—the state's Racketeer Influenced and Corrupt Organization Act and its Civil Remedies for Racketeering Activity Act (CRRA)—in the companion cases of *Fort Wayne Books, Inc. v. Indiana* and *Ronald Sappenfield v. Indiana*.[14]

Indiana's RICO law defined "pattern of racketeering activity" as being involved within a five-year period in at least two incidents of "committing, attempting to commit or conspiring to commit or aiding and abetting" a series of predicate offenses, including obscenity. An individual may be subject to criminal prosecution under RICO as well as civil action under CRRA, which also entitled the prosecution to initiate a forfeiture action. "Upon a showing by a preponderance of the evidence that the property in question was used or intended for use, derived from, or realized through racketeering activity, the court may order the property seized and forfeited to the state." And, since CRRA did not require the state to set a trial date, seizure could last indefinitely without a judicial determination on the merits of the complaint or on whether obscene materials were even involved.[15]

Justice White, writing for the Court, said that the RICO statute was constitutional, but that the pretrial seizure of books under CRRA was not. White focused on a line of cases, beginning with *Marcus v. Search Warrant*, that held that "rigorous procedural safeguards must be employed before expressive materials can be seized as 'obscene.'" He emphasized the importance of adversarial hearings before permitting pretrial seizures as a way of focusing the judicial inquiry on the essential issue—the alleged obscenity of the materials in question. He concluded that until there is a determination of obscenity following a hearing, it was unconstitutional to remove a publication completely from circulation. White continued:

> While the general rule, under the Fourth Amendment is that any and all contraband, instrumentalities, and evidence of crimes may be seized on probable cause (and even without a warrant in various circumstances), it is otherwise when materials presumptively protected by the First Amendment are involved. It is the risk of prior restraint, which is the underlying basis for the special Fourth Amendment protections accorded searches for and seizures of First Amendment materials that motivates this rule. These same concerns render invalid the pre-trial seizure at issue here.[16]

Fort Wayne Books arose in March 1984 when a county prosecutor started a civil action against the operator of an adult bookstore in Fort Wayne, claiming that the store had engaged in a pattern of racketeering activity by repeatedly violating the state's obscenity laws. In April 1985, an investigation of adult bookstores in Howard County, Indiana, led prosecutors there to charge Ronald Sappenfield with several counts of distribution of obscene matter. The U.S. Supreme Court sustained Sappenfield's conviction but reversed the Fort Wayne seizure order.

The trial court agreed with the district attorney that there was probable cause to believe that Fort Wayne Books was violating the state RICO law and directed the immediate seizure of the real estate, publications, and personal property and ordered the sheriff to padlock the stores. Decisive was an affidavit by a local police officer recounting thirty-nine prior criminal convictions of the company for selling obscene books and films. The Indiana Court of Appeals held that the relevant RICO/CRRA provisions violated the U.S. Constitution, but the state supreme court reversed.[17]

Justice White was joined by an interesting mix of justices. Regarding the Court's acceptance of obscenity as a predicate offense under RICO, he was joined by Chief Justice Rehnquist and Justices Blackmun, Scalia, and Kennedy. With regard to holding that Indiana's CRRA pretrial seizure-provision created an unconstitutional prior restraint, he was joined by Rehnquist, Brennan, Blackmun, O'Connor, Scalia, and Kennedy, who were joined in concurrence by Marshall.

White rejected the argument that the "inherent vagueness" of the *Miller v. California* requirements meant finding RICO unconstitutional. Because *Miller* was not vague, he said, the RICO provisions incorporating *Miller* were not vague. While the justices agreed that RICO laws could define obscenity as a category of racketeering activity and that bookstore inventories could be forfeited like other property, they rejected the state court's conclusion that "expressive property" lacked First Amendment protection against the CRRA forfeiture provision.

Justice Stevens, in partial dissent and joined by Brennan and Marshall, agreed that the seizure of property was unconstitutional. Yet he would have taken the case much further. Stevens argued that the Indiana statutory scheme, because of its vagueness and its broad application of criminal sanctions and wide-ranging civil penalties, failed to ensure that only unprotected speech would be suppressed.

> Whatever harm society incurs from the sale of a few obscene magazines to consenting adults is indistinguishable from the harm caused by the distribution of a great volume of pornographic material that is protected by the First Amendment. Elimination of a few obscene volumes or videotapes from an adult bookstore's shelves thus scarcely serves the State's purpose of controlling public morality.[18]

Stevens's basic complaint, however, was that Indiana's RICO/CRRA scheme was not finely enough tuned to the suppression of truly obscene materials to pass constitutional muster. The nature of the scheme, he asserted, made it impossible to seize legally obscene materials without also seizing protected ones: "The Indiana RICO/CRRA statutes allow prosecutors to cast wide nets and seize, upon a showing that two obscene materials have been sold, or even just exhibited, all a store's books, magazines, films, and videotapes—the obscene, those nonobscene yet sexually explicit, even those devoid of sexual reference." Stevens also appeared to suggest that the federal RICO statute and those of most states are invalid. He agreed that pretrial seizures were unconstitutional, but he also implied that posttrial seizures were too. "I would extend the Court's holding to prohibit the seizure of these stores' inventories, even after trial, based on nothing more than a 'pattern' of obscenity misdemeanors."[19]

When the justices next encountered a community's efforts to regulate obscenity, or, as Justice Scalia called such attempts under RICO, "Draconian sanctions for obscenity which make it unwise to flirt with the sale of pornography," it was a licensing scheme in Dallas. In *FW/PBS Inc. v. Dallas*, announced early in January 1990, a majority of the Court concluded that the city's licensing scheme for regulating sexually oriented businesses was unconstitutional, but the justices split over the issue of whether all of the procedural safeguards enunciated in *Freedman v. Maryland* should be applied to the Dallas ordinance. Under the ordinance, all "sexually oriented businesses" were required to be inspected by the city and to obtain a license after the inspection. The ordinance specified that the license shall be issued within thirty days, but it failed to ensure that the business would be inspected within that time frame.[20]

Justice Sandra Day O'Connor, writing the plurality opinion, said that because the scheme in Dallas did not present the grave "dangers of a censorship system," as was the case in *Freedman*, "the full procedural protections" set forth in that decision are not required. However, O'Connor said, "The first two safeguards" enunciated in *Freedman* "are essential: the licensor must make the decision whether to issue the license within a specified and reasonable time period during which the status quo is maintained and there must be the possibility of prompt judicial review in the event the license is erroneously denied."[21]

The Dallas ordinance, O'Connor said, "does not provide for an effective limitation on the time within which the licensor's decision must be made. It also fails to provide an avenue for prompt judicial review so as to minimize suppression of the speech in the event of a license denial." Thus, the justice said, "the failure to provide these essential safeguards renders the ordinance's licensing requirement unconstitutional insofar as it is enforced against those businesses engaged in First Amendment activity."[22]

Justice Brennan, joined by Marshall and Blackmun, concurred in the ruling. All three of the procedural protections set down in *Freedman* should be applied, Brennan said, not just two of them. "We have never suggested that our insistence on *Freedman* procedures might vary with the particular facts of the prior restraint before us," Brennan wrote. The city of Dallas should "bear the burden of going to court and proving its case before it may permissibly deny licenses to First Amendment–protected businesses."[23]

Justice White, with Chief Justice Rehnquist, asserted that *Freedman* "is inapplicable to the Dallas scheme." The ordinance "regulates who may operate sexually oriented businesses, including those who sell materials entitled to First Amendment protection; but the ordinance does not regulate content and thus it is unlike the content-based prior restraints that this court has typically scrutinized very closely." In this case, White opined, the licensor is not vested with unbridled discretion, and thus "the basis for applying *Freedman* is not present here."[24]

There is "no realistic prospect that the requirement of licensing will have anything more than an incidental effect on the sale of protected materials," White said. "Perhaps Justice O'Connor is saying that those who deal in expressive materials are entitled to special procedures in the course of complying with otherwise valid, neutral regulations generally applicable to all businesses. I doubt, however, that bookstores or radio or television stations must be given special breaks in the enforcement of general health, building, and fire regulations."[25]

Justice Scalia, concurring in part and dissenting in part, noted that communities seeking to eradicate sexually explicit businesses have been forced to adopt oblique approaches, such as zoning ordinances or RICO prosecutions. "It does not seem to me desirable to perpetuate such a regime of prohibition by indirection," he said. "I think the means of rendering it unnecessary is available under our

◆ SYNDICATED SEX

precedents and should be applied in the present." He continued:

> That means consists of recognizing that a business devoted to the sale of highly explicit sexual material can be found to be engaged in the marketing of obscenity, even though each book or film it sells might, in isolation, be considered merely pornographic and not obscene. It is necessary, to be sure of protecting valuable speech, that we compel all communities to tolerate individual works that have only marginal communicative content beyond raw sexual appeal; it is not necessary that we compel them to tolerate businesses that hold themselves forth as specializing in such material.[26]

Scalia lamented the fact that Dallas's effort was but one example of an increasing number of attempts throughout the country, by various means, "not to withhold from the public any particular book or performance, but to prevent the erosion of public morality by the increasingly general appearance of . . . 'sexually oriented businesses.' " Indeed, he said, as a case the Court heard in the previous term demonstrated, they reach even the smallest of communities via telephonic "dial-a-porn." Scalia was alluding to *Sable Communications of California Inc. v. FCC*, in which the justices, voting six to three, said that the Federal Communications Commission could regulate obscene telephone messages but, unanimously, they said the agency could not extend those controls to indecent messages as well. Shortly afterwards, Congress enacted more limited legislation requiring, among other things, written consent in advance before such messages can be played to a caller. The new law, sponsored by Senator Jesse Helms of North Carolina, finally passed the Court's constitutional scrutiny in January 1992.[27]

Meanwhile, controversy continued at the Supreme Court over the federal and state RICO laws. In the 1992–1993 term, in *Alexander v. United States*, the justices addressed the free-speech question they had left dangling in *Fort Wayne Books*. The Court held, but not without serious disagreement among the justices, that the use of RICO's forfeiture provisions to seize "presumptively protected" expressive materials did not violate the First Amendment. Chief Justice Rehnquist, writing for himself, White, O'Connor, Scalia, and Thomas, upheld the forfeiture of an entire bookstore chain and the destruction of more than 100,000 nonobscene books, magazines, and videotapes as punishment for the sale and distribution of seven obscene magazines and videocassettes. Justice Kennedy, joined by Blackmun, Stevens, and, in part, Souter, said simply that such use of RICO was an exercise in government censorship and control of speech protected by the First Amendment. Souter, while agreeing with the majority's judgment, wanted the case remanded to see if the forfeiture violated the Eighth Amendment's excessive fines clause.

In 1989, the federal government brought obscenity and RICO charges against Ferris J. Alexander, the owner and operator of more than a dozen adult bookstores and theaters in the Minneapolis area. A jury, after a four-month trial, convicted Alexander of selling and transporting four obscene magazines and three videotapes and, predicated solely on these seven obscenity offenses, found him guilty of three RICO offenses. The district court imposed a prison sentence and a $100,000 fine and also ordered the forfeiture of Alexander's entire chain of bookstores and video shops, including an inventory of more than 100,000 presumptively nonobscene books and tapes. The combined value of Alexander's forfeited assets amounted to more than $9 million.

Alexander claimed that the seizure of his protected expression violated the First Amendment, but the Eighth Circuit Court of Appeals rejected this argument and held, in part, that the Constitution permitted the RICO confiscation of nonobscene expressive materials because the materials were seized not for their speech content but for their connection to racketeering activity. The court also rejected Alexander's claim that the forfeiture of his ten media businesses violated the Eighth Amendment's prohibition of excessive fines and of cruel and unusual punishments. After the circuit court's decision, but while a request for rehearing was still pending, the government destroyed Alexander's three tons of films and printed materials.[28]

194

The Supreme Court remanded for reconsideration the decision of the Eighth Circuit on the excessive fines but affirmed on the First Amendment issue. Rehnquist first rejected Alexander's argument that the forfeiture constituted a prior restraint on speech and, therefore, was subject to the highest level of scrutiny. He said the forfeiture order was a "subsequent punishment," not a prior restraint on speech, because it merely deprived Alexander of existing assets without forbidding him from engaging in future expression. "He is perfectly free to open an adult bookstore or otherwise engage in the production and distribution of erotic materials," the chief justice said. "He just cannot finance these enterprises with assets derived from his prior racketeering offenses." Rehnquist's brief interpretation of the RICO forfeiture statute is important because it is the more prevalent view:

> It calls for the forfeiture of assets because of the financial role they play in the operation of the racketeering enterprise. The statute is oblivious to the expressive or nonexpressive nature of the assets forfeited; books, sports cars, narcotics, and cash are all forfeitable alike under RICO. Indeed, a contrary scheme would be disastrous from a policy standpoint, enabling racketeers to evade forfeiture by investing the proceeds of their crimes in businesses engaging in expressive activity.[29]

Rehnquist next held that "under normal First Amendment standards," the RICO forfeiture at issue fell "well short" of constitutional violation. "Our cases . . . establish quite clearly that the First Amendment does not prohibit either stringent criminal sanctions for obscenity offenses or forfeiture of expressive materials as punishment for criminal conduct." He recognized that seizure of protected materials could chill free speech but then, citing *Fort Wayne Books*, asserted that the threat of forfeiture "had no more of a chilling effect" than other punishments for obscenity, such as "a prison term or a large fine," both of which the Court had previously judged constitutional.[30]

In a fiery dissent, Justice Kennedy decried the Court's decision as "a deplorable abandonment and grave repudiation of fundamental First Amendment principles." Believing that the forfeiture of Alexander's inventory did in fact constitute a prior restraint on speech, Kennedy admonished the majority for elevating form over substance by simplistically labeling the forfeiture a subsequent punishment without examining its practical effect. "The First Amendment is a rule of substantive protection," he said, "not an artifice of categories."[31]

Kennedy stated that, even if the forfeiture of Alexander's protected expression had not constituted a prior restraint requiring heightened scrutiny, it nevertheless violated the First Amendment. "The rights of free speech and press in their broad and legitimate sphere cannot be defeated by the simple expedient of punishing after in lieu of censoring before." The "destruction of books and films that were not obscene and not adjudged to be so is a remedy with no parallel in our cases," he argued. "What is happening here is simple: Books and films are condemned and destroyed not for their own content but for the content of their owner's prior speech," Kennedy asserted. "Our law does not permit the government to burden future speech for this sort of taint." Pointing to a line of pretrial search-and-seizure cases in which the Court mandated special protections for presumptively protected materials, Kennedy noted that "we have been careful to say that First Amendment materials cannot be taken out of circulation until they have been determined to be unlawful."[32]

For sheer eloquence, as well as its persuasiveness, Kennedy's defense of the First Amendment is comparable in this category of law to Justice Harlan's spirited endorsement of speech in *Cohen v. California* in 1971. For instance, one is hard-pressed to find a more compelling, and concise, argument than that conveyed in the following passages from *Alexander*:

> In a society committed to freedom of thought, inquiry, and discussion without interference or guidance from the state, public confidence in the institutions devoted to the dissemination of written matter and films is essential. That confidence erodes if it is perceived that speakers and the press are vulnerable for all of their expression in the past. Independence of speech and press can be just as

compromised by the threat of official intervention as by the fact of it.

The threat of a censorial motive and of ongoing speech supervision by the state justifies the imposition of First Amendment protection.[33]

In the persistent debate over which is more important, the government's interest in combating crime and obscenity, which always risks infringing on free expression, or free speech itself, which has never garnered absolute protection in the Court, the periodic winner seems to depend upon the goal to be achieved. The *FW/PBS* decision, which sought to regulate but not destroy obscene matter, was a serious effort to devise a single adequate rule of law for governing prior restraint. All of the justices in that case pointed to *Freedman v. Maryland* for safeguards for determining the constitutional validity of a restraint. Dallas's licensing scheme was not safeguarded enough, the justices asserted.

The Supreme Court has never found a prior restraint on *pure* speech to be constitutional. But it has said that some speech may be restrained prior to its utterance by, for example, the rules governing the context of speech found acceptable in *Young v. American Mini Theatres* and *Renton v. Playtime Theatres*. The plurality in *FW/PBS*, while solicitous of First Amendment rights, also tried to balance the competing interests by insisting on procedural safeguards against unbridled censorship.[34]

In its dealings with RICO laws and crime of the organized variety, however, the Court has been less concerned about balancing the competing interests. Justice Kennedy alluded to this when he suggested that the Attorney General's Commission on Pornography was somewhat to blame for the zealousness with which the government moved against certain types of disfavored speech when it advocated the use of RICO and similar statutes to "substantially handicap" or "eliminate" pornography businesses. "The constitutional concerns raised by a penalty of this destructive capacity are distinct from the concerns raised by traditional methods of punishment."[35] That concern did not seem to stir the *Alexander* majority, led by Chief Justice Rehnquist, who chose to rely upon *Arcara* rather than either *Freedman* or, even more relevant, *O'Brien*, the draft-card burning case that established a four-part test for determining the "overreaching effect" of curtailing protected speech.

The *Arcara* Court held that the penalty of closing a bookstore for allowing solicitation by prostitutes did not require *O'Brien* scrutiny because prostitution was completely unexpressive and the burden on bookselling activities was "dubious at best." The *O'Brien* test was designed to assess the constitutionality of content-neutral, context-based restrictions. First, the regulation must be "within the constitutional power of the Government"; second, it must further "an important or substantial governmental interest"; third, that interest must be "unrelated to the suppression of free expression"; and, fourth, "the incidental restriction on alleged First Amendment freedoms [must be] no greater than is essential to the furtherance of that interest." *O'Brien* is applicable to the RICO cases because, as the ruling itself stipulated, "content-neutral laws with an impact on speech" trigger its "intermediate scrutiny" test. And, clearly, the penalized acts in *Alexander* were speech offenses.[36]

Analyzed under *O'Brien*, the RICO forfeiture provisions as applied to obscenity convictions fail to satisfy the third and fourth part, both of which require that an indirectly restrictive law be "narrowly tailored" to accomplish the government's goal. While there is no question that the government has serious interest in combating crime and regulating obscenity, protecting nonobscene speech is at least as important. Most RICO laws, as reinforced by the seizure provision, are more than is necessary for the government to realize its goal. In a case decided one year before *Alexander*, the Ninth Circuit stated that "at the very least, those assets or interests of the defendant invested in legitimate expressive activity being conducted by parts of the enterprise uninvolved or only marginally involved in the racketeering activity may be forfeited."[37]

Limiting the scope of RICO in this manner would be in keeping with the principle that because, as Justice Brennan declared in 1963, a "dim and uncertain line" separates protected from unprotected speech, "freedoms of expression

198

must be ringed about with adequate bulwarks." It would allay the fear of the *Alexander* majority that racketeers of all types could launder their ill-gotten gains by investing them in speech enterprises because, consistent with *Arcara*, only obscenity and other speech-related offenses would trigger limitations on RICO forfeiture.[38]

In *Fort Wayne Books*, the Court recognized the perils of using RICO's *pre*judgment seizure provisions by striking down that part of the statute authorizing such conduct. When dealing with the issue of *post*judgment forfeitures of expressive materials, the justices could build upon the Indiana case to find that such use of RICO is a prior restraint equally as violative of the First Amendment.

Justices Kennedy and Souter got it right when they recognized the First Amendment violation. The majority could have availed itself of a number of tests, the most relevant being *O'Brien*, that would have restricted the reach of RICO and rendered the forfeiture provisions even more efficient in the fight against organized crime. Instead, as one commentator has said in denouncing the opinion as "legerdemain by which book burning has now . . . been made legal in America," the Court upheld the confiscation of protected expression. RICO and similar laws may now be used, in the words of another commentator, "to suppress enterprises bold enough to deal in disfavored expression yet unfortunate enough to cross the 'uncertain line' that separates protected speech from obscenity."[39]

XI

◆

Viewpoint Discrimination

◆

If this Court were to extend to this case the rationale in Ferber to uphold the Amendment, it would signal so great a potential encroachment upon First Amendment freedoms that the precious liberties reposed within those guarantees would not survive.

—Judge Sarah Evans Barker,
American Booksellers Association v. Hudnut

THE CASE, *American Booksellers Association v. Hudnut*, was the first for U.S. district judge Barker, who had been appointed by President Reagan and sworn in on 30 March 1984, and the only case on pornography as sex discrimination against women ever to reach the U.S. Supreme Court. Judge Barker's ruling, issued on 19 November 1984, was upheld on 27 August 1985 by the U.S. Court of Appeals for the Seventh Circuit and affirmed by the Supreme Court without an opinion on 24 February 1986. Seldom has a case been so controversial and received so much publicity, but also, seldom have all of the judicial determinations been so uniform in support of unfettered speech. Thus, *Hudnut*, as a history lesson on free expression, affords the opportunity to review and, at the same time, close our discussion of the justices' intractable obscenity problem.[1]

The 1984 Indianapolis ordinance, signed into law on 1 May by William H. Hudnut III, the Republican mayor and a former Presbyterian minister, was supposed to help stem the spread of adult bookstores, movie theaters, and massage parlors. More to the point, however, it was designed specifically to penalize pornography as discrimination against women and a violation of their civil rights. The law defined pornography as "the graphic sexually explicit subordination of women, whether in pictures or words," if it showed them enjoying "pain or humiliation" or in "positions of servility or submission or display" or as "sexual objects who experience sexual pleasure in being raped." Mayor Hudnut heralded the law as "a sensible solution to a problem that has boggled legal minds for a long time."[2]

But hardly an hour after Mayor Hudnut's signing, the ordinance was challenged in federal district court by bookstores, trade associations, and a cable television station. Judge Barker issued a preliminary injunction that stopped enforcement of the law until the suit was resolved. The plaintiffs included the American Booksellers Association, made up of more than 5,000 bookstores and chains; the Association of American Publishers; and an Indianapolis seller and renter of videocassettes, Video Shack. Also joining the suit against the ordinance were the American Civil Liberties Union, its Indiana affiliate, and the Indiana Library Association, who opposed the proposed law as a violation of the First Amendment's guarantee of free expression.

The idea that pornography is a violation of women's rights got its start in Minneapolis with Catharine A. MacKinnon, at the time a law professor at the University of Minnesota, and Andrea Dworkin, a New York feminist and author of the powerful *Pornography: Men Possessing Women*, which appeared in 1981. They taught a course on pornography at the university, and, at the urging of a city council member, collaborated on the draft of an ordinance for Minneapolis. They drew upon the research of Edward I. Donnerstein, Daniel Linz, and Steven Penrod, whose findings suggested that men exposed to movies fusing sex and violence tended to become less sensitive to the violence and degradation of women. When they served as jurors in a reenactment of a rape trial, the men were less prone to believe the rape victim and more likely to believe she was to blame. However, the researchers did not claim that men who are exposed to pornography are more likely to rape and murder women, but proponents of the bills in both Minneapolis and Indianapolis frequently made such causality arguments.[3]

The MacKinnon-Dworkin proposed law made its first official appearance before the Minneapolis City Council in December 1983. Following two days of hearings, the council approved it by a margin of one, but Mayor Donald M. Fraser vetoed it in January, saying that it impinged upon the First Amendment. His veto set off a war of words between Harvard law professors Alan M. Dershowitz and Laurence H. Tribe. Dershowitz praised Mayor Fraser for his action, while Tribe chastised him for not allowing the courts an opportunity to decide upon "what may eventually be found to be the first sensible approach to an area which has vexed some of the best legal minds for decades." Fraser's veto caught the eye of Mayor Hudnut, whose Indianapolis ordinance was to be an adaptation of the Minneapolis effort, except that Andrea Dworkin was not invited to participate because, apparently, her feminist views were too radical for conservative Indiana.[4]

Judge Sarah Evans Barker, meanwhile, heard oral arguments on the Indianapolis ordinance on 30 July 1984 and on 19 November issued a strong decision against the proposed law, pointing to its ideological and political elements. She disagreed with the ordinance's defenders, who maintained that the type of expression that it proscribed was in keeping with those categories held previously by the Supreme Court not to be entitled to First Amendment protection, e.g. libel or fighting words.

Judge Barker dismissed the analogy with fighting words, which "by their very utterance inflict injury or tend to incite an immediate breach of the peace." She said the ordinance's defenders had read this passage from *Chaplinsky v. New Hampshire* out of context, because the "words" of pornography do not by their very nature carry the immediate poten-

202

tial for injury. Barker further noted that, while obscenity might not be protected, the defendants themselves "concede that the 'pornography' they seek to control goes beyond obscenity, as defined by the Supreme Court and excepted from First Amendment protections." Accordingly, the judge observed, "it becomes clear that what defendants actually seek by enacting this legislation is a newly-defined class of constitutionally unprotected speech, labeled 'pornography' and characterized as sexually discriminatory."[5]

The defendants identified three cases to support the creation of the new category: *New York v. Ferber*, the child pornography case; *FCC v. Pacifica Foundation*, in which the Court said that patently offensive, but nonobscene, words in a regulated context were not protected by the Constitution to the degree that similar speech in a nonregulated context was; and *Young v. American Mini Theatres Inc.*, in which the Court determined that a zoning law affecting nonobscene pornography did not violate the First Amendment unless it was too restrictive.[6]

Barker held that none of the cases nor the rationales used by the Court applied to the Indianapolis situation. *Ferber* pertained solely to child pornography, and the justices recognized the state's compelling interest in safeguarding the physical and psychological well-being of a minor. Children, unlike adult women, could not be presumed to consent voluntarily to being subjects in pornography. The judge explained:

> Adult women generally have the capacity to protect themselves from participating in and being personally victimized by pornography, which makes the State's interest in safeguarding the physical and psychological well-being of women by prohibiting "the sexually explicit subordination of women, graphically depicted, whether in pictures or in words" not so compelling as to sacrifice the guarantees of the First Amendment.[7]

Pacifica dealt only with broadcasting, a historically regulated area of communication law that has never enjoyed as much First Amendment coverage as publishing and filmmaking. The reasons for the rule in *Pacifica*, Judge Barker

Viewpoint Discrimination ◆

pointed out, were not present in *Hudnut*. "If an individual is offended by 'pornography,' as defined in the Ordinance, the logical thing to do is avoid it, an option frequently not available to the public with material disseminated through broadcasting." Barker added that the ordinance was not adopted as a way of protecting the "well being of [its] youth."[8]

American Mini Theatres, the third proof that the *Miller v. California* standard was not applicable, was essentially a time, place, and manner restriction on the location of movie theaters featuring erotic films. The Indianapolis ordinance, however, prohibited completely the sale, distribution, or exhibition of material depicting women in a sexually subordinate role "at all times, in all places and in every manner." This, Judge Barker implied, would amount to outright censorship.[9]

Because the ordinance went beyond the established categories of unprotected expression, Judge Barker said that the court had to apply the strict scrutiny required for proposals to limit speech within protected categories. Therefore, "the Court must . . . examine the underlying premise of the Ordinance: that the State has so compelling an interest in regulating the sort of sex discrimination imposed and perpetuated through 'pornography' that it warrants an exception to free speech."[10]

Judge Barker observed that the ordinance sought not only to protect specific, identifiable victims from the direct harms of pornography but also to protect women as a class, or group, from sociological harm. To Barker, this had the sound of group libel, which courts have found suspect in recent years because of the number of constitutional problems such vague and broad categorizations invoke. She refused to grant the defendants their "novel theory," which, if accepted, could lead to special group preferences at the expense of the public good, as in, for example, legislation barring uncomplimentary or oppressive literary depictions of handicapped persons on the grounds that they cause discrimination against that group of people.[11] Barker continued:

> If this Court were to extend to this case the rationale in
> *Ferber* to uphold the Amendment, it would signal so great

◆ VIEWPOINT DISCRIMINATION

a potential encroachment upon First Amendment freedoms that the precious liberties reposed within those guarantees would not survive.

To permit every interest group, especially those who claim to be victimized by unfair expression, their own legislative exceptions to the First Amendment so long as they succeed in obtaining a majority of legislative votes in their favor demonstrates the potentially predatory nature of what defendants seek through this Ordinance and defend in this lawsuit.[12]

Finally, Judge Barker addressed other constitutional requirements, which she said had to be satisfied in order for the ordinance to be upheld, e.g., vagueness, overbreadth, and prior restraint. She said that the ordinance was filled with vagueness problems in, for instance, the definition of *pornography* itself and, more specifically, the phrase "subordination of women." Nothing in the ordinance suggested whether the forbidden phrase related to a physical, social, psychological, religious, or emotional subordination or "some other form or combination of these." The judge concluded that persons subjected to the law could not "reasonably steer clear between lawful and unlawful conduct" to know with confidence what its terms prohibited. And the ordinance was overbroad because it regulated nonobscene material normally protected by the First Amendment.[13]

A prior restraint is not unlawful per se, Judge Barker said, but enforcement of the ordinance through a government agency, the Equal Opportunity Advisory Board, amounted to prior restraint as well as a form of administrative harassment. Findings and conclusions may be appealed, but the burden of taking the appeal is upon the party against whom the decision had been made, Judge Barker said. This type of procedure was prohibited by *Freedman v. Maryland* and constituted an unlawful prior restraint, despite the fact that some due process measures had been met. "Because the *Freedman* procedural . . . standard is not satisfied *in toto*, the entire Ordinance fails for imposing an unconstitutional prior restraint on First Amendment expression."[14]

Indianapolis filed notice of its appeal on 19 December

1984 to the U.S. Seventh Circuit Court of Appeals in Chicago. The case was argued on 4 June 1985. Judge Frank Easterbrook's decision, announced on 27 August 1985, confirmed Judge Barker's holding in every respect and was just as critical and forceful. Easterbrook, like Judge Barker, a recent Reagan appointee, had been criticized for his economic interpretations and conservative applications of law, the influence perhaps of his senior colleague on the circuit bench, Judge Richard A. Posner. Posner, the author of *The Economics of Justice* and *Economic Analysis of Law*, is a leading proponent of the thesis that judicial reasoning, properly understood, is really like economic reasoning, that the procedure used by judges is actually reasoning that seeks to maximize society's wealth. Economics, along with evolutionary biology, also infuses Posner's recent book, *Sex and Reason*, where the author advances a libertarian theory of sexual legislation, defending the rights of individuals to regulate their own sexual conduct except in those cases where it can be shown to cause harm or to infringe on the rights of others.[15]

Judge Easterbrook, meanwhile, began his assessment of the Indianapolis ordinance with a quote from the famous 1943 flag salute case, *West Virginia State Board of Education v. Barnette*, in which the Supreme Court set down the principle that has evolved as *the* fundamental doctrine of government and content neutrality:

> If there is any fixed star in our constitutional constellation, it is that no official, high or petty, can prescribe what shall be orthodox in politics, nationalism, religion, or other matters of opinion or force citizens to confess by word or act their faith therein.[16]

To this, Easterbrook added:

> Under the First Amendment the government must leave to the people the evaluation of ideas. Bald or subtle, an idea is as powerful as the audience allows it to be. A belief may be pernicious—the beliefs of Nazis led to the death of millions, those of the Klan to the repression of millions. A pernicious belief may prevail. One of the things that sepa-

206

rates our society from theirs is our absolute right to propagate opinions that the government finds wrong or even hateful.[17]

Judge Easterbrook, in aphoristic fashion, said that the Indianapolis ordinance underscored such ideological dogma, which, as such, undermined the First Amendment. While the authors of the ordinance presented the view that pornography is not an idea and, therefore, not protectable speech, Easterbrook argued that pornography's alleged affect on men's thoughts itself demonstrates the power of pornography as speech. Nor was the judge satisfied that the ordinance conformed to traditional obscenity law:

> Under the ordinance graphic sexually explicit speech is "pornography" or not depending on the perspective the author adopts. Speech that "subordinates" women and also, for example, presents women as enjoying pain, humiliation, or rape, or even simply presents women in "positions of servility or submission or display" is forbidden, no matter how great the literary or political value of the work taken as a whole. Speech that portrays women in positions of equality is lawful, no matter how graphic the sexual content. This is thought control. It establishes an "approved" view of women, of how they may react to sexual encounters, of how the sexes may relate to each other. Those who espouse the approved view may use sexual images; those who do not, may not.[18]

"If pornography is what pornography does, so is other speech," Easterbrook said. "Many people believe that the existence of television, apart from the content of specific programs, leads to intellectual laziness, to a penchant for violence, to many other ills."[19] He added:

> Racial bigotry, anti-semitism, violence on television, reporters' biases—these and many more influence the culture and shape our socialization. None is directly answerable by more speech, unless that speech too finds its place in the popular culture. Yet all is protected as speech, however insidious. Any other answer leaves the government in

control of all the institutions of culture, the great censor and director of which thoughts are good for us.[20]

Easterbrook framed his denouement around the concept that government neutrality in matters of speech regulation is the best policy. Even if the court accepted the city's basic contention that pornography conditions "unfavorable responses to women," he said, the ordinance was still unconstitutional.

Indianapolis appealed the decision to the U.S. Supreme Court, where Easterbrook's ruling was affirmed without an opinion. The action came in a brief order that also noted that Chief Justice Burger and Justices Rehnquist and O'Connor wanted to hear the case, but they made no comment on the correctness of the appellate decision. It traditionally takes the votes of four of the nine justices to grant review.

"By upholding the decisions below, the court has removed any doubt that this type of statutory scheme is unconstitutional," said Michael Bamberger, a lawyer who represented a group of publishers and publishers fighting the ordinance. "This should bring to a halt the misguided attempts of various groups to regulate sale of legitimate works in the name of upholding the civil rights of women."[21]

Andrea Dworkin disagreed: "It shows that the legal system protects the pornography industry and anything that the pornography system does to women is all right." Mayor Hudnut, too, expressed disappointment. "We don't feel it is a wasted effort, because we have focused attention on a way to deal with pornography." Perhaps the most prophetic understatement was voiced by Indianapolis City-County Council member Beulah A. Coughenour, a sponsor of the overturned law: "I don't think this will be an end of the attempt to find pornography not protected by the First Amendment. I am sure someone will take up the cry, because pornography is such a degrading force in our lives, especially to minors."

The whole issue of pornography as an attack on the civil rights of women has not met with widespread endorsement and has many feminist critics as well. But it is neither a gender issue nor a political battle between conservatives and lib-

◆ VIEWPOINT DISCRIMINATION

erals. Catharine MacKinnon, in a letter to the editor of the *New York Times* criticizing "so-called research on the politics of pornography [that is] made up of the favorite fantasies and fabrications of its defenders," denies any political leanings one way or the other on the part of those who have joined her in the fight against pornography. "Our 'sin' is in building a women's politics that is as indifferent to left and right as pornography's harm to women is."[22]

As Judith Butler points out, it becomes a "political *problem*" when one assumes that the category of "women" can be subsumed under a "common identity." For MacKinnon, *all* women, no matter what their race, culture, class, or beliefs are *automatically* subordinated under a male patriarchy. It is a "universal basis for feminism" in which all women are "*sexually*" oppressed by men. Butler and Denise Riley both point out the risk of essentialism that is inherent in such approaches taken by feminists like MacKinnon. The notion of a "universal patriarchy" and the generic category "women" are not always helpful, for they limit women's "political practice." As Butler notes, "If one is a woman, that is surely not all one is."[23]

MacKinnon by her own theory and in her own writing reinforces a binary (male/female) opposition that relegates women to a subordinated position, reifies gender relations, and assumes that gender identities are stable and perhaps normal. In the process, she reproduces that which she wishes to fight against. And she reinforces those notions of gender that support masculine hegemony and heterosexist power rather than exploring ways in which these may be contradicted and subverted. As Mary Poovey argues, to maintain that "all women necessarily occupy the position of the other to man and that social oppression follows from this binary split is to risk reducing position to essence, because it retains both the concept of unified identity and the oppositional logic that currently dictates our 'knowledge' of sex difference and the nature of women." Or, as Sallie Tisdale puts it more succinctly, "Feminists against pornography have done a sad and awful thing: *they* have made women into objects."[24]

Varda Burstyn calls it the "censorship trap," which will

do nothing to ease the real problems in women's lives, that is, the social and economic conditions surrounding them. "Sexist pornography is a product of the economic and social conditions of our society—not vice versa. Societies that are not based on profit, industrialization and male dominance have sexual culture—but this looks and functions nothing like pornography." So it is these conditions, Burstyn argues, that need to be changed. Ellen Willis, a leading feminist in New York City, said, "Pornography that gives sadistic fantasies concrete shape—and, in today's atmosphere, social legitimacy—may well encourage suggestible men to act them out. But if *Hustler* were to vanish from the shelves tomorrow, I doubt that rape or wife-beating statistics would decline."[25]

Pornography as sexual discrimination and, as such, a potential exception to First Amendment protection, raises eyebrows as did the existing categories of proscribable speech when they first acquired Supreme Court endorsement. But none of them—fighting words, libel, obscenity, child pornography—would so severely alter our national commitment to open and robust debate as would the overbroad and underinclusive ordinances proposed to abate pornography that hurts women.

We do not know how Justice Stevens would have voted had the Court accepted *American Booksellers Assoc. v. Hudnut* on appeal, though he was among the six justices who did not feel the need to hear the case. But one can speculate on the basis of his other opinions, and especially the evolution of his theory, stated crisply in *Smith v. United States*, that so long as the government did not *totally suppress* protected speech and was faithful to its *paramount obligation* of *complete neutrality* with respect to the *point of view* of a protected message, there was no reason why regulation of certain types of speech might not take into account obvious differences in *subject matter*. The key phrases are underscored so as to make clear the *conditional* nature of Stevens's theory of First Amendment values. "Even within the area of protected speech, a difference in content may require a different governmental response," he said. Within Stevens's the-

◆ VIEWPOINT DISCRIMINATION

ory, it would be difficult to see the subject matter of women and pornography, as expressed in *Hudnut*, as sufficiently viewpoint-neutral to pass constitutional muster.[26]

Discrimination on the basis of viewpoint worries Judge Easterbrook's fellow Seventh Circuit judge Richard Posner, who, as clerk to Justice Brennan twenty-five years before, influenced the Court's decision in *Jacobellis* and the *Tropic of Cancer* case. In response to the "feminist attack" on pornography, Posner, in *Law and Literature: A Misunderstood Relation*, writes:

> A group of radical feminists, opportunistically supported by social and religious conservatives, invites us to consider the obscene less as a matter of excessive frankness in the portrayal of sex than as a point of view harmful to women, and to suppress as obscene some works that would not flunk the *Miller* test of obscenity.

More important, Posner explains why the juridical system is perhaps not the best, certainly not the most sensitive, arena for literary works to be scrutinized:

> The danger to literary values comes from the fact that much of the world's great literature, though not sexually explicit by modern American standards, portrays with approval the subordination, often by force, of women to men (though this is not the same thing as depicting women enjoying that subordination—the particular concern of the feminist opponents of pornography).
>
> The Bible contains many instances of what by contemporary standards is misogyny; so do *Paradise Lost* and *The Taming of the Shrew*, not to mention *Eumenides*—the list is endless. Because literature is by definition the writing that survives a protracted competitive process, most literature is old and much of it therefore reflects, and some of it approves, values that modern readers find offensive—such as anti-Semitism or belief in racial inferiority of blacks or in the natural subordination of women. Maybe the values in some works of literature will become so repulsive that the works themselves disappear from the body of literature.

But this process should be left to the competition of the literary marketplace rather than hurried along by politicians, prosecutors, judges, and jurors.[27]

Stevens and Brennan are two justices who have spent more time than the others, with the possible exception of Harlan, trying to resolve the intractable obscenity problem. But only Douglas and Black, with the occasional sympathy of Marshall, ever advocated absolute protection short of action. Rather, from *Roth-Alberts* in 1957 to the RICO cases in the 1990s, the Court has endorsed the two-value, or two-level, approach, as defined and defended by Brennan and Stevens, to controlling pornography. Justice Frank Murphy set the tone in 1943 in the "fighting words" case, *Chaplinsky v. New Hampshire*, when he said that "certain utterances" were "no essential part of any exposition of ideas" and were "of such slight social value as a step to truth that any benefit to be derived from them was clearly outweighed by the social interest in order and morality." Among such utterances were the "lewd and obscene."

Nine years later, Justice Felix Frankfurter, writing for a five-to-four Court in the group libel case, *Beauharnais v. Illinois*, drew upon Murphy's opinion when he ruled that no constitutional problem was raised by proscribing certain "narrowly limited" classes of speech, including the obscene, the lewd, and the libelous. But the dissenters were not passive. Hugo Black, joined by William O. Douglas, criticized the majority for the "expansive scope" it had accorded libel, making it punishable "to give publicity to any picture, play, drama, or any printed matter which a judge may find unduly offensive to any race, color, creed or religion." Justice Stanley Reed turned his view on the vagueness of the words under question, noting that such words possessed neither general nor specific meanings "well enough known to apprise those within their reach as to limitations on speech." Douglas wrote that the "peril of speech" must be clear and present to override the "plain command of the First Amendment." Justice Robert Jackson, questioning the very concept of group libel, opined: "No group interest in any particular prosecu-

◆ VIEWPOINT DISCRIMINATION

tion should forget that the shoe may be on the other foot in some prosecution tomorrow."[28]

So, when it became Brennan's turn in the *Roth-Alberts* decision, he relied, not unpredictably, on *Chaplinsky* and *Beauharnais*. However, he altered Murphy's rationale by asserting that the reason obscenity was excluded from First Amendment protection was not that it had only "slight social value as a step to truth" but that it did not communicate "ideas having even the slightest redeeming social importance." Expression was disqualified from protection not because, as Murphy and Frankfurter had said, it had only *slight* value, but because it had *none*. Proving no value would be easier than proving some value, Brennan thought. Brennan's doctrine, some authorities believe, was meant to replace the nebulous "order and morality" rationale with "utterly without" value or importance because the latter is more specific and, perhaps, more protective of literary works. The premise in *Roth-Alberts*, as explained by Edward de Grazia, an attorney who has represented numerous authors and their works, served to extend constitutional protection to literature and the arts, while at the same time, in Brennan's typical balancing fashion, it established some guidelines for determining obscene material.[29]

One of the ironies in the Indianapolis case was the city's use of *Beauharnais*, long since repudiated by a string of rulings protecting libelous utterances and making "group libel" anachronistic. For example, in *New York Times v. Sullivan* of 1964, Brennan, writing for six justices in the unanimous decision, said that "misstatements of fact" about public officials—later to be extended to public figures and public events—were protected unless the false material was published with "actual malice," that is, with knowledge of its falsity or with reckless disregard of whether it was true or false.

In *Collin v. Smith* of 1978, which affirmed the striking of laws meant to block parades such as that by American Nazis, the U.S. Seventh Circuit Court of Appeals said that *Sullivan* had so washed away the foundations of *Beauharnais* that it could not be considered authoritative. Judge Easterbrook, in a footnote to *American Booksellers Assoc. v. Hudnut*, added: "It is not clear that depicting women as subordinate in sexually explicit ways, even combined with a depiction of pleasure in rape, would fit within the definition of group libel. The well-received film *Swept Away* used explicit sex, plus taking pleasure in rape, to make a political statement, not to defame."[30]

Meanwhile, Brennan, in putting together a coalition of five justices for the *Roth-Alberts* ruling, which included Harold Burton, Tom Clark, Stanley Reed, and Felix Frankfurter (Chief Justice Warren concurred separately), simply elaborated on Justice Murphy's two-value, or two-level, approach to freedom of expression. Of greatest value on the upper level were the traditionally protected kinds of speech, such as political and religious ideas, which are entitled to full protection. Of lowest value on the lower level were the unprotected varieties, such as profane, obscene, and libelous speech, and fighting words.

After the liberal Arthur H. Goldberg, a Kennedy appointment, replaced the unpredictable Frankfurter on the Court in 1962, Brennan's coalition was able to elevate to protected status more "low-value" expression. Justice Goldberg's first obscenity case was *Jacobellis v. Ohio*, handed down in June 1964. Brennan, joined only by Goldberg, established a credo worth recalling and, especially, remembering:

> It follows that material dealing with sex in a manner that advocates ideas, or that has literary or scientific or artistic value or any other form of social importance, may not be branded as obscenity and denied the constitutional protection. Nor may the constitutional status of the material be made to turn on a "weighing" of its social importance against its prurient appeal, for a work cannot be proscribed unless it is "utterly" without social importance.[31]

Two years later, in 1966, Justice Brennan wrote three more leading opinions, one on John Cleland's erotic *Fanny Hill* and the second and third concerning publications by Ralph Ginzburg and Samuel Mishkin. The *Fanny Hill*, or *Memoirs*, case demonstrated the limits of the "utterly without social importance," or "social value," doctrine. Brennan

214

insisted in *Memoirs* that the three-part test of *Roth-Alberts* must coalesce, that each must be met independently in determining obscenity. Thus, as Professor Harry Kalven Jr. observed at the time, "The concession to censorship is minimal and very little material is left within the reach of the law."[32]

But, as we also learned earlier, Justices White and Clark disagreed with Brennan, the former saying that if "social importance" were to prevail, "obscene material, however far beyond customary limits of candor, is immune if it has any literary style, if it contains any historical references or language characteristic of a bygone day, or even if it is printed or bound in an interesting way." Clark added that the "utterly without" condition "rejects the basic holding of *Roth* and gives the smut artist free rein to carry on his dirty business."[33] Pandering and deviance, therefore, became additional creations of the Brennan-influenced Court, imaginative methods to get rid of the publications of the annoying Ginzburg and Mishkin, but they are hardly ways to deal with obscenity and pornography over the long haul.

Brennan joined Chief Justice Warren in what may be called the "intent" theory for establishing unprotected obscene speech, contrasted with the Harlan-Stewart "content" theory that disallowed only hard-core pornography. Brennan also in the 1960s began talking about the legitimacy of limiting the control of obscenity to that directed at unwilling recipients and juveniles, a concept borne of frustration and elaborated on in *Paris Adult Theatre* in 1973.

On 30 September 1970, the chairman of the President's Commission on Obscenity and Pornography, William B. Lockhart, former dean of the law school at the University of Minnesota, submitted the commission's report to President Nixon and the Congress. The Johnson administration had instructed the commission in 1968 to evaluate and recommend definitions of obscenity and pornography, to explore the nature and volume of traffic in such materials, to study the effect of obscenity and pornography on the public, and to recommend advisable, appropriate, effective, and constitutional means to deal effectively with the flow of such traffic. One year earlier, in 1969, Warren Burger, a conservative federal judge, had been named by Nixon to replace Earl Warren as chief justice after Abe Fortas was forced to withdraw his candidacy under Lyndon Johnson. Fortas himself was replaced on the Court by Harry Blackmun in 1970.

In *Miller v. California* in 1973, Chief Justice Burger announced: "Today, for the first time since Roth was decided in 1957, a majority of the Court has agreed on concrete guidelines to isolate 'hard core' pornography." Thus, the term *pornography* became part of the definition of *obscenity*, further muddying, in the words of Attorney Edward de Grazia, "the metaphysical waters for the legal community and giving anti-porn feminists and right-wing fundamentalists a new epithet with which to belabor merchants of filth."[34] Burger's new coalition of five discarded the permissive *Memoirs* test, replacing the "utterly without" phrase with "without literary, artistic, political, and social value" and abandoning the national community standard by which obscenity had been judged since *Jacobellis*.

Next, in *Pope v. Illinois*, decided in 1987, William Brennan joined the dissenting opinion of Justice John Paul Stevens, who pointed out that Justice Byron White's seeming "rejection of the community values test" with respect to artistic value concealed a "standard [that] would still, in effect, require a juror to apply community values, unless the juror were to find that an ordinary member of his or her community is not 'a reasonable person.'" And that's not likely to happen. Stevens's dissent in *Pope* emphasized the threat that White's gloss on the "serious value" standard posed for unpopular or misunderstood art. The glossed standard "will provide room," according to Stevens, "for juries to disregard the testimony of experts such as art critics; a jury might conclude that the experts represent an unreasonable minority, and that the majority of the population, who are less likely to see the work as valuable, are more reasonable than the critics."[35]

President Ford picked the "professorial Stevens" to replace Justice Douglas, the "fiery liberal," in 1975. Stevens won a unanimous confirmation from the Senate on 17 December. While moderate to conservative, Stevens, a nonpolitical appeals court judge from Chicago, nonetheless shares a

216

fierce individualism with the late Justice Douglas. Some justices heavily edit or substantially rewrite their clerks' writing, but according to David G. Savage, who covers the Court for the *Los Angeles Times*, only a few justices—notably Scalia and Stevens—turn out opinions that feature their own characteristic style. "If there is one member of the Court who can match wits with Scalia, or any attorney appearing before the Court, it is the bow-tied Stevens."[36]

Justice Stevens's approach to freedom of speech may be summarized by his pig-in-the-parlor majority opinion in *FCC v. Pacifica Foundation* in 1978 and in his strong dissenting opinion in *R.A.V. v. City of St. Paul* in 1992. (Stevens actually concurred in the judgment of the Court, written by Justice Scalia, but scolded his colleagues for veering from the principle that certain categories of expression are unprotected.) In *Pacifica*, he recalled Justice George Sutherland's earlier allusion: "A nuisance may merely be a right thing in the wrong place—like a pig in the parlor instead of the barnyard." Stevens said, "Words that are commonplace in one setting are shocking in another." Or, as he paraphrased Justice Harlan, one occasion's lyric is another's vulgarity. It is commonplace for Stevens to assert that government may regulate speech according to its content and its context, which is to say, in other words, pigs *versus* people, or people *instead of* pigs.[37]

Stevens said in dictim in *Pacifica*: "A requirement that indecent language be avoided will have its primary effect on the form, rather than the content, of serious communication. There are few, if any, thoughts that cannot be expressed by the use of less offensive language." He referred to Justice Oliver Wendell Holmes's classic exposition of the proposition that both the content and context of speech are critical elements of First Amendment analysis. "The character of every act depends upon the circumstances in which it is done," Holmes wrote in *Schenck v. U.S.* in 1919. He continued:

> The most stringent protection of free speech would not protect a man in falsely shouting fire in a theater, and causing a panic. The question in every case is whether the

Viewpoint Discrimination ◆

words used are used in such circumstances and are of such a nature as to create a clear and present danger that they will bring about the substantive evils that Congress has a right to prevent. It is a question of proximity and degree.

Stevens is not fearful of restraining speech on the basis of proximity and degree—but not without some safeguards. "There are, in fact, many situations in which the subject matter, or, indeed, even the point of view of the speaker, may provide a justification for a time, place, and manner regulation," he said in 1980 in *Consolidated Edison v. Public Service Commission*. Stevens continued to explain his approach:

> Any student of history who has been reprimanded for talking about the World Series during a class discussion of the First Amendment knows that it is incorrect to state that a time, place, or manner restriction may not be based upon either the content or subject matter of speech. As is true of many other aspects of liberty, some forms of orderly regulation actually promote freedom more than would a state of total anarchy.[38]

Justice Harlan, in *Cohen v. California*, distinguished between a speaker's *word* choice and the *method* of communication. Paul Robert Cohen's word choice for expressing his opposition to the draft was "Fuck the Draft," instead of, let's say, "Screw the Draft," as Chief Justice Burger would have preferred. Cohen's method was to print the message on his jacket, instead of with a handbill or sound truck. The *Cohen* decision said that regulation of a speaker's method of communication implicates different and stronger interests than regulation of word choice. Stevens reiterated this concept when he said in *Consolidated Edison*: "Independently of the message the speaker intends to convey, the form of his communication may be offensive—perhaps because it is too loud or too ugly in a particular setting." Other speeches, he said, even though elegantly phrased in dulcet tones, are offensive simply because the listener disagrees with the speaker's message. He continued: "The fact that the offensive form of some communication may subject it to appropriate regulation surely does not support the conclusion that the offensive

◆ VIEWPOINT DISCRIMINATION

character of an idea can justify an attempt to censor its expression."[39]

Stevens and Harlan part company, however, over the role message content plays in regulation, Harlan believing that the government engages in content regulation when it proscribes the form of a speaker's words just as much as when it proscribes the content of the message itself. For Harlan, word choice was an indispensable part of a vital and durable First Amendment. He stressed that "words are often chosen as much for their emotive as their cognitive force."[40] Stevens tried to combine word choice with method of communication in an effort to allow for some restraint on speech. The New York state regulation banning utility bill inserts that discussed controversial issues was not reasonable in *Consolidated Edison* because it was based on the content of the inserts. In Stevens's view, the "offensive form" of content may be a proper basis for regulation—even content with a point of view. But, since the state Public Service Commission justified its action on the basis of "idea expression," and not simply content across the board, or a narrow category of speech, he joined the Court in striking down the regulation. It was neither content-based nor even viewpoint-based; it favored a *particular* viewpoint over others.

Contrary to the broad declaration in *Police Department of Chicago v. Mosley*, that content-based regulations of speech are "never permitted," Stevens said that distinctions based on content, "far from being presumptively invalid, are an inevitable and indispensable aspect of a coherent understanding of the First Amendment." He reiterated that belief in the "hate speech" decision in 1992 in *R.A.V. v. St. Paul*, written by Justice Scalia. Stevens agreed with the judgment but from a substantially different angle.[41]

Scalia's majority of Chief Justice Rehnquist, Kennedy, Souter, and Thomas based its holding on Robert A. Viktora's contention "that in [punishing only some fighting words and not others], even though it is a subcategory, technically, of unprotected conduct, [the ordinance] still is picking out an opinion, a disfavored message, and making that clear through the State." More precisely, the justices held that the ordinance was "facially unconstitutional" because it regulated speech on the basis of its content, i.e., expression of group hatred. "The First Amendment," Scalia said, "does not permit St. Paul to impose special prohibitions on those speakers who express views on disfavored subjects." In its practical operation, he said, the ordinance goes even beyond mere content discrimination to actual viewpoint discrimination.[42]

Stevens agreed with Viktora's overbreadth argument but not with Scalia's obsession with content. "The Court today goes beyond even the overstatement in *Mosley* and applies the prohibition on content-based regulation to speech that the Court had until today considered wholly 'unprotected' by the First Amendment—namely, fighting words." This new absolutism, according to Stevens, severely contorted the fabric of settled First Amendment law. He explained that heretofore the Court's First Amendment decisions had created a rough hierarchy in the protection of speech. "Core political speech occupies the highest, most protected position; commercial speech and nonobscene, sexually explicit speech are regarded as a sort of second-class expression; obscenity and fighting words receive the least protection of all."[43]

By prohibiting the regulation of fighting words on the basis of subject matter, the Court in *R.A.V.* provided the same protection to this category, or level, of expression as is provided in core political speech. Stevens went on to explain his view:

> Whether the selective proscription of proscribable speech is defined by the protected target ("certain persons or groups") or the basis of the harm (injuries "based on race, color, creed, religion, or gender") makes no constitutional difference: what matters is whether the legislature's selection is based on a legitimate, neutral, and reasonable distinction.[44]

Stevens also attacked the "quest for doctrinal certainty" through the definition of categories and subcategories, which in his opinion, are destined to fail. For one thing, the concept of categories fits poorly with the complex reality of expression. "Few dividing lines in First Amendment law are straight and unwavering, and efforts at categorization inevi-

220

tably give rise only to fuzzy boundaries," the justice said. Nor does the categorical approach, which Justice White subscribed to in *R.A.V.*, take seriously the importance of context, for the meaning of any expression and the legitimacy of its regulation can only be determined in context. Stevens borrowed Justice Holmes's immortal phrase:

> A word is not a crystal, transparent and unchanged, it is the skin of a living thought and may vary greatly in color and content according to the circumstances and the time in which it is used.

[To which Stevens added:]

> Whether, for example, a picture or a sentence is obscene cannot be judged in the abstract, but rather only in the context of its setting, its use, and its audience.
>
> In short, the history of the categorical approach is largely the history of narrowing the categories of unprotected speech.[45]

While Justice Brennan sought to *limit* regulation of obscene matter to that which involves minors and is foisted upon unconsenting adults, Stevens seeks to *broaden* First Amendment protection on the basis of content and context case by case, adhering to traditional and well-settled categories of proscribable speech and following long-established precedents. Both justices turn out to be realists.

XII

Afterword

Hand's Insight

THE METAPHOR of the carousel—what goes around, comes around—applies to this attempt to resolve—though not necessarily solve—the Supreme Court's intractable obscenity problem. Discussion began with references to early obscenity decisions by Judge Learned Hand, and it ends, not surprisingly, with the relevance of his speech-protective approach to questionable matter.

In the 1913 ruling, *United States v. Kennerley*, Judge Hand wrote: "I question whether in the end men will regard that as obscene which is honestly relevant to the adequate expression of innocent ideas, and whether they will not believe that truth and beauty are too precious to society at large to be mutilated in the interests of those most likely to pervert them to base uses." This was in reaction to the prevailing Victorian English decision, *Regina V. Hicklin*, which said that the obscenity of a book may be determined by its isolated passages rather than as a whole.[1]

Hand's feelings also stand as an early warning against the still-existing belief that obscene matter *causes* obscene behavior. Hand argued that there should be no prosecution for the sole purpose of protecting a susceptible, immature group in the potential audience. He allowed, however, that the standards of the community should prevail and that a jury could ascertain those standards.

Judge Hand's prescription for protecting speech was more fully developed in 1917 in a case regarding political dissent, *Masses Publishing Co. v. Patten.* He said that it was a highly questionable function of the courts to second-guess legislators and administrators on the probable consequences of dissident speech. As interpreted by Gerald Gunther, author of a magnificent biography of Hand, "A legal standard inviting speculation about the consequences of words—whether immediate or remote—would allow judges and juries to succumb to majoritarian, speech-repressive sentiments."[2]

Hand's solution, instead, focused on the speaker's words, not on the probable consequences of the words. Rather than asking in each case if the words had a tendency to induce unlawful conduct, the judge tried to fashion a more "absolute and objective test," focusing on the words only, the language used. What he urged, Gunther explains, was "a test based upon the nature of the utterance itself," an "incitement" test: If the words constituted solely a counsel to violate the law, solely an instruction that it was the listener's duty or interest to violate the law, they could be forbidden; in a democratic society, all other utterances had to be protected. As he wrote: "To assimilate agitation, legitimate as such, with direct incitement to violent resistance, is to disregard the tolerance of all methods of political agitation which in normal times is a safeguard of free government." Predictions about the possible effects of speech, even if empirically plausible, could not form a legal standard consistent with the safeguarding of free speech, Hand maintained. "Direct incitement" to illegal behavior was for Hand a standard that focused on the content rather than the effect of speech.[3]

James Joyce's *Ulysses* was under attack the next time Judge Hand participated in an obscenity case, in 1934, which came after his elevation to the U.S. Second Circuit Court of Appeals. He was joined in the decision by his cousin Augustus Hand and Martin T. Manton, the chief judge and "a staunch defender of established morals," according to Gunther. Learned Hand, by contrast, had acquired since the *Kennerley* and *Masses* cases a reputation as a strong defender of freedom of expression. Augustus wrote the majority opinion, finding *Ulysses* nonobscene, though Learned's influence was said to be powerful.[4] With *Ulysses*, *Hicklin* was dead once and for all.

Next for Learned Hand in the realm of obscenity was *United States v. Levine* in 1936. The decision, while it served mainly to throw more dirt on *Hicklin*'s grave, presented Hand with another opportunity to reiterate his speech-protective view. "The work must be taken as a whole, its merits weighed against its defects; if it is old, its accepted place in the arts must be regarded; if new, the opinions of competent critics and published reviews or the like may be considered; what counts is its effect not upon any particular class, but upon all those whom it is likely to reach." *Levine*, Gunther believes, was the apex of the most speech-protective position for which Hand could find support, which is a challenge any pioneer thinker faces.[5]

Brennan's Lesson

William J. Brennan Jr. was the first Supreme Court justice to measure obscenity against the First Amendment. Yet he never went as far as Justices Douglas and Black, who argued routinely that, since obscenity is a form of speech and speech is protected by the First Amendment, laws punishing obscene speech are unconstitutional. Brennan believed that some speech, such as obscenity, fell outside the First Amendment. This notion became Court doctrine in *Roth v. United States*, for which Brennan wrote the majority opinion during his first year on the Court. A companion case, *Alberts v. California*, was decided the same day.

In the *Roth-Alberts* decisions, Brennan emphasized that "sex and obscenity are not synonymous," and he tried to make as small as possible the area of speech that could be penalized. The Court decided that "obscenity is not within the area of constitutionally protected speech or press." Brennan, writing for the Court, found "implicit in the history of

◆ AFTERWORD

the First Amendment . . . the rejection of obscenity as utterly without redeeming social importance." He concluded that material having a *tendency* to incite lustful thoughts may be suppressed without proof that it would induce antisocial conduct. The test, "whether to the average person, applying contemporary community standards, the dominant theme of the material taken as a whole appeals to prurient interest," was said to define obscenity clearly enough that discussion of sex would be safeguarded. Thus, the words *obscene, lewd, lascivious*, and *filthy*, though imprecise, were held to give sufficient notice of what conduct was criminal.[6]

Brennan believed he had set a reasonable course for the Court, keeping to some degree Judge Hand's speech-protective approach and drawing a line between obscenity and protected speech. Such was not the case, however, as "the intractable obscenity problem," described by Justice John Marshall Harlan, only got worse. Ten years after *Roth-Alberts*, Justice Harlan observed: "The subject of obscenity has produced a variety of views among the members of the Court unmatched in any other course of constitutional adjudication." By then, the Court had decided thirteen obscenity cases and the justices had written fifty-five separate opinions. Harlan remained convinced, as he wrote a friend only months before his death, that the problem was "almost intractable, and that its ultimate solution must be found in a renaissance of societal values."[7]

In a 1966 case, *Memoirs v. Massachusetts*, Justices William Brennan, Earl Warren, and Abe Fortas used as a test of obscenity that the questionable material be "utterly without redeeming social value" and that community standards continue to be national in scope, as defined in a 1964 case, *Jacobellis v. Ohio*. Justices William O. Douglas, Hugo Black, and Potter Stewart concurred in *Memoirs*. All this changed in 1973 with *Miller v. California*, when Chief Justice Warren Burger's conservative majority discarded the "utterly without redeeming social value" criterion and, in effect, removed the burden of proof from the prosecutor. It was left to the defense to convince a judge or a jury that the material had "serious literary, artistic, political, or scientific value."

The *Miller* ruling came down the same day as *Paris Adult*

Theatre I v. Slaton. In his dissent, which also served as his dissent in *Miller,* Brennan confessed that his long effort to figure out the difference between obscenity and protected speech had been a failure. "I am convinced that the approach initiated 16 years ago in *Roth v. United States . . .* and culminating in the Court's decision today, cannot bring stability to this area of the law without jeopardizing fundamental First Amendment values, and I have concluded that the time has come to make a significant depature from that approach." He said that the Court had been unable to provide "sensitive tools" to separate obscenity from other sexually oriented but constitutionally protected speech. He added that judicial attempts to follow the lead of the Supreme Court had often ended in "hopeless confusion." Brennan's "lesson" then followed:

> I am reluctantly forced to the conclusion that none of the available formulas . . . can reduce the vagueness to a tolerable level while at the same time striking an acceptable balance between the protections of the First and Fourteenth Amendments, on the one hand, and on the other the asserted state interest in regulating the dissemination of certain sexually oriented materials.[8]

Brennan said that, at least in the absence of distribution to juveniles or "obtrusive exposure" to unconsenting adults, the First and Fourteenth Amendments prohibited state and federal governments from attempting wholly to suppress sexually oriented materials on the basis of their allegedly obscene contents.

Stevens's Solution

Justice John Paul Stevens's content-based solution, while not without serious risks, takes us from Learned Hand's early views on the need for protecting as much speech-as-speech as possible, to beyond Brennan's feelings of desperation. Brennan's lesson, the result of a kind of judicial pragmatism, may be traced to Hand's pioneering views. Both jurists may have influenced Stevens. Brennan, for one, found especially appealing Hand's rewriting, and refining, of Oliver Wendell

226

Holmes's "clear and present danger" test. "In each case [courts] ... must ask whether the gravity of the 'evil,' discounted by its improbability, justifies such invasion of free speech as is necessary to avoid danger." Hand established a higher, and more explicit, threshold than had Holmes, which Brennan, in the end, did not think the government could meet when suppressing most obscenity.[9]

We get more than a hint of Stevens's approach in a 1978 ruling, *FCC v. Pacifica Foundation*, the so-called "dirty words" case: "A requirement that indecent language be avoided will have its primary effect on the form, rather than the content, of serious communication. There are few, if any, thoughts that cannot be expressed by the use of less offensive language." Earlier, in *Smith v. United States* (1977), the justice stated crisply that so long as the government did not totally suppress protected speech and sticks to its obligation of complete neutrality with respect to the point of view of a message, some speech may be regulated on the basis of its subject matter. "Even within the area of protected speech," Stevens said, "a difference in content may require a different governmental response." The key words and phrases in this formula are obvious, and they make clear the *conditional* nature of Stevens's theory of sliding-scale First Amendment values.[10]

Stevens's approach to freedom of speech may be characterized, and summarized, by his use of the pig-in-the-parlor metaphor in the *Pacifica* decision. He recalled Justice George Sutherland's earlier allusion: "A nuisance may merely be a right thing in the wrong place—like a pig in the parlor instead of the barnyard." Stevens added, "Words that are commonplace in one setting are shocking in another." Or, as he once paraphrased Justice Harlan, one occasion's lyric is another's vulgarity. It had become commonplace for Stevens to assert that government may regulate speech according to its content and context, which is to say, in baser terms, "pigs *versus* people, or, what's better, people *instead of* pigs."

In 1976 in *Young v. American Mini Theatres*, Stevens said that the government has a "paramount obligation of neutrality" in matters of speech, and that it could not ever regulate speech on the basis of a particular point of view. The justice drew upon the Court's rulings on libel and commercial speech, where constitutional protection is limited by the content of the speech.

His strongest argument appears in *R.A.V. v. City of St. Paul* in 1992. The Court struck down St. Paul's Bias-Motivated Crime Ordinance, a disorderly conduct law banning displays of symbols—including, as in this case, the burning of a cross—that arouse anger in others on the basis of race, color, creed, religion, or gender. Justice Antonin Scalia, writing for five members, said the ordinance was unconstitutional because it regulated speech on the basis of viewpoint content. John Paul Stevens agreed with those justices who thought the law overbroad but criticized the majority for ruling that proscrible speech cannot be regulated on the basis of subject matter. He accused the Court of giving fighting words speech and obscenity the same degree of protection accorded core political speech. Justice Byron White, who also said the St. Paul ordinance was simply overbroad, accused the Scalia majority of breaking with precedent. He, like Stevens, affirmed the Court's long-standing categorical approach to limiting speech protection. "Should the government want to criminalize certain fighting words," White said, "the Court now requires it to criminalize all fighting words."[11]

Stevens accused the majority of succumbing to the "allure of absolute principles." He said that Scalia had revised the Court's categorical approach by stating that certain elements of expression were wholly proscribable. "Even within categories of protected expression," Stevens said, "the First Amendment status of speech is fixed by its content." Content makes a difference, but Stevens believed the Court in *R.A.V.* had invalidated the selective regulation of speech based on content. He supported the Court's traditional categorical approach because it had been an effort, he believed, to narrow the categories of unprotected speech.

A state would be acting neutrally, according to Stevens, if it singled out cross burning for special fighting words punishment. But a state cannot decide that cross burning is worse than, let's say, an attack on a person's political views, as the Scalia majority said. It is the severe social consequences of cross burning, as in the St. Paul instance, that

228

made it fit the fighting words category, not, as the majority said, because the law singled out speech on certain specified topics. In the case of obscenity, therefore, Stevens allows for such a proscribable category to exist so long as regulation is applied neutrally. Obscene matter, as defined generally, may be regulated; as described in specific viewpoint terms, it may not.

The extent to which Justice Stevens believes in neutrality may be seen, "somewhat amazingly," as Margaret Blanchard notes, in his majority opinion in the 1987 case, *Meese v. Keene*. When the Justice Department categorized three Canadian films as political propaganda, California state senator Barry Keene retorted that such labeling was prejudicial. Justice Stevens, however, found "political propaganda," as used in the Foreign Agents Registration Act, had a neutral meaning. "The term," he said, "does nothing to place regulated expressive materials 'beyond the pale of legitimate discourse.' " He said the statutory definition of political propaganda had been on the books for more than four decades. "We should presume that the people who have a sufficient understanding of the law to know that the term . . . is used to describe the regulated category also know that the definition is a broad, neutral one rather than a pejorative one." Inside the courts, the "notion of neutrality," as described by Cass R. Sunstein, a legal theorist, is "designed to ensure that judges do not simply implement whatever intuitions they happen to have, but that they order and make coherent those intuitions through reasoning by analogy." However, such neutral indifference to "whose ox is gored," can be used for, as well as against, the suppression of obscenity.[12]

Baker's Liberty

C. Edwin Baker's views are the most applicable of the legal scholars who address First Amendment issues. First, he rejects both the marketplace of ideas and the market failure theories, the latter a liberal attempt to correct the deficiencies or imbalances of the former. Second, he rightfully questions the usefulness of the expression-action dichotomy: "Unfortunately, neither identifying protected 'expression' by determining the conduct's contribution to the purposes of the system or by using common sense to distinguish between expression and action works." Behavior viewed objectively is neither expression nor action but a combination of both. Sunstein argues for a distinction between emotive and cognitive speech, the latter closer to the center of First Amendment concern. But they are so intertwined, as Baker recognizes, that dividing them for purposes of protection seems ludicrous.[13]

Freedom of speech may be defensible not because of the market's supposed capacity to discover truth, but because freedom of speech, Baker says, "embodies respect for the liberty or autonomy and responsibility of the participants." What is important is not that everything worth saying be said, as most libertarian theorists have urged, but rather, the important concern is that society deny no one the right to speak. Liberty of the speaker is the focus of Baker's theory. Motive, content, and effects of speech are not the important considerations; what is, he argues, is the coercive or noncoercive nature and context of an act in determining whether or not it is protected by the First Amendment—but not pornographic speech, which Baker contends may have more to do with ribald entertainment than with robust debate. "If pornography degrades sexual intimacy or contributes to the subordination of women it does so more by being an undersirable activity and a corrupting experience, not by being an argument."[14]

From the perspective of the liberty theory, pornographic communications or even pornographic materials produced and pursued by a solitary individual, contribute—whether in good or bad fashion—to building the culture. As Justice Douglas pointed out, Baker reminds us, materials that most people view as pornographic may play an important role in some people's self-fulfillment and self-expression. Even if obscene publications do not contribute to the marketplace of ideas, they promote these key First Amendment values. According to Baker, the First Amendment, therefore, should protect the listener's or reader's interest in obscenity. In sum, Baker's position is that speech deserves protection so long as it represents the freely chosen expression of the

◆ AFTERWORD

speaker, depends for its power on the free acceptance of the listener, and is not used in the context of a violent or coercive activity. If these conditions preside, "freedom of speech represents a charter of liberty for noncoercive action."[15]

One jurist who might agree is Richard A. Posner, whose views on artistic expression are presented in chapter 9. Judge Posner, a Reagan appointee, along with Judge Frank Easterbrook, to the U.S. Court of Appeals for the Seventh Circuit, admonishes those lawyers and judges who would dismiss popular culture as unworthy of legal protection, as for example, a photograph by Robert Mapplethorpe, which most viewers would think pornographic: "The issue of obscenity as it is posed in court cases requires the balancing of the offensiveness of the work in question against its social value, or in my terms the balancing of its aphrodisiacal properties against its formal, informational, and ideological ones," writes Posner. "The metaphor of balancing is misleading here, however, because it gives an exaggerated impression of the distinctness of the things being compared." The judge explains that it is important to distinguish (as best we can) between an offensiveness generated by a perception of the aphrodisiacal character of an erotic work and the offensiveness of its ideology. The First Amendment, as we have seen in a number of Supreme Court rulings, has long been held to protect the right of an author or artist to preach disfavored ideologies, even sexual immorality. Yet it was precisely Mapplethorpe's ideology, his sexual preference, that has been unconstitutionally censored.[16]

Between *Roth-Alberts* and *Miller v. California*, Justice Brennan changed from focusing on the marketplace of ideas rationale to giving primacy to the notion of individual liberty and autonomy. His *Roth-Alberts* solution turns out to have been clumsy and restrictive. He argued that the "right to receive information and ideas, regardless of their social worth . . . is fundamental to our free society" and "is closely tied . . . to 'the right to be free except in very limited circumstances, from unwarranted governmental intrusions into one's privacy' " and to "the right of the individual, married or single, to be free from unwarranted governmental intrusion into matters so fundamentally affecting a person as the decision whether to bear or beget a child." Adopting the typical liberty emphasis on consenting adults, Brennan suggested that it may "follow that a State could not constitutionally punish one who undertakes to provide this information to a willing, adult recipient."[17]

In the end, the mood of the Court at any given time, influenced by public opinion and precedent will determine the degree to which pornography will be tolerated legally. But the hope is that the Court may be influenced by Judge Hand's insight, Justice Brennan's lesson, Justice Stevens's solution, and the First Amendment theories of Baker and other legal scholars. From the judge, the justices, and the scholars, we could say that it will behoove the Court in future obscenity rulings to give less time to *defining* obscenity—the problem Justice Stewart spotted—and even less time limiting speech protection on the basis of possible *effects*. Since we will never know obscenity unless we see it, and because social science results are so inconclusive, it is more to the point to limit speech on the basis of speech-as-speech, as Hand urged, and not on the basis of harm, alleged or otherwise. Stevens, too, allows for the categorization of words, so long as there is neutrality in the *content* of the message they convey. Baker is not as concerned with content or context as he is with personal liberty and autonomy. Obscenity is an issue for the individual, not the collective. Hence, Brennan's lesson becomes feasible: let the government protect minors and unconsenting adults; the rest is up to the individual.

Notes

Index

Notes

◆ I. Isolated Passages

1. Richard S. Randall, *Freedom and Taboo: Pornography and the Politics of a Self Divided* (Berkeley: Univ. of California Press, 1989), 160.

2. Randall, 90–91.

3. Randall, 28–29. Also see Steven Marcus, *The Other Victorians: A Study of Sexuality and Pornography in Mid-Nineteenth-Century England* (New York: Basic Books, 1974), 241; and Peter Gay, *The Bourgeois Experience: Victoria to Freud*, vol. 1, *Education of the Senses* (New York: Oxford Univ. Press, 1984).

4. Randall, 5.

5. Randall, 5. Also see President's Commission on Obscenity and Pornography, *Report* (New York: Bantam, 1970).

6. Randall, 115.

7. John D'Emilio and Estelle B. Freedman, *Intimate Matters: A History of Sexuality in America* (New York: Harper & Row, 1988), 277.

8. Norman Dorsen, Paul Bender, and Burt Neuborne, *Emerson, Haber, and Dorsen's Political and Civil Rights in the United States*, 4th ed., vol. 1 (Boston: Little, Brown, 1976), 351–52. Also see Walter Kendrick, *The Secret Museum: Pornography in Modern*

Culture (New York: Viking, 1987); and *Regina v. Hicklin*, L.R. 3 Q.B. 360 (1868).

9. Frederick Schauer, *The Law of Obscenity* (Washington, D.C.: Bureau of National Affairs, 1976), 15–16.

10. Schauer, *Law of Obscenity*, 15–16.

11. D'Emilio and Freedman, 131.

12. D'Emilio and Freedman, 156–57.

13. D'Emilio and Freedman, 157.

14. In John J. Watkins, *The Mass Media and the Law* (Englewood Cliffs, N.J.: Prentice Hall, 1990), 359.

15. Kendrick, 135.

16. *Rosen v. U.S.*, 161 U.S. 29 (1896).

17. *Swearingen v. U.S.*, 161 U.S. 446 (1896) at 446 n.

18. Thomas L. Tedford, *Freedom of Speech in the United States* (New York: Random House, 1985), 55–56.

19. D'Emilio and Freedman, 279.

20. *U.S. v. Kennerley*, 209 F. 119 (S.D.N.Y. 1913).

21. *U.S. v. One Book Called "Ulysses,"* 5 F.Supp. 182 (D.N.Y. 1933).

22. at 182.

23. *U.S. v. One Book Entitled Ulysses by James Joyce*, 72 F.2d 705 (2d Cir. 1934).

24. Ben Ray Redman, "Obscenity and Censorship," *Scribner's Magazine*, May 1934, 341.

25. Redman, 343, 344.

26. *U.S. v. Levine*, 83 F.2d 156 (2d Cir. 1936).

27. *Chaplinsky v. New Hampshire*, 315 U.S. 568 (1942) at 572; and *Near v. Minnesota*, 283 U.S. 697 (1931).

28. *Chaplinsky* at 572; and *Commonwealth v. Gordon*, 66 D.&C. 101 (1949), cited in Tedford, 164–65.

29. Charles Rembar, *The End of Obscenity: The Trials of Lady Chatterly, Tropic of Cancer and Fanny Hill* (New York: Harper & Row, 1986), 3.

30. Felice Flanery Lewis, *Literature, Obscenity, & Law* (Carbondale: Southern Illinois Univ. Press, 1976), 158–61.

31. D'Emilio and Freedman, 280–84. Also see Loren Baritz, *The Good Life: The Meaning of Success for the American Middle Class* (New York: Knopf, 1989), 189–90.

32. D'Emilio and Freedman, 284.

33. Anne Lyon Haight and Chandler B. Grannis, *Banned Books 387 b.c. to 1978 a.d.* (New York: R. R. Bowker, 1978), 76–77.

34. Morton Moskin, "Criminal Law: Legislation: Inadequacy of Present Tests As to What Constitutes Obscene Literature," 34 *Cornell Law Quarterly* 442 (1949).

35. "Cases Noted," 47 *Columbia L. Rev.* 686 (May 1947).

36. Transcript Record at 78, *People v. Doubleday*, 297 N.Y. 687, 77 N.E.2d 6 (1947), cited by Morton Moskin.

37. Sumner was quoted in the *New York Times*, 28 Nov. 1946, pp. 1, 25.

◆ II. Dominant Theme

1. *Butler v. Michigan*, 353 U.S. 380 (1957).

2. See James C. N. Paul and Murray L. Schwartz, *Federal Censorship: Obscenity in the Mail* (New York: Free Press of Glencoe, 1961), 142.

3. Paul and Schwartz, 142.

4. *Kingsley Books Inc. v. Brown*, 354 U.S. 436; and *Roth v. United States* and *Alberts v. California*, 354 U.S. 476 (also known as *Roth-Alberts*).

5. *Kingsley Books Inc. v. Brown*, 1 L.Ed.2d 1469 at 1474.

6. Paul and Schwartz, 148; *Near v. Minnesota* at 697; and *Kingsley Books Inc.* 1 L.Ed.2d at 1474.

7. *Kingsley Books Inc.*, 1 L.Ed.2d at 1477.

8. at 1478.

9. Donald M. Gillmor, "The Puzzle of Pornography," 42 *Journalism Quarterly* 363, 368 (Summer 1965).

10. Dorothy Ganfield Fowler, *Unmailable: Congress and the Post Office* (Athens: University of Georgia, 1977), 173.

11. Paul and Schwartz, 82–83, 144.

12. *Alberts v. California* at 476.

13. *Roth-Alberts* at 487.

14. at 489.

15. at 504.

16. at 504.

17. at 510.

18. at 512–13, 514.

19. Fowler, 175.

20. *Roth-Alberts* at 510.

21. *Kingsley International Pictures Corp.*, 360 U.S. 684 (1959); and *Smith v. California*, 361 U.S. 147 (1959).

22. *Mounce v. U.S.*, 355 U.S. 180 (1957); *One Inc. v. Olesen*, 355 U.S. 371 (1958); and *Sunshine Book Co. v. Summerfield*, 355 U.S. 372 (1958).

23. *Kingsley International Pictures Corp.* at 685.

24. at 689, 690.

25. at 708, 691–92.

26. See D.A.B. [Douglas A. Boeckmann], "Constitutional Law—Freedom of Speech—Lack of Scienter Element in City Ordinance Against Obscenity Violates First Amendment," 2 *William and Mary L. Rev.* 491 (1960) for discussion.

27. *Smith v. California* at 152, 154.

28. at 159–60, 168.

29. at 165–67.

30. at 171.

31. Gillmor, "The Puzzle of Pornography," 369.

32. Paul L. Murphy, *The Constitution in Crisis Time* (New York: Harper & Row, 1972), 351.

33. See David M. O'Brien, *Storm Center: The Supreme Court in American Politics*, 2d ed. (New York: Norton, 1990).

34. *Times Film Corp. v. Chicago*, 365 U.S. 43.

35. Tinsley E. Yarbrough, *John Marshall Harlan: Great Dissenter of the Warren Court* (New York: Oxford University Press, 1992), 219; and Harlan to Clark, 3 Nov. 1960, Harlan Papers, Box 113, Seeley G. Mudd Manuscript Library, Princeton University (MLPU).

36. *Times Film Corp.* at 51, 67. See also *The Student's Milton*, ed. Frank Allen Patterson (New York: Appleton-Century-Crofts, 1933), 742.

37. *Times Film Corp.* at 75.

38. *Freedman v. Maryland*, 380 U.S. 51 (1965); and *Teitel Film Corp. v. Cusack*, 390 U.S. 139 (1968).

39. *Marcus v. Search Warrant*, 367 U.S. 717.

40. *Kingsley Books* 354 U.S. at 436; *Marcus* at 737.

41. *Manual Enterprises Inc. v. Day*, 370 U.S. 478.

42. Comstock Act, 18 U.S.C. Sec. 1461.

43. *Manual* at 482, 488.

44. at 488. See also Kenneth Mott and Christine Kellett, "Ob-

238

scenity, Community Standards, and the Burger Court: From Deference to Disarray," 8 *Suffolk Univ. L. Rev.* 14 (1979).

45. *Jacobellis v. Ohio*, 378 U.S. 184 (1964).

46. Correspondence in Harlan Papers, Box 583, MLPU. O'Meara letter dated 30 Aug. 1962; Harlan response dated 19 Sept. 1962.

47. *Bantam Books v. Sullivan*, 372 U.S. 58 (1963).

48. at 59–61.

49. at 68–69, 72.

50. at 76.

51. Yarbrough, 221–22.

◆ III. Community Standards

1. *A Quantity of Books v. Kansas*, 376 U.S. 205 (1964); and *Grove Press v. Gerstein*, 378 U.S. 577 (1964).

2. *Jacobellis* at 191.

3. at 190, 188.

4. at 193.

5. at 193, 195.

6. at 200, 203.

7. at 203–4

8. at 196.

9. Leslie Crocker, "Recent Decisions," 16 *Western Reserve L. Rev.* 780, 787–88 (1965).

10. Baritz, 228.

11. D'Emilio and Freedman, 256.

12. *Griswold v. Connecticut*, 381 U.S. 479 (1965); and *Poe v. Ullman*, 367 U.S. 497 (1961).

13. Baritz, 272–73.

14. *Freedman v. Maryland* at 51.

15. Randall, 228–29.

16. *Memoirs v. Massachusetts*, 383 U.S. 413 (1966); *Ginzburg*, 383 U.S. 463 (1966); and *Mishkin*, 383 U.S. 502 (1966).

17. *Memoirs* at 426.

18. Rembar, 223–24.

19. Rembar, 333.

20. Felice Flanery Lewis, 218–19.

21. Rembar, 391.

22. Rembar, 341, 394.

23. Rembar, 410, 204–5; Felice Flanery Lewis, 209.

24. Rembar, 454–55.

25. Felice Flanery Lewis, 219.

26. John Cleland, *Memoirs of a Woman of Pleasure* (New York: G. P. Putnam's Sons, 1963), 43–44.

27. Randolph Trumbach, "Erotic Fantasy and Male Libertinism in Enlightenment England," in *The Invention of Pornography: Obscenity and the Origins of Modernity, 1500–1800*, ed. Lynn Hunt (New York: Zone Books, 1993), 266–67.

28. *Memoirs v. Massachusetts* at 418–19.

29. Rembar, 440–41, 457.

30. *Memoirs* at 420.

31. at 428.

32. at 431–32.

33. at 445–46.

34. Cited in Bernard Schwartz, *Super Chief: Earl Warren and His Supreme Court—A Judicial Biography* (New York: New York Univ. Press, 1983), 620–21.

35. *Memoirs* at 451–53.

36. at 461.

◆ IV. Variable Obscenity

1. *Ginzburg v. U.S.* at 463, 481–82; Fowler, 181.

2. *Ginzburg* at 464, 467, 470; and *Roth v. U.S.* at 476, 495, 496.

3. *Ginzburg* at 465.

4. at 481, 482.

5. at 482.

6. at 494–95.

7. at 494–95, 497.

8. at 499 n. 3.

9. at 501.

10. *Roth-Alberts* at 495, 496.

11. *Kingsley Books Inc.*, 354 U.S. at 446. See also Bernard Schwartz, 619–23. After oral argument on a case, the Court discusses it at its conference later in the same week. Conferences are closed to all but the justices. The chief justice presides and starts discussion on each case. The associate justices, beginning with the most senior, present their own views and votes. The writing of opinions is also assigned when the conference(s) end. For more in-

formation on this and other technical procedures governing the Supreme Court, see Lawrence Baum, *The Supreme Court*, 3d ed. (Washington, D.C.: CQ Press, 1989).

12. Bernard Schwartz, 621–22.

13. Fred P. Graham, "The Fortas Liberalism," *New York Times*, 22 June 1966, p. 19.

14. *Mishkin v. New York* at 502.

15. at 509.

16. Bernard Schwartz, 622–23.

17. *Mishkin* at 518.

18. *Ginzburg* at 472. See also Leon Friedman, "The Ginzburg Decision and the Law," 36 *American Scholar* 71, 77 (Winter 1966–67).

19. As reported in Rembar, 484–85.

20. Robert Shogan, *A Question of Judgment: The Fortas Case and the Struggle for the Supreme Court* (New York: Bobbs-Merrill, 1972); Bruce Allen Murphy, *Fortas: The Rise and Ruin of a Supreme Court Justice* (New York: William Morrow, 1988); and Laura Kalman, *Abe Fortas: A Biography* (New Haven: Yale Univ. Press, 1990); Fred P. Graham, "High Court Rules Ads Can Be Proof of Obscene Work," and "Publisher of Erotica," *New York Times*, 22 Mar. 1966, p. 1; *The Nation*, 4 Apr. 1966, 379–80; *The New Republic*, 3 Apr. 1966, 5–6; and Rembar, 484.

21. Reported in Rembar, 484–85. Also see Paul L. Montgomery, "Booksellers Here Staging a Cleanup," *New York Times*, 23 March 1966, p. 1; Irving Spiegel, "Clergymen Hail Obscenity Bans," *New York Times*, 2 May 1966, p. 30.

22. Reported in Rembar, 484–85. Also see Russell Baker, "Observer: Some Advice to the Supreme Court," *New York Times*, 24 Mar. 1966, p. 38.

23. Rembar, 488–89.

24. Rembar, 490.

25. *Redrup, Austin*, and *Gent*, 386 U.S. 762; Fortas memo in Bernard Schwartz, 623. Also see "Obscenity Ruling Argued in Court," *New York Times*, 11 Oct. 1966, p. 33; " 'Witch Hunt' Feared on Obscenity Issue," *New York Times*, 12 Oct. 1966, p. 23.

26. Donald M. Gillmor, Jerome A. Barron, Todd F. Simon, and Herbert A. Terry, *Mass Communication Law: Cases and Comment*, 5th ed. (Minneapolis: West Publishing Co., 1990), 657; Dwight L. Teeter and Don R. Pember, "The Retreat from Obscenity: *Redrup v. New York*," 21 *Hastings L. J.* 175 (Nov. 1969).

27. Reported in Bernard Schwartz, 653.

28. Schwartz, 653.

29. Schwartz, 655.

30. Schwartz, 656.

31. Teeter and Pember, "Retreat from Obscenity," 175.

32. *Interstate Circuit Inc. v. Dallas*, with *United Artists Corp. v. Dallas*, 390 U.S. 676; and *Ginsberg v. New York*, 390 U.S. 629.

33. *Ginsberg* at 674.

34. at 674.

35. Kalman, 344.

36. *Ginsberg* at 673.

37. Schauer, *Law of Obscenity*, 92–95. Also see Schauer, "Speech and 'Speech'—Obscenity and 'Obscenity': An Exercise in the Interpretation of Constitutional Language," 67 *Georgetown L.J.* 899 (1979).

38. William B. Lockhart and Robert C. McClure, "Censorship of Obscenity: The Developing Constitutional Standards," 45 *Minnesota L. Rev.* 85 (1960); and *Ginsberg* at 636.

39. Lockhart and McClure, "Censorship of Obscenity," 77.

40. Lockhart and McClure, "Literature, the Law of Obscenity, and the Constitution," 38 *Minnesota L. Rev.* 341 (1954). See also Harold Leventhal, "An Empirical Inquiry into the Effects of *Miller v. California* on the Control of Obscenity," 52 *NYU L. Rev.* 838 (1977).

41. *Ginsberg* at 639.

42. Willard M. Gaylin, "The Prickly Problems of Pornography," 77 *Yale L. J.* 579 (1968).

◆ V. Politics and Pandering

1. *Ginsberg v. New York* at 655–56. On the effort to identify obscenity, Douglas once explained "with considerable glee" why his venerable brethren had so much more difficulty agreeing on a definition of pornography any more precise than Justice Potter Stewart's insistence that he knew it when he saw it. "The legal test," he said to his friend Harry Ashmore, "is whether the material arouses a prurient response in the beholder. The older we get, the freer the speech." See Ashmore, "Doubling the Standard," 62 *Va. Quarterly Rev.* 70–71 (Winter 1986).

2. *Ginsberg* at 650.

3. Quotes in this and the following paragraph are from *Interstate Circuit v. Dallas* (with *United Artists Corp. v. Dallas*) at 684.

4. at 707.

5. William Manchester, *The Glory and the Dream: A Narrative History of America, 1932–1972* (New York: Doubleday, 1974), 1357.

6. Cass R. Sunstein, *Democracy and the Problem of Free Speech* (New York: Free Press, 1993), 122. Also see Catharine A. MacKinnon, *Only Words* (Cambridge: Harvard Univ. Press, 1993).

7. *Interstate Circuit* at 706.

8. at 707.

9. at 704–8, 710–11.

10. *Ginsberg* at 672, 674–75.

11. Bruce Allen Murphy, 215.

12. Murphy, 215; and Kalman, 320, 349.

13. Manchester, 1375–1410; and Clark Clifford, *Counsel to the President: A Memoir* (New York: Random House, 1991), 554.

14. David M. O'Brien, *Storm Center: The Supreme Court in American Politics*, 2d ed. (New York: Norton, 1990), 125.

15. Bruce Allen Murphy, 376.

16. O'Brien, 125.

17. Manchester, 1395.

18. Clifford, 555–56.

19. Kalman, 329; and Shogan, 171.

20. *Schackman v. California*, 388 U.S. 454 (1967).

21. Bruce Allen Murphy, 442.

22. Shogan, 172; and Bruce Allen Murphy, 443–44.

23. *The Report of the Commission on Obscenity and Pornography*, 319; excerpts in Dorsen, Bender, and Neuborne, 365–75 here and in following paragraph. See *Schackman v. Arnebergh*, 258 F.Supp. 983 (1966) for descriptions of films.

24. Bruce Allen Murphy, 449.

25. Shogan, 172–73; and Bruce Allen Murphy, 442.

26. *Landau v. Fording*, 388 U.S. 456 (1967) and 245 Cal.App.2d 820, 54 Cal.Rptr. 177 (1966); and *Grove Press v. Maryland*, 401 U.S. 480 (1971).

27. Bruce Allen Murphy, 456–57.

28. Murphy, 530–31.

29. Kilpatrick, "Proposal Suggested to Save Time in Fortas Argument," *Washington Star*, 13 Aug. 1968, cited in Murphy, 456–62.

See also Kalman, 342–45. The Williams letter appeared in the *Washington Star* on 23 Aug. 1968, and the deans' letter in the *Washington Post* on 11 Sept. 1968.

30. Reported in Bruce Allen Murphy, 507.

31. The McClellan comment is in Kalman, 353.

32. Letter, 14 May 1969, Harlan Papers, Box 606, MLPU.

33. Clifford, 559.

34. *Stanley v. Georgia*, 394 U.S. 557.

35. *Report of the Commission on Obscenity and Pornography*, 169, 171. Also reported in Walter Kendrick, chap. 8.

36. Cited by Kendrick, 216.

37. Kendrick, 219; and *New York Times*, 25 Oct. 1970, p. 71.

◆   VI. Social Importance

1. *Miller v. California*, 413 U.S. 15 (1973) at 32.

2. *Rowan v. U.S. Post Office Department*, 397 U.S. 728 (1970). Title III of the Postal Revenue and Federal Salary Act of 1967, 81 Stat. 645, 39 U.S.C. Sec. 4009.

3. Quotes in this and the following paragraph can be found in *Rowan* at 737–38.

4. *Cain v. Kentucky*, 397 U.S. 319 (1970); and *Walker v. Ohio*, 398 U.S. 434 (1970).

5. *Hoyt v. Minnesota*, 399 U.S. 524 (1970).

6. *Hoyt* at 524.

7. *U.S. v. Reidel*, 402 U.S. 351 (1971) at 355; and *U.S. v. Thirty-Seven Photographs*, 402 U.S. 363 (1971).

8. *Stanley v. Georgia* at 557.

9. *Thirty-Seven Photographs* at 376.

10. Black's dissent, *Thirty-Seven Photographs* at 381, 382. Marshall's dissent, which follows, is in *Reidel* at 360.

11. *Stanley* at 568.

12. Bob Woodward and Scott Armstrong, *The Brethren: Inside the Supreme Court* (New York: Simon and Schuster, 1979), 195.

13. Quotes here and in the following paragraph are found in *California v. LaRue*, 409 U.S. 109 (1972) at 114, 118.

14. *Paris Adult Theatre I v. Slaton*, 414 U.S. 49.

15. See *Rabe v. Washington*, 405 U.S. 313 (1970) at 316 for dis-

cussion here and following. Also see Woodward and Armstrong, 200.

16. *Kois v. Wisconsin*, 408 U.S. 229 (1972) at 232.

17. *Miller v. California* at 29.

18. *Miller v. California* at 23, 24–25; *Paris Adult Theatre* at 57–60; *Kaplan v. California*, 413 U.S. 115 at 119; and *Paris Adult Theatre* at 68.

19. Woodward and Armstrong, 201.

20. Anthony Lewis, "Sex . . . and the Supreme Court," *Esquire*, 1 June 1963, 82.

21. Woodward and Armstrong, 200–204.

22. *Miller v. California; Paris Adult Theatre; Kaplan; U.S. v. Twelve 200-Ft. Reels of Super 8mm Film*, 414 U.S. 123; and *U.S. v. Orito*, 413 U.S. 139.

23. *Miller v. California* at 23, 24.

24. Margaret A. Blanchard, *Revolutionary Sparks: Freedom of Expression in Modern America* (New York: Oxford Univ. Press, 1992), 388.

25. *Miller v. California* at 25–26.

26. at 30–34.

27. Douglas's comments here and following can be found in *Miller v. California* at 44–46.

28. *Jacobellis* at 204.

◆ VII. Consenting Exposure

1. *Paris Adult Theatre I v. Slaton* at 73.

2. *Memoirs v. Massachusetts* at 447.

3. *O'Brien*, 114–15; *Memoirs* at 451; and President's Commission on Obscenity, 32.

4. *Interstate* at 707.

5. Dorsen, Bender, and Neuborne, 357.

6. *Pope v. Illinois*, 95 L.Ed.2d 439 (1987) at 448.

7. *Paris Theatre* at 59, quoting Bickel, "On Pornography II: Dissenting and Concurring Opinions," 22 *Public Interest* 33 (1971).

8. Discussion here and in following paragraph is taken from *Griswold v. Connecticut* at 479.

9. See Richard F. Hixson, *Privacy in a Public Society: Human Rights in Conflict* (New York: Oxford Univ. Press, 1987), 75–77.

10. Bickel, "On Pornography II," 25–26; Woodward and Armstrong, 245–46.

11. Woodward and Armstrong, 246.

12. *Palko v. Connecticut*, 302 U.S. 319 (1937); *Roe v. Wade*, 410 U.S. 113 (1973); and *Paris Theatre* at 65.

13. Milton R. Konvitz, "Privacy and the Law: A Philosophical Prelude," 31 *Law & Contemporary Problems* 279 (1966).

14. *Lamont v. Postmaster General*, 381 U.S. 301 (1965) at 308.

15. *Martin v. City of Struthers*, 319 U.S. 141 (1943).

16. *U.S. v. Thirty-Seven Photographs* at 382. Also see C. Edwin Baker, *Human Liberty and Freedom of Speech* (New York: Oxford Univ. Press, 1989), 299 n.

17. *Roth v. U.S.* at 494–96.

18. *Roth* at 495; and *Ginzburg v. U.S.* at 465, 467.

19. *Paris Theatre* at 57; and Bickel, "On Pornography II," 25–26.

20. *Paris Theatre* at 64, 63.

21. Dorsen, Bender, and Neuborne, 365; and Act of 3 Oct. 1967, Pub. L. No. 90-100, 81 Stat. 254.

22. Rodney A. Grunes, "Obscenity Law and the Justices: Reversing Policy on the Supreme Court," 9 *Seton Hall L. Rev.* 448–51 (1978).

23. *Paris Theatre* at 58.

24. at 69.

25. at 62–63.

26. Nat Hentoff, "Profiles: The Constitutionalist," *New Yorker*, 12 Mar. 1990.

27. *Paris Theatre* at 84.

28. at 92.

29. at 98.

30. at 70–73.

31. Woodward and Armstrong, 280; and *Jenkins v. Georgia*, 418 U.S. 153 (1974).

32. Woodward and Armstrong, 280–81; and *Hamling v. U.S.*, 418 U.S. 87 (1974).

33. Edward John Main, "The Neglected Prong of the Miller Test for Obscenity: Serious Literary, Artistic, Political, or Scientific Value," 11 *Southern Illinois Univ. L. J.* 1159 (1987).

34. *Hamling* at 93.

35. at 94.

36. at 105.

37. at 115 here and following paragraphs.

◆ VIII. Content Restriction

1. *Young v. American Mini Theatres Inc.*, 427 U.S. 50 (1976) at 70.

2. at 63.

3. *Police Dept. of Chicago v. Mosley*, 408 U.S. 92 (1972).

4. *Schenck v. U.S.*, 249 U.S. 49 (1919) at 52–53.

5. *Schneider v. Irvington*, 308 U.S. 147 (1939) at 161.

6. at 160.

7. Steven H. Shiffrin, *The First Amendment, Democracy, and Romance* (Cambridge: Harvard Univ. Press, 1990), 20.

8. Ely, "Flag Desecration: A Case Study in the Roles of Categorization and Balancing in First Amendment Analysis," 88 *Harvard L. Rev.* 1485 (1975); Schauer, "Codifying the First Amendment: *New York v. Ferber*," *The Supreme Court Review* 285–317, 300 (1982).

9. *American Mini Theatres* at 70.

10. at 70, 72.

11. at 66.

12. at 66.

13. at 68–69, for quotes here and following paragraph.

14. at 69–70.

15. Stevens's argument here and Powell's argument, which follows, are found in *American Mini Theatres* at 70, 79–84.

16. *American Mini Theatres* at 84–88.

17. *Erznoznik v. City of Jacksonville*, 422 U.S. 205 (1975) at 211.

18. *Erznoznik* at 218.

19. at 223.

20. at 84.

21. *Village of Euclid v. Ambler Realty Co.*, 272 U.S. 365 (1926). See Alfred C. Yen, "Judicial Review of the Zoning of Adult Entertainment: A Search for the Purposeful Suppression of Protected Speech," 12 *Pepperdine L. Rev.* 651 (1985).

22. *Smith v. U.S.*, 431 U.S. 291 (1977); *Splawn v. California*, 431 U.S. 595 (1977); and *Ward v. Illinois*, 431 U.S. 767 (1977).

23. Comstock Act, 18 U.S.C. Section 1461.

24. *Miller v. California* at 25; and *Smith v. U.S.* at 302.

25. *Smith v. U.S.* at 312, 316.

26. at 317, 324.

27. *Smith v. U.S.* at 313–18; *Manual Enterprises Inc. v. Day*; *Jacobellis v. Ohio*; and *Miller v. California.*

28. *Smith v. U.S.* at 318–19.

29. at 319.

30. *Splawn v. California* at 602–4.

31. at 603–4.

32. at 603, 604 nn. 2, 3.

33. Schauer, *Law of Obscenity*, 167.

34. *Marks v. U.S.*, 430 U.S. 188 (1977).

35. at 191.

36. at 198; and *Stanley v. Georgia* at 557.

37. *Ballew v. Georgia*, 435 U.S. 223 (1978); *Pinkus v. U.S.*, 436 U.S. 293 (1978); and *FCC v. Pacifica Foundation*, 438 U.S. 726 (1978).

38. See *Pinkus v. U.S.* at 296–98, 298–301, 305–6 for arguments of Burger, Stevens, and Brennan.

39. *FCC v. Pacifica Foundation.*

40. "The original seven words were shit, piss, fuck, cunt, cocksucker, motherfucker, and tits," *Pacifica* at 753, Transcript of the Monologue. Also 92 *Harvard L. Rev.* 148 (1978). Robert Wolff, "*Pacifica*'s Seven Dirty Words: A Sliding Scale of the First Amendment," *Law Forum* 969 (1979).

41. Wolff, "*Pacifica*'s Seven Dirty Words," 972; federal obscenity law, 18 U.S.C. Sec. 1464 (1976); and 47 U.S.C. Sec. 303 (1970).

42. Stevens, *Pacifica* at 748–51. See *Hamling v. U.S.* at 114, interpreting 18 U.S.C. Sec. 1471. Also see *U.S. v. 12 200-ft. Reels of Super 8mm Film* at 130; and *Manual Enterprises Inc. v. Day* at 484.

43. *FCC v. Pacifica* at 743 n. 18.

44. at 746, 747.

45. at 749, 750.

46. at 761.

47. at 770, 771.

48. at 773.

49. at 762, 775, 776, 777; and *Towne v. Eisner*, 245 U.S. 418 (1918) at 425 for the Holmes quotation.

50. *Young v. American Mini Theatres* at 79–84.

248

◆ IX. Expressive Activity

1. *Schad v. Borough of Mount Ephraim*, 452 U.S. 61 (1981); *Renton v. Playtime Theatres Inc.*, 475 U.S. 41 (1986); and *Barnes v. Glen Theatres Inc.*, 501 U.S. 560 (1991).

2. *New York v. Ferber*, 458 U.S. 747 (1982); *Massachusetts v. Oakes*, 491 U.S. 576 (1989); and *Osborne v. Ohio*, 495 U.S. 103 (1990).

3. *Schad v. Borough of Mount Ephraim* at 65–66.

4. *Schneider v. Irvington* at 161. White, *Schad* at 61. See also Justice Stevens's opinion in *American Mini Theatres* at 71 n. 35.

5. *Schad* at 67.

6. Beackmun, *Schad* at 78, quoting *Schneider* at 163 and *Terminiello v. Chicago*, 337 U.S. 1 (1949) at 4–5.

7. *Schad* at 80, 83, 84.

8. at 86.

9. *California v. LaRue* at 118 (emphasis added to quotation); *Southeastern Promotions Ltd. v. Conrad*, 420 U.S. 546 (1975), protection for the rock musical *Hair*; and *Doran v. Salem Inn Inc.*, 422 U.S. 922 (1975), topless dancing by women protected.

10. *Doran* at 933.

11. *New York State Liquor Authority v. Bellanca*, 452 U.S. 714 (1981) at 718–19.

12. *Barnes v. Glen Theatre Inc.*, 115 L.Ed.2d 504 (1991).

13. Rehnquist is quoted in *Barnes*, 115 L.Ed.2d at 511. See also *U.S. v. O'Brien*, 391 U.S. 367 (1968).

14. *Barnes*, 115 L.Ed.2d at 512.

15. at 521, 522, 523 n. 2.

16. at 528.

17. *Texas v. Johnson*, 491 U.S. 397 (1989).

18. *Barnes*, 115 L.Ed.2d at 527.

19. at 525 n. 1.

20. at 517, 530.

21. T. C. Donnelly, "Protection of Children From Use in Pornography," 12 *J. of Law Reform* 2 (Winter 1979).

22. Protection of Children from Sexual Exploitation Act, 18 U.S.C. Sec. 2252 (1979).

23. *New York v. Ferber* at 757, 761.

24. at 759–60.

25. at 775.

26. at 781, 778.

27. Attorney General's Commission on Pornography, *Final Report* (Washington, D.C.: Government Printing Office, 1986), 416.

28. See Patricia Chock, "The Use of Compters in the Sexual Exploitation of Children and Child Pornography," 7 *Computer L. J.* 386 (Summer 1987).

29. *New York Times,* 29 Sept. 1988; *Washington Post,* 6 Sept. 1988; *Publishers Weekly,* 2 Dec. 1988; and *New York Times,* 13 Mar. 1989.

30. *Brockett v. Spokane Arcades Inc.,* 105 S.Ct. 2794 (1985).

31. at 2799.

32. *Renton* at 41.

33. at 50, 49 n. 2, 48.

34. at 54.

35. *American Mini Theatres* at 70.

36. *Pope v. Illinois,* 481 U.S. 497, 95 L.Ed.2d 439 (1987).

37. Pope, 95 L.Ed.2d at 445 n. 3.

38. at 448.

39. at 445 and n. 3 at 445.

40. Stevens's comment at 452, 453.

41. at 456.

42. See *Smith v. U.S.* at 301.

43. *Pope,* 95 L.Ed.2d at 452, 453 n. 5. See also Steven G. Gey, "The Apologetics of Suppression: The Regulation of Pornography As Act and Idea," 86 *Michigan L. Rev.* 1564 (June 1988).

44. Gey, "Apologetics," 1580–81; and *Chaplinsky* at 572.

45. *Philadelphia Inquirer,* 9 May 1987, p. 8-A.

46. *Virginia v. American Booksellers Association Inc.,* 484 U.S. 383 (1988).

47. *Massachusetts v. Oakes* at 576; *Osborne v. Ohio,* 495 U.S. at 103; and *Jacobson v. U.S.,* 118 L.Ed.2d 174 (1992).

48. *Oakes* at 578. Mass. General Laws, Chap. 272, Sec. 29A (1986).

49. *Osborne,* 109 L.Ed.2d 98 (1990) at 108.

50. at 109.

51. at 110.

52. at 123, 131–32.

53. Child Protection Act, Pub. L. 98–292, 98 Stat. 20, 18 U.S.C. Sec. 2252(a)(2)(A). *Jacobson v. U.S.,* 118 L.Ed. 2d at 181.

54. *Newark Star-Ledger,* 23 Apr. 1991, p. 6.

55. Daniel L. Milhalko, a postal inspector who supervised the investigation, said the agents "would have been remiss" not to pursue the case of "a man who was around children daily" in his job as a school bus driver. On the fact that at least four men committed suicide after being charged, Mihalko said investigators could hardly be blamed for the suicides. "It is not unusual for people to commit suicide after some kind of arrest or charge" (*New York Times*, 19 Apr. 1992).

56. *Miller v. Civil City of South Bend*, 904 F.2d 1081 (7th Cir. 1990); and *Barnes v. Glen Theatre Inc.*, 115 L.Ed.2d at 504.

57. *Miller v. South Bend* at 1091, 1092.

58. at 1096, 1098, 1100.

◆ X. Syndicated Sex

1. One notable RICO case is *Fort Wayne Books Inc. v. Indiana*, 489 U.S. 46 (1989). For the development of RICO laws and their implications for obscenity prosecutions, see Matthew D. Bunker, Paul H. Gates, and Sigman L. Splichal, "RICO and Obscenity Prosecutions: Racketeering Laws Threaten Free Expression," 70 *Journalism Quarterly* 692 (Autumn 1993). Also see Andrew J. Melnick, "A 'Peep' at RICO: *Fort Wayne Books Inc. v. Indiana* and the Application of Anti-Racketeering Statutes to Obscenity Violations," 69 *Boston Univ. L. Rev.* 389 (1989); and Gerald E. Lynch, "RICO: The Crime of Being a Criminal, Parts I and II," 87 *Columbia L. Rev.* 661 (1987).

2. Bunker, Gates, and Splichal, "RICO and Obscenity Prosecutions," 693.

3. Attorney General's Commission on Pornography, 1053, 1051–52, 1042.

4. Attorney General's Commission, 1349–50.

5. Bunker, Gates, and Splichal, "RICO and Obscenity Prosecutions," 693. See also Melnick, "A 'Peep' at RICO."

6. Organized Crime Control Act of 1970, Pub. L. No. 91-452, Sec. 1, 84 Stat. 922, 923. See also Melnick, "A 'Peep' at RICO."

7. Melnick, "A 'Peep' at RICO," 393. The Racketeer Influenced and Corrupt Organization Act ("RICO"), codified as amended at 18 U.S.C. Sec. 1461–64 (1982). For Helms's statement from the floor of the Senate see 130 *Cong. Rec.* S434 (daily edition, 30 Jan. 1984).

8. Melnick, "A 'Peep' at RICO," 393.

9. *Arcara v. Cloud Books Inc.*, 478 U.S. 697, 92 L.Ed.2d 568 (1986) at 578.

10. *U.S. v. O'Brien* at 367; and *Arcara*, 92 L.Ed.2d at 575–76, 576–77.

11. *Arcara*, 92 L.Ed.2d at 580.

12. at 577 n. 2. See also Tod R. Eggenberger, "RICO vs. Dealers in Obscene Matter: The First Amendment Battle," 22 *Columbia J. of Law and Social Problems* 71 (1988).

13. *Marcus v. Search Warrant* at 717. Also Eggenberger, "RICO vs. Dealers," 111.

14. *Ronald Sappenfield v. Indiana*, 489 U.S. 46 (1989). See also for explanation Ken Nuger, "The RICO/CRRA Trap: Troubling Implications for Adult Expression," 23 *Indiana L. Rev.* 109 (1990).

15. *Fort Wayne Books*, 103 L.Ed.2d 34 at 51–54.

16. *Marcus v. Search Warrant* at 717; *Fort Wayne Books*, 103 L.Ed.2d at 51.

17. See Nuger, "Rico/CRRA Trap," 126.

18. *Fort Wayne Books*, 103 L.Ed.2d at 62–63.

19. at 63, 65.

20. Scalia, *FW/PBS Inc. v. City of Dallas*, 493 U.S. 215 (1990) at 252; and *Freedman v. Maryland* at 51.

21. O'Connor, *FW/PBS* at 228.

22. at 229.

23. Brennan at 239, 240.

24. White at 244, 245–46.

25. at 248.

26. Scalia at 253.

27. *FW/PBS Inc.* at 251, 252. *Sable Communications of California v. FCC*, 492 U.S. 115 (1989). The new 1989 law amended the Telephone Decency Act, 47 U.S.C. Sec. 223 (1988). Earlier legislative efforts also included the Child Protection and Obscenity Enforcement Act, 102 Stat. 4502, Sec. 7524 (1988).

28. *Alexander v. U.S.*, 125 L.Ed.2d 441 (1993). In 1970, Alexander was convicted of interstate transportation of obscene material in federal court, along with Samuel Manarite, a member of the Vito Genovese Family and Richard J. Portela. In 1972, Alexander was sentenced to Sandstone Penitentiary where he served nine of eighteen months and paid a $20,000 fine.

29. Rehnquist, *Alexander* at 450, 451.

30. at 453, 454.

31. Kennedy at 468, 457, 460.

32. at 464, 465, 467.

33. at 459.

34. For a discussion see Andrew B. Bloomer, "Sex, Speech and Videotape: Prior Restraint and *FW/PBS Inc. v. City of Dallas*," 1991 *Wisc. L. Rev.* 707.

35. *Alexander* at 459.

36. *O'Brien* at 377.

37. *Adult Video*, 960 F.2d at 791 (1992) as reported in "The Supreme Court—Leading Cases," 107 *Harvard L. Rev.* 244–54 (1993).

38. Brennan quoted from *Bantam Books Inc. v. Sullivan* at 66. *Alexander* at 451.

39. Jed S. Rakoff, "Will the Supreme Court Restrain Forfeiture?" *N.Y. L. J.*, 8 July 1993, 3, 7. See also "The Supreme Court—Leading Cases," 107 *Harvard L. Rev.* 244, 254 (1993).

◆ XI. Viewpoint Discrimination

1. *American Booksellers Assoc. Inc. v. Hudnut*, 771 F.2d 323 (7th Cir. 1985), summarily aff'd. 475 U.S. 1001 (1986).

2. Mayor Hudnut, quoted in *Philadelphia Inquirer*, 25 Feb. 1986, p. 11-A.

3. Donnerstein, Linz, and Penrod, *The Question of Pornography: Research Findings and Policy Implications* (New York: Free Press, 1987). See also the earlier Neil M. Malamuth and Donnerstein, eds., *Pornography and Sexual Aggression* (New York: Academic Press, 1984). For a book-length scholarly treatment of the Minneapolis and Indianapolis ordinances see Donald Alexander Downs, *The New Politics of Pornography* (Chicago: Univ. of Chicago Press, 1989).

4. *New York Times*, 15 May 1984 and 10 June 1984, both news accounts by E. R. Shipp.

5. *Hudnut* at 1331, 1332.

6. *New York v. Ferber* at 747; *FCC v. Pacifica* at 726; and *American Mini Theatres* at 50.

7. *Hudnut* at 1334.

8. at 1334.

9. at 1335.

10. at 1335.

11. at 1335–36; and *Beauharnais v. Illinois,* 343 U.S. 250 (1952).

12. *Hudnut* at 1336, 1337.

13. at 1338.

14. at 1341. In *Freedman,* the Court upheld state requirements that all films be submitted for advance approval so that obscene and, therefore, constitutionally unprotected movies could be prohibited. But it also ruled that such screening must include certain safeguards. In order to pass muster, a statute or ordinance providing for administrative approval of films prior to their exhibition must: (1) place on the censorship body the burden of proof; (2) require that the censor, within a very brief time period, either issue a license or seek a court order to stop the film from being shown; and (3) assure a prompt final judicial decision on whether the film is obscene. The Maryland statute was subsequently amended to include these safeguards, and it was repealed altogether in 1981.

15. Posner, *The Economics of Justice* (Cambridge: Harvard Univ. Press, 1981); *Economic Analysis of Law* (Boston: Little, Brown, 1986); and *Sex and Reason* (Cambridge: Harvard Univ. Press, 1992).

16. *West Virginia State Board of Education,* 319 U.S. 624 (1943) at 642.

17. Easterbrook, *Hudnut* at 327–28.

18. at 328.

19. at 329.

20. at 330.

21. Quotes here and in the following paragraph are from *Newark Star-Ledger,* 25 Feb. 1986.

22. The letter appeared in the *New York Times,* 11 Mar. 1990.

23. Butler, *Gender Trouble: Feminism and the Subversion of Identity* (New York: Routledge, 1990), 3.

24. Poovey, "Feminism and Deconstruction," 1 *Feminist Studies* 113; and Tisdale, "Talk Dirty to Me: A Woman's Taste for Pornography," *Harper's Magazine,* Feb. 1992, 37–46.

25. Varda Burstyn in Burstyn, ed., *Women Against Censorship* (Vancouver: Douglas and McIntyre, 1985), 24; and Willis, *Beginning to See the Light: Pieces of a Decade* (New York: Knopf, 1981), 221–22.

26. *Smith v. U.S.* at 318–19; and *Young v. American Mini Theatres* at 66.

27. Posner, *Law and Literature: A Misunderstood Relation* (Cambridge: Harvard University Press, 1988), 334–35.

28. *Beauharnais v. Illinois*, Reed at 283–84, Black at 273, and Jackson at 304–5.

29. De Grazia, *Girls Lean Back Everywhere: The Law of Obscenity and the Assault on Genius* (New York: Vintage Books, 1992), 411–16.

30. *New York Times v. Sullivan*, 376 U.S. 254 (1964); *Collin v. Smith*, 578 F.2d 1197 (7th Cir. 1978) at 1205; and *Hudnut* at 331–32 n. 3.

31. *Jacobellis v. Ohio* at 191.

32. Harry Kalven Jr., *A Worthy Tradition: Freedom of Speech in America*, ed. Jamie Kalven (New York: Harper & Row, 1987), 38.

33. *Memoirs v. Massachusetts* at 461.

34. De Grazia, 580.

35. *Pope v. Illinois*, 481 U.S. 497 (1987) at 512 and n. 5. Also see Amy M. Adler, "Post-Modern Art and the Death of Obscenity Law," 99 *Yale L.J.* 1359 (1990).

36. Savage, *Turning Point: The Making of the Rehnquist Supreme Court* (New York: John Wiley, 1992).

37. *Pacifica* at 742 n. 18 here and following; and *Schenck*, 63 L.Ed. 470 (1919) at 473–74 in the extract.

38. *Consolidated Edison v. Public Service Commission*, 447 U.S. 530 (1980) at 545, 544, 546.

39. *Consolidated Edison* at 548.

40. *Cohen v. California*, 403 U.S. 15 (1971) at 26.

41. *Police Dept. of Chicago v. Mosley* at 99; and *R.A.V. v. City of St. Paul*, 120 L.Ed.2d 305 (1992) at 342.

42. *R.A.V.* at 316 n. 3, quoting Transcript of Oral Argument at 8.

43. *R.A.V.* at 343, 344.

44. at 345.

45. at 346 n. 5 for Holmes quote from *Towne v. Eisner*, 245 U.S. at 425 (1918); Stevens, *R.A.V.* at 346, 347.

◆ XII. Afterword

1. *U.S. v. Kennerley* at 119. See also Matthew J. Bruccoli, *The Fortunes of Mitchell Kennerley, Bookman* (San Diego: Harcourt Brace Jovanovich, 1986).

2. Gerald Gunther, *Learned Hand: The Man and The Judge*

(New York: Knopf, 1994), 157; and *Masses Publishing Co. v. Patten*, 244 F. 535 (S.D.N.Y. 1917), *rev.* 246 F.2d 24 (2d Cir. 1917).

3. Gunther, 157–58.

4. Gunther, 333.

5. *U.S. v. Levine* at 157.

6. *Roth v. U.S.* at 489, the test drawn from the Model Penal Code.

7. Yarbrough, *John Marshall Harlan*, 220.

8. *Paris Adult Theatre I v. Slaton* at 73–74, 84.

9. Holmes's test is enunciated in *Schenck v. U.S.* at 47; Hand's test is in *Dennis v. U.S.*, 183 F.2d 212 (2d Cir. 1951).

10. *FCC v. Pacifica Foundation* at 742 n. 18; and *Smith v. U.S.* at 316–18 for this and following paragraph.

11. Quotes from Stevens here and following can be found in *R.A.V. v. City of St. Paul* at 339–52.

12. Blanchard, *Revolutionary Sparks*, 453.

13. Baker, "Scope of the First Amendment Freedom of Speech," 25 *UCLA L. Rev.* 986 (1978); and Sunstein, "Pornography and the First Amendment," 1986 *Duke L.J.* 602–8 (1986).

14. Richard F. Hixson, "C. Edwin Baker: A Review Essay on Free Speech," unpublished manuscript, Rutgers Univ., 1989.

15. C. Edwin Baker, *Human Liberty and Freedom of Speech*, 69.

16. Richard A. Posner, *Sex and Reason* (Cambridge: Harvard Univ. Press, 1992), 375.

17. *Paris Adult Theatre I v. Slaton* at 85–86, 86 n. 9. See also C. Edwin Baker, "Of Course, More Than Words," 61 *Univ. Chicago L. Rev.* 1181 (1994).

Index

264

pornography, 176–77; and commerce, 103, 148–49; as concept, 119–20; and criminality, 101; and definition of obscenity, 106–7; and mail, 100–101; and possession, 123–24; and public acts, 123, 141–42; right to, 104–5, 123; zones of, 122–23, 124

prostitution, 185–86, 198

Protection of Children from Sexual Exploitation Act, 166

prurient interest, 21, 24–27, 43, 49, 55–59, 97, 103, 113, 115, 125, 128, 146, 225; and audience, 68; definition of, 170; and indecency, 152; and violence, 82

Quantity of Copies of Books v. Kansas, A, 41, 42, 45

questionable material, 114–15

R. A. V. v. City of St. Paul, 217, 219–21, 228–29

Rabe v. Washington, 108

Racketeering Influence and Corrupt Organizations Act (RICO), 182–85; Civil Remedies for Racketeering Activity Act (CRRA), 182–85; Indiana version of, 185, 188; penalties, 183–84; and seizure, 187–88, 190, 193–94

Radich v. New York, 103

radio broadcasts, 150–56

Randall, Richard S., 3–6, 48–49

reasonable person, 144, 171–74, 216

Redman, Ben Ray, 12–13

Redmond v. United States, 119

Redrup v. New York, 72–75, 91, 92, 102, 106, 110, 111; and privacy, 119

Reed, Stanley, 212

Regina v. Hicklin, 7–8, 9, 11, 13, 18, 24, 68, 77, 126, 222, 224

regulation, 27; content-based, 138, 142–46, 153; and expressive activity, 161, 162–63; of radio, 152–53; and sliding scale (two-level) theory, 142–43

Rehnquist, William H., xi, 100, 132, 133, 146, 162; on context, 109–10; on regulation, 142, 161; on RICO laws, 194, 195

Rembar, Charles, 14–15, 50–51, 52–53, 55, 59, 70–71

Renton v. Playtime Theatres, 197

Roberts, Owen, 137

Roe v. Wade, 112, 119

Ronald Sappenfield v. Indiana, 188

Rosen v. United States, 9, 10

Roth-Alberts-Memoirs test, 62, 74–75, 82, 84, 114; as definitional, 108–9; reformulation of, 110

Roth-Alberts test, 27, 29, 41, 97, 99, 111, 124–25, 157; and community standards, 31–32, 145; and conduct, 66; and customs, 103; and dominant theme, 42–43; and literature, 212, 213, 215; and pandering, 63, 73; and privacy, 96–97, 104; refinements of, 35,

RICHARD F. HIXSON, a member of the Rutgers University faculty since 1960, is a professor in the Department of Journalism and Mass Media. He specializes in the history of American journalism, especially the early years, and the laws and regulations governing the mass media. His books include *Mass Media and the Constitution, Privacy in a Public Society,* and *Isaac Collins: A Quaker Printer in 18th-Century America.* He is also the author of several entries in the *Dictionary of American Biography.* His current work includes "The Fourth Estate," which will look at the U.S. Supreme Court's treatment over time of the First Amendment's press clause.

BURLINGTON COUNTY COLLEGE
COUNTY ROUTE 530
PEMBERTON NJ 08068